*A sound accomplishes nothing; without it life would
not last out the instant.*

John Cage

*It is the tradition of the fortunate seekers never to
be content with partial practice.*

Milarepa

*To Aaron and Isaiah
who brought me my books*

EXILE AND THE PROPHETIC
volume one

THE
heartbeat
OF THE **PROPHETIC**

MARC H. **ELLIS**

WIPF & STOCK · Eugene, Oregon

Wipf and Stock Publishers
199 W 8th Ave, Suite 3
Eugene, OR 97401

The Heartbeat of the Prophetic
By Ellis, Marc H.
Copyright©2015 by Ellis, Marc H.
ISBN 13: 978-1-5326-1906-9
Publication date 3/20/2017
Previously published by New Disapora Books, 2015

TABLE OF CONTENTS

Preface   i

PART ONE

The Beach Mezuzah	1
Tighter Than Tight	5
South Africa in the Mirror	9
Chosen / Kairos	13
Traveling Jewish	19
The Jewish Wheel of Fortune	23
Jewish (Empire) Geography	29
How Deep is (Y)our Colonial Mentality?	35
Squandered. Beginning Again.	41
The Jewish Pandora's Box	47
Tell Me, Have You Ever Been Fed by Ravens?	53
Birthright Prophetic	59
Overcoming Partial Practice	63
Helicopter Gunships in the Ark of the Covenant	69
Prying Eyes	75
The Heartbeat of the Prophetic	79
Mezuzah (God) Watch	83
They Left Me With Nothing	87
The Edward Said I Knew	91
Gathering Light	95
Revered to Radioactive	99
Chief Last Night	103
Prophet Gray	107
Rejected! Jewish 'Common Sense' Religion	113
Reading the Torah Out Loud (No Rabbis Allowed!)	117

PART TWO

No Prophet Spoken Here	123
Genocide - Donate Now	127
After Genocide, No Justice	131
Exporting the Holocaust	135
Jewish (Holocaust) Missionaries	139
Plan B	143
I'm Leaving on a (Nazi / German) Jet Plane	147

Henry's Letter	153
Decolonizing the Holocaust	157
On Both Sides of the Congo Line	161
The Ever-Expanding World of the Bereaved	165
Have You Been Conquered by the Bible?	169
Uprooted Jew	173
Imagine There's No Prophetic, I Wonder If You Can	177
Collecting (Palestinian) Books	181
Israel's 'Never-Again' Drones in German Uniforms	185
Normalizing the Hitler Youth	189
BGS / BDS - It's Never Easy on the Jewish Front	193
Jewish (Re)Education	199
Romero Rising	203
Where Will Jews Rise?	207
(Jewish) Birth Certificate in the New Diaspora	211
Dancing with Wolves	217
A (Jewish) Pedagogy for / of the Oppressor	221
Romney's Romero Blood Money	225

PART THREE

When the Jewish Student is Ready	231
Archipelago Palestine	235
On Empty Suits and Olive Trees	241
Rachel Corrie Rising	247
Rachel Corrie, Righteous Gentile	253
Shoah Business	259
Rachel Corrie - On the Field of Battle	265
War Crimes	269
What About an Encyclopedia Prophetica?	275
Zen and the Art of Special Book Collections	281
Now Isaiah Knows	287
Zen and the Art of Star of David Helicopter Gunship Maintenance	291
Preparing our Defense for the Coming Days of Awe	295
Einstein on (My) Beach	301
Plus Suffering	305
Rabbis for Jewish Rights	311
Sounding the Prophetic Gong	315
A Cross on the Beach	319
Missing Muna	323
Our Jewish Anechoic Chamber	329
Mahatma Condi	333

Living in the Oprasphere	337
James Baldwin's Coalition is Ours	341
If Rosh Hashanah Returns	345
The Prophetic Under the Banyan Tree	349
David Gregory Came to My Seder	351
The Next Four Years	355
Researching the Jewish Future	361
The Americanization of Israeli Power	365
The Jewish Civil War Interviews	369
My (un)Invited Exchange with John Mearsheimer	375
B'Tselem and the End of Jewish History	383
The Day Without a Future	387

PREFACE

In an interview days before his eightieth birthday, the famed Jewish musician, Leonard Cohen, quoted from his recent song: 'There's truth that lives and truth that dies. I don't know which, so never mind. There is no need that this survive, there's truth that lives and truth that dies.' Cohen reflected on his lyrics: "It's one of those phrases that resonates in some corner of the heart. And I don't think it serves us well to explain it or to analyze it or to interpret it. It sounded right to me. There are certain truths that are in a dormant stage that you can't always locate or be nourished by. But they're there."

I thought of Cohen's words as I reread my commentaries of July through September, 2012. Since I had recently taken early retirement from my university faculty position and come to live in Cape Canaveral, Florida, the context was central to my writing. The transition wasn't smooth or easy. But when corruption reigns at the highest level of the institution where you work, when conspiracy and paid testimony become part of a cover-up and those involved pursue a lie as if it is God's truth, then it's time to move on.

More and more universities are led by the miseducated and, if truth be known, uneducated "educators," as my former university is now. Committed thinkers and committed thought are thus hamstrung. Free speech is aborted. The prophetic is strangled.

That's the immediate backdrop of these commentaries. But the road less traveled goes back decades before, indeed from the moment I became conscious of the world. For reasons I cannot account for, the prophetic has always been central to my existence. My Jewishness no doubt points to this. Individual personality may play a part as well. The result of such consciousness is obvious. My entire life has been shadowed by a sense of exile and too often the physical reality of exile as well.

More and more, people around the world are experiencing the same sense of dislocation and the call to speak truth to power. I am not alone.

Within exile there are periodic bursts of energy, times when the overall arc of the prophetic becomes more urgent and expressive. My arrival in Cape Canaveral occasioned such an outpouring.

When I arrived at the Cape, Adam Horowitz, a co-editor of a website on the Middle East called, after its founder, Philip Weiss, Mondoweiss, came to mind. I wondered if he might be interested in publishing a daily commentary I was thinking of writing. When I approached Adam, I had thought little of how I would fashion such commentaries for the web. Blogging was a new venture for me.

After consulting with Philip, Adam welcomed me into the Mondoweiss staple of writers. Since I proposed a series they asked for a title. The theme which had been continually present in my life – *Exile and the Prophetic* – came to mind.

What I began then continues to this day, though with a twist. In my first commentaries, the first 75 of which are published here, I had little idea how to write for the internet. For an academic, the audience for my books had been significant. I don't write in stilted language – at least for an academic – but I soon discovered the internet audience to be different. Over time I learned the blog ropes and became more topical. I now use the news of the day and write shorter pieces that are more easily read and understood.

The commentaries here fall short of that internet ideal and for this I am grateful. Instead, these original blogs are more like commentaries. They often pick up from one another and generally neglect the news of the day. More often they feature excursions on the beach and books I was reading on such diverse luminaries as the musician, John Cage, and the artist, Mark Rothko. Throughout, the underlying theme is the prophetic. In exile, I am once again attempting to sort out the mysterious heartbeat of the prophetic.

Can one be grateful for exile? This isn't the first time I've asked this question nor is it the first time this question has been asked. After survival, gratitude is the most difficult question that exiles wrestle with. As a Jew, I inherit a history of exile. Still, present-day Jewish exile is quite different. The prophetic, too, is a Jewish distinctive but the contemporary Jewish prophetic, like exile, is up against a curious set of circumstances. Among them is the Holocaust and an ever-expanding and militaristic Israel.

In these commentaries I explore the heartbeat of the prophetic. What exactly is the heartbeat of the prophetic? Where is the prophetic heartbeat to be found? If we cannot define it completely, how can we approach the prophetic, which is so powerful and vulnerable at the same time?

I seek to unravel this mystery as an act of self-understanding and as a gift to all those who struggle with the prophetic in their lives. Since I continue to write daily, obviously I have yet to solve the puzzle of puzzles.

This I know: Without the prophetic there is no meaning in history – or our lives; there may be no meaning in history or our lives; the prophet embodies the possibility of meaning in our history – and in our lives.

The prophet also embodies the possibility of God in history – and our lives.

Throughout I emphasize "possibility." I have not found certainty in the realm of meaning or God.

What I do know is that we Jews, along with others, must testify to what we see and the future we want to bring into being. Periodically, too, we must collect our testimony lest it become scattered and lost. The virtual world spreads our messages around the globe but in the end we must focus our sensibilities. We wait expectantly for the moment when history opens and a new path becomes possible.

Gathering these commentaries in one place might seem retro to some in our day and age. However, depth is often found in the archaic. The way forward won't only be modern.

In these pages I collect my individual witness within the broader arc of Jewish history.

Other Jews and other communities need to collect their own witness. Collecting our mutual witness - for ourselves and to each other. This is a *novum* in history, the face of a new interfaith solidarity coming of age.

Have I given away the end of my exploration, or at least part of the end?

Yes, unless you understand that at the end of the prophetic, we return to the beginning.

Exiled, I started again, now with you the reader.

EXILE AND THE PROPHETIC
part one | *volume one*

Living Labyrinth
CAPE CANAVARAL

The Rabbi's Weekend Home
CAPE CANAVERAL

JULY 5

THE BEACH MEZUZAH

Jewish – a concept I have struggled with my entire life. As in – what does it mean to be Jewish? Of course this is a perennial question in Jewish history. It's never solved once and for all. Each generation responds. Each generation's response is their answer. What is ours?

After the Holocaust, the question arose again. Extreme times heighten the "what does it mean to be Jewish" question. Now there is another after: after Israel, and what Israel has done and is doing to the Palestinian people.

In Cape Canaveral, I hoped to put this question behind me for a while. After all, everyone needs some time to rest, especially after a harrowing year of fighting against the powers-that-be. But then, on my first walk to the beach, I notice that the last house on the street has a huge mezuzah affixed to the door. Later I learned the home is owned by the local congregation. The rabbi stays there on weekends.

Or so it seems. As far as I can tell there isn't a synagogue in town. The closest synagogues are in Melbourne and Orlando, at least 30 some miles away. But, strangely enough, there is a Jews for Jesus storefront just a few blocks from where I am staying. I pass by it on the way to the grocery store.

The mezuzah was part of my childhood. Wherever I have lived I affix them to my doorposts. But to be honest, when I see one now – and right on my way to the beach! – I feel a sense of pain. As if violence is about to come my way. I don't know the rabbi who stays there so it may be unfair, but in my own experience a mezuzah on the door often means that the occupant of the home is an Israel Firster. Most Israel Firsters don't want the likes of me around. (This, of course, doesn't mean that Israel Firsters knows anything about Israel. It is the idea of Israel that is the point. No doubt, it makes undying loyalty easier too.)

What happens when a religious symbol of such importance becomes a sign of violence against you – or at least when that is your first thought when the symbol appears? As if the mezuzah is following you!

Perhaps it's like the Cross for my Christian friends – a sign of historical contradiction, or what Palestinians feel when they see Jewish sacred symbols. I would think that they experience what I do when I see a Cross. It seems logical since the Cross became a sign of our oppression and things Jewish are signs of Palestinian oppression.

Speaking of Jews for Jesus, I've noticed such a strong antipathy toward these "wayward" Jews that blinds our own waywardness. Perhaps this is purposeful. We deflect outward what we don't want to see within.

Where I lived previously, the local congregations would get up in arms when Jews for Jesus came to town. Voices were raised. On the Israel front, though, whatever was done to Palestinians was alright, even necessary. Arabs in general were included in this "necessary." I often wondered if their voices would be as loud if Israel dropped a nuclear bomb on Cairo – or, more immediately, Tehran. I wondered but my wonderment was rhetorical. I knew the answer.

That's how far we Jews have come. What an arrival! After the Holocaust, we needed power. Now we have it. What do we do with it? Want more power. Has power healed the trauma of the Holocaust? Not at all. The trauma festers. Meanwhile Jewish dissenters are confused and often abused by those who wield power in the Jewish community. So much so that the mezuzah on the door has become a sign of contradiction. To others. To ourselves.

Lift Off
CAPE CANAVERAL

JULY 6

TIGHTER THAN TIGHT

Just a few days after I arrived at the Cape, as a rocket was lifting off nearby my apartment, the news of Yitzhak Shamir's death crossed the wires. When a rocket lifts off, I hear the rumble in my apartment. It's so loud, the apartment shakes. It feels like a minor earthquake, at least that's the sensation as I hear it from others who live in earthquake zones.

At first, I experienced Shamir's death as an afterthought. As in, is he still around? But in his prime Shamir was important. As prime minister of Israel in the late 1980s, early 1990s, Shamir sealed the deal against a Palestinian state. Under his leadership, the settlement explosion in Jerusalem and the West Bank continued. Then he ordered the crushing of the first Palestinian Uprising which was carried out courtesy of his cabinet minister and recently minted saint, Yitzhak Rabin. On crushing Palestinian aspirations, the right and left-wing of Israeli parties have always come together. Rhetoric differs. Actions are virtually identical.

Shamir was an early and controversial terrorist against the British in Mandate Palestine. His early career as a terrorist didn't disqualify him from political leadership in the state of Israel. On the contrary, his terrorist credentials promoted it, like the other prime ministers before and after him.

Who of the early prime ministers of Israel could have served if terrorism or ethnic cleansing disqualified them? This includes Rabin, who was honest enough to admit his role in "removing" Palestinians from their homes to create a Jewish state. There is no use singling him out though. The whole pantheon of Israel's heroes is involved. This answers the current question I'm often asked as to whether Jews can be ethnic cleansers. Since Jews have experienced similar horrors so often at other's hands, it seems like a contradiction. Like the mezuzah on the door post?

As I say, in history practice trumps theory. In theory, Jews cannot be ethnic cleansers. In fact, we are. Can Jews participate in ethnic cleansing? The answer – "Yes."

I remember Shamir vividly because I was often on the road during those years speaking on the first Palestinian Uprising. For me the uprising was our last possibility as Jews to forge an ethical future. Israel and Jews around the world faced a clarion call: "Stop oppressing the Palestinian people!" The Jewish response (at least from those in power): "Crush them! Teach the Arabs a lesson in the only way they know – through force."

That was part of Benjamin Netanyahu's eulogy of Shamir. His refrain was, more or less: "The Arabs are as they are." Does this also mean: "The Jews are as they are?" How often this is said about Jews. Now we specialize in saying it about others. Curiously, we seem to have become what we say others are. We have become frozen into the image and reality of empire

builders and enablers. Without admitting this to ourselves, of course. This is what Shamir was. What Netanyahu is. Is this our fate as Jews? Is this what our history boils down to?

Traveling during these years, I had the sense that this was our last chance to turn around. Today I am even more certain that the uprising years were the last possibility. Shamir wanted to close that door shut, tighter than tight. He did.

Another memory during those uprising years: wherever I went to speak, the most hostile groups, especially at universities, were progressive Jews. They also wanted to close the door shut, tighter than tight, on any Jewish dissent that was to the left of them.

This is a lesson we should ponder. The problem wasn't only the identifiable ethnic cleansers of Palestinians. They knew what they had done and why. One might even admire their clarity while disagreeing with their policies. Shamir didn't have a doubt in his mind that what he did was right.

If Progressive Jews have second thoughts, they keep them to themselves. They want everyone else to keep it to themselves as well. Thus they are part of the problem. Progressive Jews fought against views that might have substantively addressed the Israel-Palestine issue. Examples abound from that time period. They were against: cutting off American aid to Israel; sending Witness for Peace delegations into the occupied territories; criticism of the Oslo Accords as too limited. What is now commonly held sometimes even by them, Progressive Jews labeled anti-Semitic and self-hating.

The ethnic cleansing/permanent occupation left the station decades ago. So why, oh why, can't Progressive Jews admit it? My own sense is that they are so involved in American and Israeli empire, so deeply dependent on and benefitting from it, that like other Jews they are blind to what has already happened to the Jewish ethical tradition. Instead, they invoke that tradition at every turn, even against those Jews who believe that its very invocation covers over its violation.

I don't exempt myself from this critique. How can I? Jewish identity today is characterized by imperial sensibilities to such an extent that they are invisible to us. As in: who, me? Us? No way.

Imperialism has penetrated so deeply into the core of what it means to be Jewish that calling it out provokes an intense reaction. It's like a traumatic wound that cannot withstand the light of day. Like the idea that Jewish history has collapsed and that our post-Holocaust era is marked by atrocity, then against us, and now others.

We live in the Golden Age of Empire Judaism. Shall we hide ourselves from this knowledge? Traveling globally, it's like a secret known all over the world. The question is our own awakening. To know and speak what is already known. By others. By us.

Dawn on the Cape
CAPE CANAVERAL

JULY 7

SOUTH AFRICA
IN THE MIRROR

Walking the beach at dawn, I marvel at the morning sky, the sun rising over the water. At these moments I feel distant from industry, all of them, including the education industry, or should I say, extending President Eisenhower's farewell address, the military/industrial/agricultural/educational/propaganda complex. I could add "Christian" to the "complex" mix since I've been there and done that. Add "Jewish" as well, since we've signed up and flourished within its ever-expanding fields of plunder and greed, it's hard to point our finger outward toward others without seeing it pointed back at us. The empire is them. The empire is us.

Unfortunately, the debris on the beach reminds me that the material world is not far from the oceanic realm. Just the opposite, it is deeply embedded there. Just a few days ago, NPR – with its annoying, predictable sound effects – reported on vast plastic plumes floating in the ocean ecosystem. Depressing.

Things change. Sometimes for the worse, other times for the better. Most often, change is mixed. We say this on the Israel-Palestine front where over the last months the Presbyterian divestment campaign ramped up. That's good. Quite belatedly, Christians are waking up to the violence of their tradition. At least some are. The committee handling the issue voted yes to divestment but the General Assembly voted it down by the smallest of margins, two votes. After the evening loss, the morning votes turned out to be more complex. Options of conscience were approved and various Israeli companies were admonished. I would call it a stalemate on one level but in the final analysis a victory for the forces of justice in Palestine.

The warfare is far from over. The violent wing of the Christian tradition still breathes fire and brimstone, but the Presbyterians on both sides of the divestment issue agreed that something is profoundly wrong with Israel's policies toward Palestinians.

A civil war within the Christian denominations is being waged over Israel and the rights of Palestinians. During the Shamir years few would have thought it possible that the interfaith ecumenical deal between Christians and Jews might be broken. Back then there wasn't any daylight between the Holocaust and the Jewish abuse of power. Christians were riding their high horse of repentance for anti-Semitism. It didn't matter that another people was suffering at Jewish hands. High level Jews didn't care. Why should they? Now all of that has changed. Christians have gone international in their justice concerns. The Empire and Progressive Jewish establishments have gone American – without a second thought.

The Uprising years were full of so much. Without romanticizing those difficult times, the mixture of despair and hope was palpable. The last chance was in the air. When the last

chance is in the air the energy is immense. Einstein time. The arc of the universe was bending toward justice.

No one stood on the sidelines. Strange as it might seem – and this includes the Presbyterian divestment debate – the lesson here is that you never know where history will take us. As Shamir sealed the fate of a Palestinian state, he planted the seeds for the explosion of the Jewish – and Christian – prophetic that we now witness.

Following the Presbyterian divestment debate online, I heard many at the microphones speaking the prophetic word on the plight of the Palestinians. It was deeply felt. I also noted the deeply divided Jewish contingent at the Presbyterian convention. Obviously the Jewish establishment was lobbying hard to keep these wayward Christians in line. But the line they sought to hold was way to the left of what anyone ever dreamed possible. Jews were also there conferring on the divestment side. They fought an uphill battle for a complete victory – but they shouldn't hang their heads. History will sort this out. Remember that the narrative of what Israel has done to Palestinians historically – what is happening today – has already been won by dissenting Jews. Few believe the "desert blooming" scenario or the "Jews are innocent/Palestinians are demons" mantra anymore. I didn't hear any of that language among the Presbyterians. Not a peep.

Crushing the Palestinian uprising ultimately sounded the death knell for the Jewish-Christian dialogue/cooperation/deal making. It has unraveled year by year. Though they continue, Holocaust memorialization – the engine of the interfaith ecumenical deal and now a major factor in trivializing the Holocaust itself – also started its downward slide then. The reasons are obvious. When it became clear that Israel as a state wasn't interested in justice for Palestinians and that Jewish leadership in America was only interested in silencing Christian misgivings about Israeli occupation policies, it was only a matter of time before the Jewish-Christian love fest came to an end.

Among the liberal Christian denominations, support for Israel is on life support. The back-up oxygen tanks, already in use, are running empty. There isn't any way of resurrecting the interfaith ecumenical deal. The "Christians are evil/Jews are innocent" genie is out of the bottle, never to return.

For the Jewish establishment, only rear-guard actions are left. They are playing the last cards in the Jewish/Christian deck. But what dissenting Jews – and Christians – hold is the prophetic wild card. That card is wholly different. It holds out the possibility of an entirely new relationship between Christians, Jews, Muslims and people of conscience wherever they are found. So we have the rear-guard. We have the novum. I choose the future.

The Christian civil war rages on. The Christian right-wing remains, of course. It has its highly paid emissaries, university presidents among them. Recently I've wondered if there ought to be an ethical bar to become president of a university. Or if there should be revised ethical guidelines for universities to receive Federal funds and for their faculty to belong to scholarly societies. Seriously, does a Christian university like the one I taught at, that is barred by charter from hiring Muslims, Hindus and Buddhists, not to mention Mormons, and has

among its stated reasons for expulsion from the university, fornication and homosexual acts – should that university be able to operate as if it is an educational institution in 21st century America?

I haven't even touched upon other political, economic and social policies supported by some educational administrators – unbridled capitalism, defense budgets beyond the ethical imagination and war waged indiscriminately. However, as an equal opportunity critic, I apply this to religious leaders as well. Many of our rabbis would do little better in a rating system involving these issues. If we're honest about it, the rabbinate has been a scandal on issues of war and peace – at least in relation to Israel and the Palestinians. Since "loving" Israel now includes a myriad of satellite issues attached to Israel's security – Iraq, Afghanistan, Pakistan and Iran is only the beginning of a wide and seemingly endless list – our rabbis are globally involved, most often on the wrong side of justice.

There are plenty of right-wing Jews eager to join the Christian right-wing chorus. They don't even have to be right-wing on any issue except Israel. Think Alan Dershowitz. How quickly he joins the empire creeds that abound. I think of these creeds as Empire doxologies, statements of faith which are objected to at one's own peril.

Do their creeds reach heaven? If so, I doubt God joins them in song. More likely God rejects them as idolatrous musings with murderous consequences. If there is a God.

The Jewish civil war is also in full bloom. It isn't only between the Empire and the Progressive Jewish contingent. Though they have their differences, in the main they share too much of the empire vision to be total adversaries. In fact, playing off one another, Empire and Progressive Jews share a stage large enough to hold them both.

While they duke it out in a staged choreography, the situation in Palestine continues to decline. The Palestinians reach bottom after bottom, until a cardinal belief emerges – at least I have held it for some time – that there is no bottom that cannot be broken through. Downward.

Thus the arrival of Jews of Conscience. The seeds for their arrival were also planted during the crucial Shamir years, after a delayed reaction. During the second Palestinian Uprising of the infamous Sharon years more than a few Jews recognized that the faux civil war between Empire and Progressive Jews was just that – fake. Jews of Conscience became serious about the high stakes in the game. It wasn't long before Jews of Conscience recognized South African apartheid in the mirror.

With apartheid staring Jews in the mirror there was no turning back.

Yasser Arafat on Star Street
BETHLEHEM

JULY 8

CHOSEN | KAIROS

Polonium – lethal stuff – and the *New York Times* reports that it was found on Yasser Arafat's clothing. "Death by poison" rumors have been around since Arafat's death in 2004. I assumed them to be true. Now, Palestinian leadership wants a full investigation. The conjecture is that Israel is the culprit. No doubt, Israel played its hand, as it often does, but there exists a history of collusion between the contesting parties. When I think through Arafat's death using a cost-benefit analysis, I arrive in some (un)expected places. How about you?

Arafat didn't know when to let go. Or he knew that letting go would mean his death. Either way it seems at some point there was no way out. Holding on to power is a full-time job. As we have seen recently, it doesn't always end well.

The blogosphere is filled with post-mortems on the Presbyterian divestment vote. It's humorous to read the anti-divestment pleas provided by Progressive Jews as – get this – providing fodder for anti-Semitism. I suppose we are to take from them that Jews who support divestment are pandering to the anti-Semites, an old canard that Empire Jews trot out to delegitimize Progressive Jews. Which, in turn, Progressive Jews then trot out to delegitimize those to the left of them. Sometimes I feel like I'm trapped in a never-ending Jewish "Wheel of Fortune:" the wheel spins, the letters are turned, then if I win – or lose – I return the next day for another round.

Shortly after Arafat's death the issue of his burial site was bantered about. Jerusalem was his preference, an obvious symbolic claim on Palestine, which Israel, of course, rejected as an obvious claim on Israel. The entire back and forth struck me in turn as demeaning and absurd. Then one night an idea struck me with particular force. It came to me in a dream which I awakened from with a jolt. A phrase ran through my mind: "Bury Arafat and Sharon together."

I wondered what this could possibly mean. Then it came to me. Why not bury Arafat in Jerusalem with his arch enemy, then Prime Minister, Ariel Sharon? Since they were so co-dependent that it was impossible for either to be understood without the other, they should be buried as they had lived – side by side. But then I thought – why stop there? Why not bury all of Israel's and Palestine's leaders together? They lived through each other, needed one another in war and peace, were visionary and corrupt together, sometimes opposed and collaborated with one another, let them rest in peace – together.

Now I wonder if the various sides of the divestment debate should be buried together too. Our final resting place is the end of our commitments and our stupidities. Knowing that we will spend eternity in adjoining plots perhaps our attitudes would be adjusted. With this

knowledge about our final resting place, would we be more just and conciliatory during our lives?

I return to yesterday's concluding image of South African apartheid in the mirror. A haunting image of what Jews have become. And what Jews could be again. Though often invoked in simplistic terms, South Africa is a complex image when viewed through the lens of Jewish history.

Last year I traveled to South Africa with my son, Aaron, to attend a conference celebrating the 25th anniversary of the Kairos Document. Written during the struggle against apartheid, the document signified an important break in South African Christianity. You see many white South African Christians saw apartheid as a Christian system. Yes it was understood that way, more or less like the slave system in the United States was or the hunger for the return of a white Christian America today. This understanding was rejected by the authors of the Kairos Document. They saw apartheid as a system of deprivation, violence and systemic injustice. The Christians of the Kairos Document named apartheid as a Christian heresy. The only way forward for Christians was to dismantle apartheid. It became part of their Christian mission.

That was then. Pervading the celebratory conference was a sense of sadness, of promises unfulfilled. The new South Africa has its own problems, mostly class and power issues rather than racial ones. Many at the conference had struggled against apartheid. Now they ask whether the new South Africa has become an oppressor state. The poor remained poor. Those in power feed themselves at the expense of others.

The complexities of revolutionary change are obvious to those who read history. Revolutionary change usually isn't revolutionary, a lesson we are learning once again with the Arab Spring. But the South African image Jews of Conscience see in the mirror has less to do with the new South Africa than with Israel as an apartheid state and the challenge to any apartheid state: one person, one vote. One person, one vote would mean the inclusion of Palestinians as equal citizens in one state. It would mean the end of the Jewish state and the birth of Israel-Palestine as a democratic, secular state.

For years Palestinians called for such a state and then, seeing that path blocked, reverted to two states for two peoples. Now, with almost no land or control in Jerusalem and the West Bank left to speak of, many Palestinians demand an undivided Palestine. This was Shamir's nightmare. This is Netanyahu's nightmare. It is also the nightmare of Progressive Jews.

The Israel-Palestine discourse scene today features conferences on the One State option, the latest being at Harvard some months ago. Incidentally, though surrounded by Alan Dershowitz's bellicose hullabaloo and even a videoed meltdown by his arch enemy, Norman Finkelstein, the conference was rather staid. No protests outside. No yelling inside.

I attended the conference and thought it interesting primarily for its political ramifications. To be honest, there wasn't much analysis to be found there. The Harvard conference mostly featured rhetorical posturings. Political talking points were the order of the day. Mostly the speakers countered political talking points they didn't agree with, even

those close to them which they judged as not quite passing muster. Though important, political talking points limit the discussion of real issues.

I've also noticed that there is a One State elite group that travels from conference to conference. The One State group features its own "universal" signage. No particularities are allowed. The Palestinian discourse features Palestinians as global citizens – only – and the Jewish discourse is likewise void of Jewishness. I agree with many viewpoints presented by this group, but really who's kidding who? There aren't two more self-involved peoples on the planet than Palestinians and Jews. Shouldn't we celebrate – and critique – where we come from, if only to understand more fully the ramifications of where we want to end up?

My sense is that the main thrust of the One State option from the Palestinian side is to limit what Palestinian leaders can do with their birthright. That is, Palestinian intellectuals fear that Palestinian leadership – mostly self-appointed and to their mind corrupt and collaborationist – will sell Palestine out for some spare land and a little spare change. They might be right.

The Jewish participants are mostly Israeli Jews who have left Israel or will do so soon. Jewish Israelis are increasingly of interest. They are the Jewish boots on the ground. They have seen and participated in what most American Jews cannot believe to be true – that Israel is thoroughly imbued with an empire mentality that sees its destiny as the Lord of the Middle East forever and ever. Amen.

Yet another Empire doxology! But increasingly, Jewish Israelis refuse to parrot a rote belief in their (fragile) empire structure. In leaving Israel, they become the vanguard of the Jewish people. When they leave Israel they deflect their identification of being Israeli or even being Jewish. Yet they are so Israeli and so Jewish!

More about these Israelis in the future. The point about South Africa is that it provides a mirror image of Jews outside Jewishness. South Africa points to what Jews have become without referencing Jews, Jewish history or Jewish destiny. Of course, Jews in apartheid South Africa were players on both sides of the Empire Divide, as Jews often are in history. On the one hand, South African Jews milked the apartheid system for everything they could find. On the other, Jews fought against apartheid, giving their treasure and blood for the cause. The mirror image that comes to Jews today has little to do with South African Jews – and everything to do with American and Israeli Jews. The haunting aspect of the image for Jews is that it is Jewless. Herein lies its liberating potential as well.

With a caveat. There is no evidence in Jewish history that Jews have ever thought of themselves as simply another people or with a destiny like others. Though it's difficult to absorb in our deceptively secular "universal" age, Jews have never thought of themselves as a randomly organized community with no destiny at all, perhaps as others might think of themselves, or at least as Jews, consciously or not, think that others think of themselves. Bear with me.

Whether justified or not, throughout history Jews have had a particular sense of themselves, first as God's chosen people, then morphing into different strands of chosenness.

This tradition continues with the Holocaust as a peculiar but, in light of Jewish history, quite understandable, sense of being singled out. The Holocaust narrative embraced by a majority of Jews is chock full of chosenness and, tied to the Holocaust, the state of Israel too has acquired this designation.

Jewish chosenness can be explained in a variety of ways. Being singled out among the nations – the same theme as chosenness with and without God language - is an intrinsic way of understanding what it means to be Jewish. Anti-Semitism, the Holocaust and Israel are modern stand-ins for the Biblical sense of a special destiny for Jews. In all, Jews are chosen/singled out. That is why strictly political language on any of these issues is by and large deflected by Jews as being beside the point. Obviously, this can be used to assume an aura of unaccountability. Nonetheless, chosenness is a deep well from which Jewish argumentation, and dissent, draws.

Whether anti-Semitism, the Holocaust or the state of Israel is unique is secondary to the embraced perception. So whether or not Jews are chosen/special/singled out is less important than the centrality of each to Jewish identity. In my view, Jews of Conscience illustrate this as much as Empire and Progressive Jews. What's different is how this perception works its way in the world. In what direction being chosen/special/singled out takes us makes all the difference.

Difference makes the world go round. The direction we take our Jewish identity means everything. It is our stake in Jewish history. It is our stake in the world.

We can argue the point of chosenness vigorously, as often happens. Yet the argument itself is the point. The challenge of chosenness is a perennial in Jewish history. The struggle over Israel and the debates about the lessons of the Holocaust confirm this understanding. So, in my view, the One State option is way more complicated than the rhetoric allows.

This isn't to imply that the Two State option is simple. After all, Shamir and his ilk made such a solution academic and regressive. It serves now as a fig leaf for Israel expansion. For decades, perhaps since 1967, there has been only one state. That state runs from Tel Aviv to the Jordan River. It is controlled by Israel. The expanded state of Israel has millions of Jews within its borders. And millions of Palestinians, too.

Which brings me back to South Africa and the image Jews see in the mirror. South Africa is us. South Africa isn't us. In the end the South Africa image cannot save us from ourselves. No one can save Jews except Jews. If it isn't too late.

Kairos is Greek, meaning a highly charged moment that must be seized. It is a point of conversion. The road ahead is blocked and there is, as well, no return to the past. We have to choose.

Though it is always risky to compare, in some ways Jews are in a more difficult place that the South Africans were decades ago. Jewish history rolled the Jewish state dice and then expanded the state until there was no way to retreat. Today, Israel is like a modern Sparta. The bridges toward a just inclusion in the Middle East as a nation among nations, recognizing a real Palestinian state, are burned.

What power Jews of Conscience have is mostly rhetorical. Does Israeli state power render a Jewish kairos moment moot?

A Kairos Moment
FLORIDA

JULY 9

TRAVELING JEWISH

Word on the Congolese street is that our intrepid French decolonizer, Victoria Fontan, who I will write about in the near future, attended a Pentecostal church service there. Being an intensely secular daughter of the French republican tradition, she was shocked by some of what she saw and heard as Jesus Christ was extolled for more than two hours. If you're not into something like that, church can feel like eternity itself. Then it got interesting. Israel entered the picture as the featured guest of all things good surrounded by all things evil, which no doubt translated into Palestinians.

As I've often thought, in the end there will only be two supporters of Israel around the world, the Jewish establishment and evangelical Christians. When you think of how evangelical Christians celebrate Israel, the (un)reality should strike fear into every living Jew and Palestinian. Along with a boatload of others, including those Americans who watched the Republican primary debates this spring. The debates were an "I love Israel more than you" competition. "And by the way, nuke Iran." So (un)real.

I can't remember whether she saw an Israeli flag in the church, as is often the case. But lo and behold, on my walk today to pick up some errant food items I noticed the American flag proudly being flown in front of a home. Then I noticed another flag right beside it – the Israeli flag. I took a picture as I have of the rabbi's home – the mezuzah on the beach. Perhaps a book cover to be, both pictures side by side.

Kairos, the right or opportune moment. If South Africa is not us but only the image we see reflected back in the mirror, as in – we are on the verge of becoming, or have become, everything we loathed about our oppressors – then as Jews who are we? If kairos is Greek and Kairos documents abound, migrating now to Palestine and recently to America as Christian responses to the heresy their co-religionists propogate, what time is Jewish time? What, Jewishly-speaking, is the right or opportune moment?

First, let's step back for a moment. It isn't clear to me at all that bad behavior on the part of Christians is aberrational or heretical. Not by a long shot. The civil war among Christians moves to the very heart of the way Christians have practiced their faith historically. So much of that history has been violent toward Jews, but that is only part of Christianity's amazingly violent history. In fact, a majority of Christians around the world were conquered by Christianity or, as I often think of it, they were "conquered by the Gospels." If violence has been with Christianity since its founding, it is a stretch to call it heretical. When does heresy become the norm? When we label actions heretical is it a call to reform a faith community or the need to create something radically new?

Perhaps this isn't the time to think about Christianity in negative terms. Let the present-day good stuff roll. It's easy for Jews to get off cheap shots at Christian history. Easy target! The hard truth is that parts of Christianity have a taken global turn for the better and are content to leave the Ken Starr's of our world to draw their million-dollar-plus salaries. Christians interested in global justice are fighting the right-wingers tooth and nail. Even if part of their fight is to prove to themselves and others that Christianity took a wrong turn eons ago, what the hell, let's root them on. Besides, there is a lesson here for Jews, since we are taking the exact same wrong turn that Christians took more than fifteen hundred years ago. This may be part of our newly acquired empire fate. Fifteen hundred years from now we may be arguing whether being Jewish isn't violence, injustice and atrocity – only.

This argument is already brewing. Wherever I travel the reception of Jewishness is difficult at best. Admittedly, I often travel off the global Jewish track. Most Jews today hardly wander beyond America's shores. Europe is as far as most will go. Even in Europe it's tough sledding. If you really want a Jewish workout try Pakistan, Malaysia, Australia, South Africa or almost anywhere else on the globe. Few want to hear about "Jewish." Fewer still about the Holocaust. Israel is considered a pariah. In relation to Israel, the most frequent word I hear applied is genocide. The reference is to Palestinians, not the Holocaust.

But what do they know, I hear the doyens of the Jewish establishment (safely tucked away in New York and Los Angeles) speak in unison. Of "Jewish" they know little, I respond. However, what they do know is not far off. It isn't fantasy or made up. I can and sometimes do advise my interlocutors of the nuances that might make some difference in their thinking. However, I don't try to turn them around. I listen to the line they've drawn in the sand. That line is freedom for Palestinians. I share that line.

Besides genocide, another word routinely applied to Israel is "colonialism." By association, colonialism is also applied to "Jewish." As in, Israel is, Jews are - colonial. Reality and myth become one. Disentangling the two without losing the main thread is almost impossible. Is it worth the time and effort?

Especially when the jetlag kicks in, I wonder. Yet when I speak the truth as a Jew, the audience's built-up anger often gives way to a hope that the Jewish community is divided and that the struggle within the Jewish community is real. Then I wonder if such a hope is real, if my own expression of what I see and want doesn't function as a panacea that serves as a cover to protect Jews and Israel. That's the modus operandi of Progressive Jews. I can't abide stupid things said about Jews. I want to avoid using a fake honesty to cover our injustice.

Parenthetically, I don't delude myself into thinking that Jews of Conscience transcend other parts of the Jewish world. I experience Empire and Progressive Jewish sensibilities within me. I want to be empowered. I want to cover over the realities of what we are doing. I want to be honest. I also want another way. The only way forward is through a brutal honesty. This is how I claim my Jewishness. But it is certainly not because I am above or have transcended the Jewish condition. Claiming my Jewishness is a choice. It also carries a cost.

The Jewish establishment has more or less given up on the world outside of America.

Years ago the newly minted countries emerging from the colonized world were lost to Israel, then more and more of Europe. Now Israel – with America by its side – stands alone in the world. Exempting, of course, Germany, Israel's great friend, who proudly provides nuclear-able submarines for Israel's navy.

What a great friend Israel has in Germany. Israel is being armed to the teeth by the country that provided industrial mass death for Jews without losing any sleep over it. Until it was over. I wonder if Germany – and America – is preparing Israel for another round of fatedness, this time through an "unbreakable" friendship.

So kairos, that Greek moment, translated into Jewish. Or is it the other way around? Regardless, we know it well. Kairos translated into Jewish is the prophetic, the indigenous of the people Israel.

Road Warnings
CAPE CANAVERAL

JULY 10

THE JEWISH WHEEL OF FORTUNE

If memory serves, it was Elie Wiesel who wrote to a Palestinian that Jews can't hate. Meaning, unlike Palestinians, of course. Read this email I received yesterday and ask if Jews can hate:

> Yes, Israel should have had ghetto Jews like you as leaders, we surely would have gone far. I just love the way you anti-Zionists portray yourselves as the epitome of Jewish ethics. So ethical, you demonize Jews every day. You are the pure Jews, we are all fascists. I am the son of an Auschwitz survivor and a former combat soldier in the IDF. To me, the lot of you, Silverstein, Weiss, are KAPOS.

I don't know which Silverstein and Weiss he refers to (although he probably refers to Phil Weiss and Richard Silverstein). They may be stand-ins for other people he knows or this may be a recycled email my email interlocutor mails various Jews whom he disagrees with. He simply forgot to change the names that are embedded in his mind. Not to get down on my email buddy, since in somewhat more sophisticated language I've heard more or less the same accusations on university campuses by super-sophisticated Jewish and Holocaust Studies folks. Local Jews also have Israel on their brain. When local Jews saunter into university president offices to have my – or your – head, academic freedom and every other civil code flies out the window. The accusatory emails are the tip of the hate iceberg. Believe me – I know what I am talking about.

Everyone has a right to their opinion. However, if you were sitting on the fence about whether there is a Jewish civil war, I hope you just fell off. As if there isn't enough evidence around us. This includes Elie Wiesel's full page paid statements in major newspapers preening about Jerusalem as the eternal capital of the Jewish people.

Credit where credit is due, though, since my email interlocutor probably didn't grow wealthy off his commentary on the Holocaust and Israel. Though he, like Wiesel, no doubt supported the invasion of Iraq, hopes for the bombing of Iran and probably supports a myriad of other covert wars to de-develop the Arab world. My email buddy also probably didn't have a fortune to lose in the Madoff scandal like Wiesel did.

The people who send these emails usually aren't high flyers. I alson wouldn't worry about Wiesel's financial situation if I were you. There is plenty of money to be made when you are on the right side of the Holocaust/Israel divide. When you lose a bundle, there is more to be had. Much more.

Demonizing Israel is my email friend's fantasy. I am not an anti-Zionist, a Zionist or a post-Zionist. My practical position is that the best solution for now is two real states, that is Israel within the 1967 borders and a Palestinian state on the West Bank and Gaza with East Jerusalem as its capital. As we know, the decision for a One State solution was made by Israel's military and settlement policies. Like most Jewish dissidents, I'm just watching Israel's wheels go round and round. I speak and write without any power to change Israel's course.

Where Auschwitz and the IDF are really taking Jews is another story. They have taken Jews into the geography of oppression. Have they also taken us into the night of our own destruction? Time will tell. We might know soon.

My favorite emails are harsher than the one quoted above. These are the ones that proffer that it would be best if I and others like me had died in the Holocaust. Other Jewish dissidents have the same experience. Ask Women in Black and the places they have been offered as their final resting place. Or check with those who demonstrate before Israeli consulates in the United States. The discussion isn't rational and, for the most part, it is conducted by the uninformed. The Israel raised up isn't the real Israel. It's a mythical place where Jews dwell somewhere outside history. For American Jews, that is, most of whom haven't even visited the country of their dreams. Why spoil the dream with an infusion of reality?

No, Israel isn't worse than other nations. It isn't better either. Notice how the Jewish establishment has used the bait-and-switch. First, Israel was better, now it is no worse. Israel is simply being attacked. Or about to be attacked. Message: Leave Israel alone. Notice that the content of Israel is no longer discussed even by its most ardent supporters. Meanwhile the critical narrative of Israel's founding in the ethnic cleansing of Palestinians written by Palestinian historians and over the last decades by the new Israeli historians is accepted around the world as the real history of Israel. We need to take note of that. It's huge for the future.

Have you noticed that with every political setback Jewish dissenters experience, the Israel-Palestine narrative victory is more assured? The narrative victory is important for a variety of reasons, but primarily because the ultimate judge of power is history. And one day soon even the Jewish community will have to accept that Israel's original sin was the ethnic cleansing of Palestine. In the very near future, Jewish identity will revolve around the Holocaust, Israel and the plight and possibility of Palestinian history. Which is to say that Jewish identity will revolve around two afters – after the Holocaust and after Israel.

By after Israel I mean after what Jews have done and are doing to Palestinians. This second after is the game changer Jews of Conscience have been waiting for – it's what Jews of Conscience are living. Embodying the two afters isn't easy. Who wants to be involved with such folks, especially when living the Holocaust after has become so easy, so successful and makes us so unaccountable. Revisiting the Presbyterian divestment debate – and all the other divestment struggles – isn't that what the argument is really about – adding the second after?

So let's get real. If you watched the Presbyterians question their financial officers, as in, how much of our money is involved in a possible divestment, according to my calculations

the sum was in the tens of millions of dollars. The entire Presbyterian investment portfolio – if I heard it correctly – was reported to be in the neighborhood of seven billion dollars. When I heard these figures in their respective order I was shocked at how little money was at stake and then how heavily invested this Christian justice-oriented denomination is in American and global capitalism.

Did anyone hearing this vast investment portfolio have the same questions I had? In the first place, the sum to be divested was symbolic in terms of the companies affected. In the second place, no matter how the vote went, Presbyterians weren't risking anything in the financial realm. Don't get me wrong, I think symbolism is important and the divestment debate is fascinating, another step in the narrative road of discovering our flaws and possibilities. Nonetheless, we can't skip over the alarming nature of Christian conformism to power and the benefits they derive therefrom.

The various industrial complexes that initially seemed far away on my beach walks are embedded in Christian and Jewish life. You cannot make a hundred grand and more a lecture, as Wiesel often does, or have a multi-billion dollar portfolio as the Presbyterians have without being part and parcel of the destruction of our planet. Of all the debating points, the Presbyterian portfolio made the biggest impression on me. How about a discussion of divesting all of that money on a variety of fronts? Wouldn't that make a huge splash around the world, including in Israel and Palestine?

And yes since I am being honest, I note that some of the divestment community – I am thinking of two leaders of European divestment I spent time with a few years ago – are unreconstructed anti-Semites. One of them wouldn't utter the word Holocaust – or Israel. The other had a Jewish world domination conspiracy model that was so retrograde and disgusting that I paid for my own hotel rather than accept his repeated invitations to bunk at his house. Interestingly, he couldn't understand my insistence on the hotel. He thought I was being a prima donna.

Just between us, I prefer crude email companions to sophisticated anti-Semites. But, of course, painting the divestment movement with the broad brush of anti-Semitism is the flip side of the sophisticated anti-Semites that think they're so above baiting Jews. Again, the Jewish Wheel of Fortune has boatloads of historical baggage. Sometimes I want to check out other community games and see if they are easier to play. Speaking of BDS, word is out of another "Norman" interview that accuses the movement of having a cult-like status. I don't see it that way at all. Some of it is deep political activism. Other parts are superficial glosses on identity formations. And Finkelstein should be aware that his own persona runs the cult danger he accuses BDS of. Veterans of dissent should know when their contribution has been made and allow history – and new voices – to emerge. New voices have a right to speak and be heard without being accused of usurpation or deviation. Finkelstein deserves respect for the work he's done. His disaffected cult-like members have their own critical reflecting to do.

Israel-Palestine has changed over these last decades. As I say, the last chance is in the air. When the Jewish Wheel of Fortune spins its last chance everyone is on edge. But look how

much we miss when we aren't paying attention. As in, the Presbyterian capitalism buy-in. As in, anti-Semitism still exists. As in, the Palestinian situation continues to deteriorate. As in, the torch is being passed to a new generation of Jews of Conscience. As in, the continual need for critical thought and evaluation.

At the local library here – mostly catering to DVD check-outs and computer use, with chattering even by librarians the rule rather than the exception – there are also good books. One I'm reading now is a biography of the American painter, Andrew Wyeth. Commenting on his use of tempera, a much rougher medium than his already popular watercolors, a critic wrote: "These are very savage paintings, scraped and beaten. I see the anger under there."

We shouldn't underestimate the amount of anger that surrounds the Israel-Palestine issue, and how that anger works itself into every nook and cranny of our lives. There's lots of anger to go around on the Jewish Wheel of Fortune. Every place the needle lands.

Rev. Jeremiah A. Wright, Jr.
CHICAGO

JULY 11

JEWISH (EMPIRE)
GEOGRAPHY

Beautiful morning. Low tide. Swimming in the ocean. Cool water. Before the heat. Dealing with anger. George Harrison's admonition running through my mind: "Beware of darkness." Translated Jewishly: beware of exile?

Again, particularity rather than the universal is important here. Though exile is also universal. So many individuals and communities have felt exile's sting. Still exile has a certain resonance in Jewish history. Or rather, it is essential to Jewish identity. Like the prophetic. Though it is secondary to the prophetic, since without the prophetic, how can we discern meaning in exile?

Jewishly speaking, exile is darkness. It can also be light. Jewishly speaking, exile is never frivolous. There's a reason for exile. Punishment is one reason. Exercising the prophetic is another.

I can hear it now and appropriately so: The issue of Palestine is not about Jews. About the Jewish ethical tradition or about the loss and possible recovery of the Jewish soul. I agree. That's Progressive Jews' naval gazing. The "politics of meaning."

But then look at the place Norman Finkelstein has landed. He's so taken with the idea of international law that he's trapped there. The argument between BDS and Finkelstein seems trapped there, too. Which side better represents the thrust of international law, as if that law had been handed down from heaven? Is international law carved on Sinai-like tablets?

The admonition here is clear, at least to me: Don't get stuck in any ism – International Law(ism), Universal(ism), Particular(ism). Why not use them all, mixing and matching, where one enhances the other, multiplying the possibilities of justice around the corner. Because none of them as they are has provided much leverage, politically speaking. Or, to be honest, all of them combined. When we realize that we have lost everything and that there is no victory on the horizon, we are free to spread our wings and fly to our next destination.

Contradictions are everywhere. Appealing to Presbyterians who aren't risking anything in their material world. Often linking with other Jews who aren't risking anything in their material world. Infighting about International Law/BDSers. Two states versus one state. Struggling together, we shouldn't demand a purity of arms. As if any of us have a lock on purity.

This infighting leaves us stuck somewhere and sometimes everywhere. Being stuck is a blind alley. You have to think again.

Being stuck encourages anger. The longer one is stuck, the more the anger. Being stuck

in anger means we argue for positions that we wouldn't ordinarily argue for. We've all been there. When it happens we need a prodding. We have to move on.

The singular and then evolving configuration of our stance on politics has to be complimented by a deeper engagement – a deeper encounter – with our backgrounds, and the primal sense of who we are and what we should be about in life. This geography of essences is disputed territory, specifically, the issue of essentialism, which in terms I can understand, means simply the question of whether or not there is some kind of enduring substructure to our identity. For example, is there an essence to Jewish identity? Are there primal areas of Jewish identity which, more or less, are unchanging or, in different contexts, orients the change that different environments demand? Like chosenness/special destiny/being singled out. Like exile. Like the prophetic.

Obviously I am going against the modernist grain here. Yet from my vantage point – and in my personal journey – it is clear that there are thoughts and actions, intentional trajectories, that are colored by our backgrounds/inheritance/history/culture/foundational texts and so on. I certainly don't agree with Harold Bloom's sensibilities that American – or Jewish – culture is in a downward spiral and that without the classics, culture is doomed. That is a superficial sense of identity formation.

What is fascinating about Jewishness is that the classics, for Jews that is usually considered to be the writings of the rabbi's gathered in the Talmud, is somehow within our Jewish being regardless of our specific "Jewish" knowledge. Rather than the rabbinic writings, our classic is the Bible, specifically the Biblical prophets. Jews "know" these prophets without having a detailed knowledge of them individually. Learning about the Biblical prophets is an add-on, a way of learning why we are like we are. This means that the prophetic is already there within Jews.

How the prophetic gets there is an interesting question. I have thought a lot about this over the years. How is it that the Jewish prophets of today are, more or less, like the Jewish prophets who roamed the earth thousands of years ago? We can try to explain it sociologically, culturally and in a myriad other ways, all of which are of interest. All need to be factored in. Taken together, however, they fall short. These reasons also cannot explain the explosion of the Jewish prophetic in our time, against the grain and against our own best interests.

After the Holocaust especially, why would Jews of Conscience rail against the abuse of Jewish power, especially when embracing that power is their gateway to affluence and acceptance? It just doesn't make sense, Jews coming out of the Jewish woodwork to say "Not In My Name!"

Most Jews of Conscience today would do extremely poorly on a Jewish "literacy" test. Equally fascinating – and telling – these Jewish literacy tests are specifically aimed at defusing the primal aspects of the prophetic Jewish identity that Jews of Conscience embody. The educational efforts of Empire Jews and Progressive Jews as well is precisely to tame the Jewish primal prophetic and convince them that the prophet's companion, exile, is not what

it is cracked up to be.

Think of the self-rabbinic coronation some years ago of Arthur Waskow and Michael Lerner. One month I flip through the pages of *Tikkun* and read the always extensive editorial of Michael Lerner. The next month I flip through the pages of *Tikkun* and read the still extensive editorial of Rabbi Michael Lerner. Voila!

Progressive Jews got caught up in the Jewish Renewal movement to improve their Jewish literacy. In doing so, they lost their prophetic edge. True, they chanted newly learned Hebrew prayers and gathered for organic Shabbat celebrations. In turn, the cutting edge of the Jewish Left was grounded into a smooth surface. They thought it was better to do "battle" with the Jewish establishment on their own turf. Huge mistake.

Establishments are not about authenticity. They're about power. All establishments. I remember being called in by Arthur Waskow when he heard I was writing a Jewish theology of liberation. He informed me that he was *the* Jewish theologian of liberation. No trespassing allowed!

In Catholic terms, playing the authentic card is like taking on the Vatican. To do this you have to become more Catholic than the Pope. Over the last decades, this has been more or less what we have witnessed: who is "really and authentically Jewish," the Empire Jewish establishment or the would-be next Jewish establishment led by Progressive Jews? How do you feel about replacing Edgar Bronfman with Michael Lerner? Or Elie Wiesel with Arthur Waskow? I'm not going there.

To my mind, the struggle over "authentic" Jewishness is a vast illusion, apes Christian piety and dulls deep thought into a return to a virtual Jewish summer camp reality show. Now everyone should do what they need to do, including improving their knowledge of Judaism, but to follow the rabbinic model of either the Empire or Progressive Jewish establishments is a dead end.

Why sign on to the elites of either of the establishments since they are both fated, one to be remembered as war mongers, the other as leading a failed movement on the verge of extinction. In the end, there will be only two major groupings in Jewish life, Empire Jews and Jews of Conscience. As well, most Jews won't be connected with either group. That's another illusion – "the Jewish community."

Which isn't to down Waskow or Lerner. They did their thing for their time. Personal and cultic excesses aside, however, they made a wrong turn and brought many people with them. The wrong turn was being more "Jewish" in a certain defined way – a kind of New Age rabbinic search for meaning and connection with a justice-edge sensibility. In practice it meant dulling the prophetic impetus, which the rabbinic system in its original formation had already accomplished. Why the Jewish renewal movement thought that dressing the old up with the new would change its dismissal of the prophetic, I have no idea. It may be related more to the cult of personality than lack of thought, though the two may be tied together. Anyway, the *Tikkun* phase of the Jewish Left is over. In the end it became the Left-wing of Empire Judaism.

Why loiter here? It's on to the next phase. But first, another memory. Several years ago, against the odds, I was asked to serve on the Board of the Society of Jewish Ethics. It's a long story but suffice to say that almost everything the SJE does programmatically is imbued with the rabbinic. This includes holding Shabbat services on Friday night and Saturday morning even though the SJE is an academic society and meets at an academic convention it shares with the much larger Society of Christian Ethics and more recently the Society of Islamic Ethics.

When I first understood that this was the way they operated I was shocked. Everyone dressed in ritual garb. Our food was catered (quite expensive) kosher. The demonstration of our Jewishness alarmed me. We wore it on our sleeves. Nonetheless I remained on the Board for three years. Most of the Board members were quite respectful of me. They even listened to my complaints.

One night I retired to my hotel room for some rest before dinner and heard noises from the street below. The conference was in Chicago. It was January 2009. When I looked out my hotel window, I saw a demonstration, several hundred strong, protesting the Israeli invasion of Gaza. At dinner that night the Board met to make sure everything was going right with the conference. We even spoke about the future. On the invasion of Gaza, silence. The Society of Jewish Ethics, good people, demonstrably Jewish. Silence.

Several years later, Reverend Jeremiah Wright was invited to speak by the Society of Christian Ethics. There wasn't silence then. In fact, all hell broke loose. The Board sent an emissary to complain about his appearance and what he said about Israel and Jewish power in the United States. A joint panel of both societies was arranged for the following year to soften the tone. As you might imagine, I wasn't asked to represent the "Jewish" point of view.

Perhaps the challenge is to decrease Jewish literacy. The most learned among us are too often the silent, the angry, the complicit. Have you noticed?

Silence on Gaza. Fury at Reverend Wright. So typical, it goes without saying. Without thinking, what in God's name is going on?

In terms of Jewish literacy, though, to end on a more positive note, did you see the new world Jewish population figures? A lesson in Jewish geography. Or a way of mapping Jewish history.

The demographics show 15.3 million Jews in the world. Can you guess the top five areas where Jews reside? The first two are obvious, the United States and Israel, followed by Argentina, with the Russian Federation ranking fifth. As Adam Horowitz points out, the fourth most populous Jewish area in the world isn't even a country. Think! Are you ready? Number four on the list is the Palestinian Authority – it is listed as such – with the citation coming from the CIA Factbook. Over 500,000 Jews in Palestinian territory. This was in 2007.

A bold step it is for the CIA to list the area as the Palestinian Authority, though this is clearly the case. What they don't say is that this particular population is a settlement population, a new nomenclature for Jewish demographics. So, just to let it sink in, after the

United States, Israel and Argentina, our most populous Jewish community is living within internationally recognized Palestine. And according to international standards these Jews are living there illegally.

So, with South Africa starring us in the mirror, let it fly: our fourth largest population concentration of Jews are illegal settlers. Now, at least from the Palestinian side, Israel's Jews might figure into that category as well. So rounding off Jewish demographics, from almost five to more than thirty percent of the world's Jewish population are illegal settlers or dominate a land that once was someone else's home. These are numbers to remember. What to do with these facts on the ground?

So often I hear both Jewish establishments talk about Palestinian demographics. The only discussion about Jewish demographics I hear relates to low birth rates and intermarriage. Should the world's Jewish demographics take on a new theme – Jews as illegal settlers?

Or how about this: counting America and Israel as empires on the global and regional scene, more than two/thirds of the world's Jewish population lives in empire. Ever heard that discussed and analyzed? No wonder Jewish identity is empire-oriented.

Map literacy. Jewish geography. Rather than Hebrew or rabbinic sources – no matter how progressive – perhaps this is the Jewish literacy we need.

Jewish professionals listen up. The title of our next conference is: "Confronting the Problem of Jewish Demographics." Topics to be discussed: Jewish birth rate, Jewish intermarriage, Jewish illegal settler population, Jews living in empire.

Divestment Writings on the Wall
WEST BANK

JULY 12

HOW DEEP
IS (Y)OUR COLONIAL MENTALITY?

There is some Presbyterian push-back on my divestment commentary. Do I, as a Jew, have a right to comment on Corporate Christianity? Some of the comments reference Jewish wealth. In the old parlance, Jewish money. It's a slippery slope, for sure, but, of course, have at it. See how you can address the question. Karl Marx wrote about Jewish finance. He did so within the broader issue of political change. The Jewish finance class was a pillar of an unjust state. Christianity had the enabling state religion part. Marx was equally critical of that pillar.

The more serious comments have to do with putting our money where our mouths are. Can't I understand the need for financial security, pension funds and the like? Besides, boat loads of money can be used for good – economic leverage, political change. If we aren't players in the larger scheme of things, we lose our power to help those on the margins. Perhaps.

Without having an answer, I am trying to think freely. I don't excuse myself from the dilemmas I can't solve. Yet the 7 billion dollar portfolio – again if I heard it right – still startles me. Especially when you balance it off the lilies of the field. I am not a Christian and don't want to be. I have been around Christians who have never had pensions or have given them up. There is something about these Christians that I take seriously. Many years ago I spent a year with Dorothy Day at the Catholic Worker house in New York City. She lived among the pensionless. She didn't have a pension.

When you are on the other side of power, even the power that seeks to rescue you, it must be difficult to understand the reluctance to give up everything to be of service to our neighbor. You can only feel this fully if you are in that position. Perhaps we've all been in that position in some aspect of our lives. I certainly have.

If I were a Palestinian listening to the Presbyterian votes on my fate – with the wonderful voting pad and colorful graphics showing the percentage of the votes cast – I wouldn't hold my breath waiting for others to come to my aid, even those with the best of intentions. Then to be betrayed by parts of your own Palestinian community, as is sometimes the case. Well, it must be somewhat like the Jews of Europe waiting on the world to act. Waiting on Jewish leadership to act. Often betrayed from within.

Remaining on the Presbyterian portfolio for another minute or two, what also struck me was how little control the Presbyterians have over their own finances. It seems that touching the portfolio is almost like tampering with the Gospels; it's safely packed away so the whims of the Christians assembled can't do anything rash. Like giving it all away. Or placing it all where justice is. As in any corporation, the foundational funds are out of anyone's controls except the delegated financial managers. Their responsibility is to a different bottom line

than what Jesus purportedly preached.

When religion goes corporate it should be analyzed in that way. Academically, the field is called the Sociology of Religion. The Sociology of Religion takes an atheological look at how religion functions. There are no sacred cows. I don't believe that how religion functions is everything we need to know about religion but without it we are stuck in pieties and prayers as another people's fate is decided.

Having said all this, I note how far parts of Christianity have advanced. How far ahead they've pulled of Jewish denominations! Or perhaps Christian and Jewish denominations are the same, split at the core, balancing money and commitment. When you're elites, you're elites. Few are willing to go the whole way. So Christians and Jews are in the same corporate boat. Like the home I passed with the American and Israeli flag flying. Missing is the Wall Street flag which, thank God, Jews and Christians can now fly together.

Yes, and now to the issue of "Jewish money." Some ask how I can criticize Corporate Christianity when there is so much Jewish money floating around the world, doing what money does, especially funding politicians of all stripes who will do their bidding in America and Israel. Too much money held by any institution or person is corrupting, Christian or Jewish. So go at it!

As we know, the notion of "Jewish money" has a long slippery-slope reality in history. Jews who don't know their place are legion and often they rub non-Jews the wrong way. Yet another slippery-slope in the historical arena. Maybe that's why the Presbyterian divestment folks voiced their love for Israel – because the Jewish thing in Christianity isn't really resolved.

Christianity has never had a real relationship with Jews or Judaism. We've either been devils or angels, either/or. Which we aren't – devils or angels. Obviously. Loved or hated, Jews remain an unresolved issue for Christians. However, I do give many Christians tremendous kudos for trying. Why not admit that Christians are ambivalent about Jews? Then we can continue to work our relationship out in honest ways.

Jews are ambivalent about Christians, too. We should admit that. After this long, dark and entangled history, ambivalent is a pretty good start on a new era.

So no free rides for Christians in their new justice garbs! And no free rides for Jews as we shed our justice garbs!

Other than the Presbyterian engagement/push back, the silence is deafening. But it's time to get over that. Any word now would be too late. It would only be a rear-guard action to deflect the necessary next step. As when Michael Lerner finally accepted that Oslo was dead after condemning anyone who didn't support it. At any rate, Progressive Jews are over. Even the Progressive Jew within us. It doesn't die easily, since that kind of Jewishness can have its cake and eat it too. It can accept its new found status in America, benefit from riding high in the economic sphere and spread the good word about us Jews being the great welcomers of all minorities and the best purveyors of justice in the history of the world. All the while, we can sponsor Jewish Renewal retreats that incorporate every Native American and Asian spiritual tradition – you name it – into Jewish ritual. As if it is ours.

I'm not exempting myself, the Zen-sitter in training. I've been sitting for many decades but at least I've kept it private. I sit by myself. And I realize that I am a Jew sitting Zen, rather than a Zen practitioner. I don't believe that Jewish ritual remains Jewish when it has become something else. Of course, most Jewish traditions come from somewhere else, they're not home grown, historically speaking. Mixing and matching isn't something new.

Historically, Jews have crossed boundaries. Crossing boundaries has been necessary if only to make sure that the various Jewish establishments didn't have the final say on what it means to be Jewish. The Jewish Renewal movement is just another example of how Jews survive the Jewish establishment and also create a Jewish way that is relevant to the time in which we live. So hats off to the Jewish Renewal movement of a (still) previous time!

In this mixing and matching of cultures and spiritual traditions, Jewish Renewal folks felt that they were honoring other peoples. No doubt they were honorable in their intentions. In practice, however, they usurped these traditions for Jewish use. The Jewish spiritual well had run dry. It's like Christian renewal movements after the Holocaust (re)appropriating their Jewishness to save them from their Holocaust credibility death knell. Some Christians now speak so lovingly about Jews and about Israel that as a Jew I can't find myself anywhere in their (parallel) Jewish universe. I suppose this is the reason that many of the Presbyterians who spoke on behalf of divestment prefaced their comments by saying how much they loved Israel.

"Loving" Israel – that's a remnant of the interfaith ecumenical deal that divestment is supposed to break. Sort of. If Christians ever let go of their love for Israel – whatever love can possibly mean in relation to a state – would they be back where they started, that is, with a fully shattered Christianity? In other words, would Christian credibility be verified only within their multi-billion dollar portfolios?

To escape the barren confines of the Jewish establishment, the Jewish Renewal movement went native. Interestingly, they didn't go Jewish indigenous. Jewish native. The unadorned, unritualized prophetic. Why did they go out when they could have gone deeper within?

When affluent and powerful cultures go native they expropriate the traditions they find so enhancing. Whatever their intentions, they ride roughshod over the native culture. The Jewish Renewal movement went colonial. They went colonial trying to escape the increasingly colonial attitudes of the Jewish establishment in Israel and America.

Colonial attitudes are found on the right and on the left. They are used to bury Others. They are used to rescue Others. Colonialism is used to distance us from Others and to bring the Other within. Regardless, Others are at our disposal. Colonial attitudes project outward because there seems to be little or nothing left within the culture that appropriates Others for its use.

As I've mentioned, there's a new book coming soon – watch for it! – by the French author, Victoria Fontan, who is still traveling in the Congo. Her working title – *Decolonizing Peace*. Her theory is that the academic field of Peace Studies and peace and development agencies around the world, including the United Nations, are so thoroughly imbued with

a colonial mentality that most of their work is thinly disguised Western missionary work.

Who does that missionary work benefit? That's another billion(s) dollar question. Fontan's answer: the West. Plus elites in non-Western societies. Anyway, the book is an indictment of "development" work in its various guises. Devastating stuff.

Right now Fontan is looking for a woman she met and spent time with during her last visit. The woman experienced the most harrowing reality of sexual violence most of us only read about in the newspapers. Real stuff. No pension plan.

Fontan draws on her experience with other Congolese women and features her other travels off the researchers' beaten track as well. And, yes, as an inheritor of that French republican tradition – also imbued with its own colonialism, of course – she doesn't pull any punches.

I've already recalled her critique of the United Nations, and my favorites bear repeating in case the reader skipped over the passages as a lark. The first is United Nation troops being supplied with trafficked girls and boys. The companies involved, the truckers paid, the night club owners welcoming, there's an entire matrix that hides the sex trade in broad daylight. It's akin to the occupation of Palestine, every corporate entity in Israel seeks the business that comes with occupation. More or less, like any occupation – or war – corporate portfolios fatten.

It's is a feat to behold. The double life there is amazing. Trafficked sex is for the night time. During the day the soldiers protect the population. Another favorite of mine is the story of a prominent female diplomat sleeping with a local leader to resolve a dispute. He even waved her panties the following day to show how the resolution kept his dignity!

So Fontan sets out to decolonize Peace Studies and development work around the globe. Bon chance, Victoria! And, of course, since she admits to being a product of the colonial mentality, she is trying to decolonize herself. Not an easy task, even for an heir of the French Revolution.

But returning to the Jewish scene, how thoroughly imbued with colonial mentalities we Jews are – on both sides of the Empire Divide. We can laugh – and should laugh – at Netanyahu's invocation of Thomas Jefferson. But have you ever read Michael Lerner on how Palestinians must guarantee Israel's security? Or how Palestinians have to demonstrate to Jews how they have reformed their retrograde culture? My personal favorite is the demilitarized Palestinian state in a region armed to the teeth. To the query of who will protect the borders of the demilitarized Palestinian state, Lerner's answer – you guessed it – the IDF!

If we wonder whether Netanyahu understands the implications of his July 4th invocation of Thomas Jefferson, how, then, can Lerner invoke Israel as the defenders of Palestine with a straight face? Indeed he does, which is a huge part of the problem. And even more, aside from my mostly unread writing, I have never read or heard this incredible assertion ever mentioned as a colonial sensibility right out of the annals of the White Man's Burden.

The Jewish White Man's Burden?

This is how acceptable colonial sensibilities are in the Jewish world. Not a peep from Jews of Conscience on this issue, who admittedly might be so fed up with Lerner and *Tikkun* that they don't want to hear his name. But, understanding that, the question still remains as to how deep the colonial is in Jewish identity, recognizing it and, depending on our explorations, what is to be done about it? It might be that the colonial is so embedded in Jewish identity that there is no way to get it out of our colonial mindset. If that is the case, which it might very well be, if we can't jettison the entire worldview, then what are we going to do with our colonial Jewish identity?

Do you remember the song, "How Deep is Your Love?" Well the refrain on the colonial level might be – very.

Karl Heinrich Marx
GERMAN PHILOSOPHER

JULY 13

SQUANDERED
BEGINNING AGAIN

Our Jewish colonial mentality. Best to admit it. Then filter it through Karl Marx, about whose life I'm reading in a new and very special book, *Love and Capital: Karl and Jenny Marx and the Birth of a Revolution,* by Mary Gabriel. The book is fascinating on a variety of levels, not the least of which is the discussion of Marx's Jewishness.

I also just picked up a biography of Thomas Paine from the local library. Paine has been one of my American – and French – revolutionary favorites since childhood. I just checked the index for his views on religion, which are, for the most part, negative, but, as with Marx, they are also complicated. Paine was against a religion that enabled state power. Good. He was also against the forced de-Christianization during the revolutionary years in France. Interesting. On the positive side of religion, Paine thought Christianity kept alive an ethical tradition that was vital to nurture republican democracy. On the Bible and the purveyors of religion he was scathing. But now, flipping through the pages, I see Paine being arrested by the French revolutionary authorities. A knock on his door during the night, then to prison he goes. A Deist on the run from the revolution! No mezuzah on Paine's door. No way. More on Paine as I delve deeper into his life.

The main theme of Gabriel's book on the Marx's is personal, combining the personal life of Marx and his family with their political writing and activities. I say "their" because his entire family was intensely political and active. The story of Marx's family history carries so much tragedy it is hard to imagine anyone surviving it. Most of his children and grandchildren didn't. Marx himself was a loving husband and father. His partnership with his wife, Jenny, is quite a ride. Their children are fascinating.

One way to understand Marx is through his attempt to decolonize his mind. By doing so he was able to cut through the layers of political and religious propaganda that limit options for justice in the world. His famous statement about religion being the opiate of the people could as well be applied to the colonial sensibility now so deeply embedded in Jewish identity. I cite again the lack of outrage over the proposal by Progressive Jews that the immediate heirs of the ethnic cleansers of the Palestinian people, Jewish Israelis, an ethnic cleansing that continues as I write, should be accepted as the protectors of the Palestinian people in their newly demilitarized state. This is accentuated by an encore performance that proposes that anyone who recognizes the obvious contradiction commits a cardinal sin. Amazing stuff, when we think more consciously about decolonizing our Jewish identity. What is obviously a colonial mentality doesn't even raise an eyebrow.

Of course, this is the major theme of any colonial mentality – the colonizer is innocent. That's how Jews think of themselves. I certainly grew up with this understanding. Most Jews

do. It's a constant battle to keep reminding ourselves, even after we have reached the aha moment, that, no, we Jews are not innocent. As importantly, we have to constantly remind ourselves that we are not going to return to that innocence. There is no way back.

The sense that Jews are innocent or could return there was the great promise held out by Progressive Jews. It is the reason they attracted so many Jews to their cause. They preserve Jewish innocence by admitting that the the post-1967 occupation is wrong. By correcting this mistake, Jews return to innocence. Jews symbolize their innocence by wearing a colorful kippah and/or by affixing a larger than life mezuzah on our door post. The IDF can protect the Palestinian borders since the IDF – in its essence – is the only fighting force in the world that is innocent. How can that be? Because Jews are innocent.

Purity of arms: Israel alone has a fighting force that doesn't want to fight, fights only when Israel is attacked and only aggresses as far as it needs to while protecting Jewish lives. You have to be my age to remember that assertion. No one makes it any more. (Un)Purity of Arms. It's true everywhere, including Israel.

Once we step back from our colonial gaze, it all becomes too obvious. And shameful. Thinking about these issues while reading Gabriel's book, she cites two quotes from Marx that bear repeating. The first relates to how our naiveté will be judged: "Hegel remarks that all facts and personages of great importance in world history occur, as it were, twice. He forgot to add: the first time as tragedy, the second as farce." Think of the history of the state of Israel. Think of the leaders of 1948 being involved in a tragic situation. Now think of present day Israeli leadership and Netanyahu as farce.

The second quote from Marx that Gabriel highlights is how history deals cards which we then have to play. Or rather, cards are dealt. We decide which cards we play in response. Here is Marx: "Men make their own history, but they do not make it just as they please; they do not make it under circumstance chosen by themselves, but under circumstance directly encountered, given and transmitted by the past." I add that in the Jewish civil war, Jews of Conscience are dealing with cards dealt by non-Jews in history, as well as with a Jewish state that acts in the name of Jews everywhere. Add to these the cards played by the various establishments that also claim to act in the interests of Jews everywhere.

Our Jewish inheritance is complicated. Our Jewish now is complicated. So I might paraphrase Marx in relation to the task of Jews today: "Jews make our own history, but we do not make it just as we please; we do not make it under circumstance chosen by ourselves, but under circumstance directly encountered, given and transmitted by Jews past and present." Or more specifically in terms of Jews of Conscience and now somewhat extended: "Jews of Conscience make our own history, but we do not make it just as we please; Jews of Conscience do not make it under circumstance chosen by ourselves, but under circumstance directly encountered, given and transmitted by Jewish history, the Holocaust, the state of Israel and the various Jewish establishments that have bequeathed an impossible situation which we must account for and work through."

Now listen to Marx on the Jewish question, a controversial issue historically. It is often

played back against Marx himself, accusing him of anti-Semitism. The Jewish question remains today, albeit in a somewhat different form. How different and in what way is an important issue. Here is how Gabriel succinctly sums up Marx on the Jewish question:

> In his treatise [on the Jewish question] Marx considered how religion was used in day-to-day affairs in Germany, whether that be Christianity in the political arena or Jewish dominance in the marketplace, and what freedom from religion would mean in nontheological terms. He argued in the case of Jews, their main activity, finance, had become integral to the state's very existence and concluded that liberating Jews from the confines of that commercial activity (which had, he felt, become the essence of Judaism), and thereby depriving the state of its benefit, would precipitate the German revolution he sought. The state could not stand if one of its pillars – in this case finance – crumbled: the government Marx and his fellows despised would collapse.

Not simple to paraphrase but taking it seriously let's see where we end up. Again thinking from the standpoint of Jews of Conscience, first we have to expand the areas of Jewish dominance, at least areas where Jews are prominent today. Finance continues unabated but Jews are everywhere in American society and, of course, in Israel. In the (extended)military/industrial complex, Jews are prominent. Including now in official political and governmental roles. "Liberating Jews from the confines of commercial activity" has to be greatly expanded. So, too, then, what is viewed as the "essence of Judaism" has to be expanded. Depriving the state of Jewish talent would be all encompassing in America. It's obviously impossible in the state of Israel.

Israel ups the ante considerably. Has it altered the Jewish question beyond what Marx could have ever imagined? In Marx's time the Jewish community dominated one pillar of the German state, finance. The American Jewish community is so integrated into the American state that pillars are more apt. But in Israel, Jews are the state. In Israel, then, Jews as pillars of the state have to distinguish between Jews who form the elite of the state in economic, military, political, intellectual and social terms and the mass of Jews who have various relations to the elite.

Thus the movement of Jews in relation to social change in America and Israel is complicated. It has to do with many factors, including where segments of Jews place themselves in relation to the societies they live in and to Jews within those societies. Then we have the empowered minority and empowered majority situation in America and Israel respectively, the interaction of Jewish elites with other elites in America and the interaction of Jewish elites in America and Israel. If the governments in America and Israel or the social and political systems which produce so much injustice in both places are to be challenged by Jews of Conscience, then first and foremost the Jewish pillars of both societies have to be transformed or replaced.

A tall order it is, especially in relation to entrenched and deeply embedded systems where Jews are privileged and powerful. Part of our historical inheritance as Jews is to think

how Jews would fare if Jewish empowerment in America and Israel were to collapse. For the most part, Jews involved in these kinds of discussions haven't lived in a time when Jews were without power. Most Jews alive today haven't experienced a time when Jews weren't becoming pillars of American society or, for that matter, when a state of Israel, however controversial, didn't exist. For most Jews alive today, unempowered Jews or a time when Jews were only an ordinary part of society, exists in history books, primarily in recitations of the Holocaust narrative. It is also the case that increasing number of Jews, perhaps a great majority of Jews alive today, have no experience of a Jewishness that isn't thoroughly imbued with colonial sensibilities.

Another German Jew, Hannah Arendt, wrote decades after Marx, this time about the Jewish question involving Palestine. Arendt insisted that in a Jewish homeland, rather than a Jewish state which she opposed, East, represented by Arabs, and West, represented by Jews, could meet in a transformative way primarily because Jews, unlike others from the West, did not have a history of colonialism. Arendt opposed the creation of the state of Israel for a number of reasons. Primary among her reasons was that the existence of a Jewish state would necessitate a dependence on colonial powers. Of necessity, in assuming colonial power, Israel and Jews in general develop a colonial consciousness. No one can have colonial power without a colonial consciousness. Not even Jews.

With Jews taking on colonialism as intrinsic to our being, Arendt believed that Jews would relinquish the most admirable attribute we had – an (un)colonial past – and one that was imperative in rebuilding the world after the Holocaust. Yet when Arendt wrote about this in 1948, it was already too late. We were already creating a colonial legacy.

How far we Jews have come from Karl Marx and Hannah Arendt! Are we or the world better off for it?

Squandering legacies. A global reality. If everyone does, why shouldn't we?

We squander our legacy in the name of those who suffered for it. Is this another inversion that isn't confined to Jews?

Sharing our squandering. Across communal lines. And don't think such squandering is limited to retro-religious folks who vote in Christian denominational assemblies or affix mezuzot to their doorposts. Think of the promise of the Enlightenment. Think of modernity despoiling the earth. Think of Apple and our newly minted saint, Steve Jobs. Don't forget the slave labor of China fueling Apple's profits and China's miraculous growth.

Squander away. It's Jewish. It's human.

The task before us: Find what is left over. Begin again. With others.

Squandering is Jewish, human, shared. So is beginning again.

Evening Stroll
CAPE CANAVERAL

JULY 14

THE JEWISH
PANDORA'S BOX

Though I walk by the beach mezuzah daily, my feelings change each time I pass by. So does the look of the mezuzah itself. When the sun shines on the dark blue door, the large wood mezuzah is highlighted. On cloudy days it recedes into the background. Did I tell you that in the foreground of the house are a number of palm trees? It's a Florida beach scene. The mezuzah on the beach is quite beautiful. Like a picture postcard.

Yesterday, two girls sat outside at a stand selling various forms of lemonade. This included a lemonade smoothie. Price – one dollar. They must be the rabbi's children. I chatted with them for a minute but didn't have any money to buy a drink. I asked them if they would be there tomorrow.

The girls are young and I've also seen the rabbi outside working in the yard. He's young, too. Things have changed over the years. Depending on the denomination and the seminary, some rabbinic students read my books. Even on occasion, I am told, writings of mine are assigned or, through a clandestine network, they are passed around. Perhaps I am misjudging. If I introduced myself to the rabbi perhaps he would know who I am and react in a positive manner. The odds aren't good, though. Not worth the risk.

I'm also not sure that I want to be known to the local rabbi even if he loved me for what I stand for. Chances are he can't announce that to his congregation anyway. Besides, somewhere in the world – with Jewish power all around us – I want to remain anonymous. If you think I'm paranoid it's okay. But then try on the life of a Jewish dissident. In public. Then report back.

I wonder what it would be like if the rabbi's house was sold and the new resident removed the mezuzah. How would I feel? The door without the mezuzah would look barren. If our history hadn't come to this, I'd miss it. Or would I? The mezuzah is a reminder of past and present. Regardless of how I feel each day, it's important. I guess. As Jewish history goes, its disappearance would be a change for the better. I suppose. Disappearing Mezuzah. An advance?

If, with the new owner, the mezuzah was tossed into the garbage – after all, the new owner might have no idea what the wooden case is – no doubt I would retrieve it. Where would I put it? In a place where I could see it on a daily basis? Or would I hide it away, taking an occasional peek at most? Perhaps I would take it, keep it and then one day toss it in the garbage. I certainly wouldn't place it on my doorpost here. I just thought about this yesterday. Though wherever I've lived I've placed a mezuzah on the doorpost, here at Cape Canaveral, I've never even thought of doing this. Not once.

As you see, I go back and forth on a daily basis. Like a surveillance video, I scope it out. Mezuzah Watch. Beach is sun and beauty. I don't need to be reminded of what we have become on a daily basis. I think.

If we hadn't squandered what Karl Marx and Hannah Arendt and others hoped for, if we hadn't squandered the Holocaust or, at least, the meaning of the Holocaust for the future, we and the world would be better off. Squandering is human. Yet the toll is tremendous.

Instead of being down on Elie Wiesel, since his witness to the Holocaust remains, look at how much he squandered. In his own life he chased dollars and hobnobbed with every elite under the sun, minus Arabs and Palestinians of course. He trivializes the Holocaust, "There's no business like Shoah business," a prominent rabbi once told me in a mocking way.

Throwing away our (un)colonial history is one thing. But doing so for a state in the Middle East with prime ministers that resemble the county commissioners I grew up with in South Florida – with an army? That's another thing entirely. Taking envelops with cash or their equivalent, under the table or in broad daylight, corruption is widespread among Israel's leaders. Though profoundly human, it's unseemly, especially with the grand claims the state of Israel makes about itself and in reference to Jewish history.

The Disappearing Mezuzah. But I also think of the mezuzah as the Colonial Mezuzah. The Colonial Mezuzah by the beach. Blue period. A rift on Picasso's blue period. Picasso had his oriental gaze, as did most Western artists of his day. Though famous, Picasso was only a painter. His Orientalism, unlike ours, was without military power. Quite a difference a state with an army makes.

Making it seems to be everything. As the Joe Paterno, Jerry Sandusky, Penn State child abuse investigation shows. But let's not limit it to Penn State. Even at my and other "Christian" universities, athletics is so marked with hypocrisy on all fronts. Just follow the news. Over the years: murder, children born out of wedlock, abuse of live-ins, rape, lesbians at the forefront when "homosexual acts" are forbidden, coaches cited for infractions and other dubious dealings – all of this where the code is "strict" – zero tolerance. What a joke when athletic structures need to be built, alums courted and revenues upped. The best thing is for all of it to be outed. Sandusky for sure. Paterno's attempt to quash the bad news. Penn State's former President's silence. More on the way.

So squandering is part of life. For everything and everyone. We pick up the pieces. That are left over. But what if the squandering goes too far that even the leftovers are tainted beyond repair? When the leftovers we collect are so toxic we become infected by just drawing near to them?

As in, Chernobyl and the land around it, fenced off. No human habitation allowed. Well, you say, it was one of those bricks falling that brought down the Soviet Union. No doubt. After having squandered Marx's vision with forced starvation and Gulags – we know that score. Good to see the Soviet Union dispatched to the dust-bin of history. Now it has been replaced with the Putin (elected) dictatorship. No doubt this structure is likewise destined to go the same way. There will still be pieces left over to collect after the next fall. I assume.

The proverbial tipping point haunts this discussion, doesn't it? There seems to be points of no return. This end time scenario confronts us on the ecological front. Have we reached that in Jewish life? Of course, "Jewish" will continue after the ethical bottom has fallen out. Like Christianity. Christianity still performs 1500 years after it conformed to state power and became the most successful imperial religion of all time, its only rival being Islam. Yes, they're both still on the march but what are they, really, other than thinly disguised agents of this imperial agent or another. All empire religions are promiscuous. Is "Jewish" any different, except smaller, now climbing into bed with every empire that will have us?

Making it. When the tipping point arrives, then what? Continue on with the same name, like an old, noted and failed company being bought for a lot of dough because the brand name is iconic. Branding is crucial in modern business. The religion business is no different.

Those who can't abide by the ethical emptiness struggle to rebrand themselves. Or refuse a brand. Or try to reclaim the ethical content so the same brand can be worn around their necks. Jewish feminism is the latest effort, along with Jewish Renewal. They say: "No, no, we simply won't allow Empire Jews to distort our namesake so out of proportion that we seem like everyone else (which we might actually be when the squandering is figured in)."

Fighting the good fight is worth it up to a point. But, then, when the discourses and corpses are piled higher than high, we have to take a deep breath, exhale and see where our breath leads us. Chernobyl-like scorched earth doesn't give us much leeway in the leftovers realm. Do we have any choice but to begin again?

Think of Jews of Conscience as scavengers after the Jewish ethical tradition has been scorched beyond recognition. That is where we start. If we are honest.

New York Times headline front page yesterday: "Abuse Scandal Inquiry Damns Paterno and Penn State." Sports: "The Paterno Legacy, Changed Forever."

Translated: "The Jewish Legacy, Changed Forever."

Notice, the lack of question mark, as in – Changed Forever?

The Jewish tipping point has been reached. Get over it. Even the leftovers are tainted.

Front page subtitle: "Fear of Publicity Cited in Effort to Conceal." Fear of airing Jewish dirty laundry?

One Penn State official was fearful of opening Pandora's box. What if there were other abused children?

The Jewish Pandora's box. If we open it will every "Jewish money" conspiracy monger in (their pre-historic) existence fly out? The idea is that if we keep the lid on, no one will know what is happening behind the establishment's Wizard of Oz curtains. Including those Jews who travel on the proverbial Yellow Brick Road.

If we just click our heels, perhaps we will be transported out of our ethical/denial dilemma.

Originally a Greek myth, today, to open Pandora's box means to create evil that cannot be undone. But translated Jewishly, it means keeping the lid on the evil we are participating in. The evil we were once experts in blowing the lid off of.

If Pandora's box opens do we fear that the maps of the disappearing Palestine will appear out of nowhere? They're known all over the global block and I hear that they're appearing on train platforms in the New York suburbs even as I ponder the end. I wonder if the suburbs referred to are upstate New York, in Croton-on-Hudson, where I used to live?

I can imagine all the execs waiting for the commuter train in the early morning eyeing the changing landscape of Palestine as they try to avoid interacting with their fellow commuters. I doubt most of them would understand what they're looking at, or care if they did.

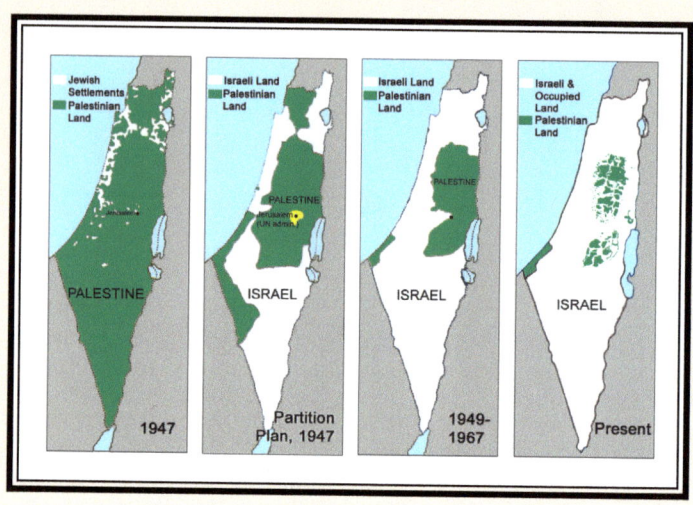

The Incredible Shrinking Palestine
ISRAEL-PALESTINE

JULY 15

HAVE YOU
EVER BEEN FED BY RAVENS?

A hoot. LOL. Leftover land. Leftover ethics. Mapping Disappearing Palestine in New York's suburbs.

Reports of the maps being at the Chappaqua Metro-North station – Hillary Clinton territory. Lots of wealth there. With the accompanying caption: "4.7 Million Palestinians are Classified by the UN as Refugees."

That should do it, shouldn't it? Not sure at all, really. Can anyone "read" these maps when we are so imbued with other, more comforting maps? Reading maps has a contextual reality. If the maps you can read are the maps you know are true, then other maps can provide a jolt to the knowledge system or be dismissed. (un)Read.

The Colonial Map of Israel – shall we show it from Tel Aviv to the Jordan River? If we read the Colonial Map of Israel then the Colonial Mezuzah appears. Or is the Disappearing Mezuzah – related to Disappearing Palestine? – our future? Both?

As Palestine disappears, Jews are enhanced. Say that it's (not) so! But the accusing images multiply on advertising billboards. Then even Jewish commuters disappear – or want to. Or get angry and accuse the images of being anti-Semitic. Mapping Disappearing Palestine, in God's name, how is that anti-Semitic?

No doubt this dark reality brings to the fore dark myths. But, then, should Jews be silent about Palestine? Should Palestinians be silent about Palestine? Because it brings all of this stuff up once again? For most American Jews and Jewish leadership the answer is yes, silence please or silence forced.

If only the trains would run on time. If only authorities would exercise their due discretion. Less time for advertising eyes to pry into actual, not mythic, Jewish history.

This reminds me of another experience during the Uprising years. I was visiting a Progressive Jew, a rabbi and an American who went to Israel after the 1967 war, one of those, who has now left Israel and lives in – of all places – Germany. Quite a journey. Back then he wore a colorful kippah but I noticed that when we traveled to the West Bank he removed it, placing it in his pocket. I asked him why he removed his kippah. He was silent. I pressed the issue. Was it because he might offend the Palestinians we visited? Out of fear we would be targeted as Jewish settlers? Or because of the shame he felt for what Israel was doing to Palestinians? After thinking for a moment, he responded – all three.

There we have it, contemporary Jewish life in a nutshell. The American, Jewish, Israeli rabbi who deepens his Jewishness by moving to Israel, then out of fear and shame doesn't

want to be identified as a Jew among the people he helped dispossess. Then he's done. Can't take it any more. He departs Israel for Germany.

Trajectory: America – Israel – Germany. White settler states. Holocaust. Empire states. Looking for refuge. Exile-time. Germany – what a place to finally lay his (now kippah (re)adorned) head!

Does that mean Jewish (Holocaust) history has come full circle? Of course, he can't escape. Germany is now our new found friend. Billions in restitution payments. Nuclear-able submarines as restitution gifts.

An omen perhaps but for the first time in more than fifty years, I see vultures on the beach here. No seagulls in sight and only a few pelicans, my favorite beach birds from youth.

Scavenging vultures. Scavenging through history. Ecological food cycle. Nothing wasted. Those on the top of the food chain. Those on the bottom. Elite eaters. Bottom feeders. Sometimes they are one and the same, at least with reference to the human.

Does it matter if "Jewish" is recycled and becomes something else? Disappearing Jewish just when we are appearing big time? Sure it happens often in history. Just when the sun will never set on this or that empire, it does. Then what? Have Empire Jews thought about the Jewish escape hatch if and when the Mediterranean Jewish sun sets?

Scavengers. The prophets might be found here. They root around in places few want to go. If there, who wants to be seen?

My memory roams back to those Uprising years again. Another rabbi. Like mezuzot, do I have rabbis on my brain?

Before you make a judgment, tell me, have you ever had a rabbi contact you and want to meet, but won't meet you in his synagogue or a restaurant or even in the lobby of your hotel for fear of being seen in your presence? This particular rabbi was willing to meet with me in my hotel room only but I thought, this is ridiculous, if he doesn't want to be seen with me, he doesn't want to share my fate, so why do him the favor of agreeing to a secret meeting?

On the brighter non-rabbinic side, during those same years I used to meet with Jewish and Palestinian students who worked side-by-side on Israel-Palestine. I remember the time when the Jewish and Palestinian editors of the University of Michigan newspaper, a quite good one, met with me in my hotel room – for convenience sake. This was after the university Hillel asked the university to ban me from campus and shut down the campus newspaper, all in one swoop. Hillel recommended the Jewish editors to their local rabbis for counseling as their parents were too divided within themselves to deal with the issues at hand. The parents didn't know what to do with the ethical impulses of their kids precisely because they didn't know what to do with their own ethical impulses. Let the rabbis sort it out, the parents agreed. But the kids didn't want to be sorted.

How prophetic the Jewish kids were. Are? I don't know what became of them. Do we have anyone following the ethical development/regression of Jewish kids who want to

do right in the world and are pressured by every side imaginable? Since the prophetic is the Jewish indigenous, this is an ongoing problem. That is, the prophetic. Exploding in our time.

The prophetic that the parents and rabbis are frightened of – where does it come from?

When I think of the Jewish prophets, I think first of the Bible, where the prophetic is introduced. The prophetic is at the very heart of the Biblical narrative, beginning with the Exodus story. The liberation of captive slaves from Egypt is so important to the Jewish canon that the origins of the universe and even the unfolding of the patriarchs appear as a Biblical second thought.

The stories in the Bible are fascinating and sometimes macabre. They all have their place. Yet the prophetic is front and center in the origins of the people Israel and in their quest to be faithful as a people. Everything revolves around the prophetic. For after all, why had God chosen this nothing of a people except for a mission that was extraordinary?

Separating Biblical fact from Biblical fiction is difficult. No, it's impossible. Whatever one can say about the historicity of the Bible, we know it isn't a history as we know history today. Instead, a narrative of formative events is placed before us, events like the Exodus, whose overall importance exceeds its mundane details. As if something happened in history that cannot be explained, or explained as a temporal event only. That is the essence of a formative event – in history/more than history.

The Bible doesn't explain or explain away these formative events as transcendent events either. Events like the Exodus are caught midway between the realm of history and a realm beyond history. That is the power of the Exodus. Parts of the Exodus narrative are believable in ordinary time while other parts aren't. Just as the Bible takes a miraculous flight of fancy we are struck by how profoundly human the hope and despair of the people Israel is. Reading the Bible, we are drawn away from history, then toward it, then away/toward. This is where the Bible finds its mark.

Entering the Promised Land, Moses issues one of his periodic dire warnings, though this particular warning has an unusual trajectory. Sure God has promised the land to the people Israel whom he led out of slavery in Egypt. Yet Moses foretells all sorts of dangers in the land that the people will naturally and almost inevitably fall prey to. We have the false Gods and the pagan Canaanites as temptations to stray. The main pitfall, however, is the injustice of the Israelites themselves.

Israel's unjust behavior is judged against the promise God has made to Israel. For God hasn't given the land to Israel for its own sake. Rather, a special task awaits Israel. The task is to create a new economic and political order over against the slave empire God brought Israel out of. Many years ago, Norman Gottwald, a Biblical scholar, wrote that the thrust of God's command to Israel was to create a "socially egalitarian decentralized tribal democracy".

Gottwald's description of Israel's destiny is an academic mouthful. Once you have digested its meaning though, think about its ramifications. Follow the Biblical story as it

unfolds. After Israel's entry into the land and as Moses predicted, Israel clamors for wealth and power, even a human king, because they mistrust the power of God and their own ethical principles to maintain a society centered on justice. Obviously, Israel's social/economic/political experiment fails. Division and oppression flourishes. The documentation of that failure – the emergence of the poor and disenfranchised.

The Bible summarizes injustice by noting the marginalization of the widow, the orphan, the poor and the stranger. In effect, God accuses Israel of recreating Egypt. As far as God is concerned, Israel might as well adopt the Egyptian Gods or some variation thereof and abandon Israel's God of Liberation. The Egyptian Gods sanction such a society. Israel's God does not. In fact, that is how the Biblical story begins to see Israel's relation with God – as a conscious abandonment of the liberation process. When Israel creates an unjust social order, she has abandoned the God that liberated Israel from bondage.

God's message of Israel's failings is brought to the people by God-commissioned prophets. The prophets in early Israelite history are legion, the more familiar ones being Jeremiah, Isaiah and Amos. My personal favorite is Jeremiah, if you can follow his plight without giving in to despair. You see, simply being commissioned by God doesn't guarantee safe passage, just the opposite. The prophets are driven pillar to post, often ending up in jail, exile or worse.

One of my favorite chapters from the prophets is found in Ezekiel, who is prone to psychedelic visions. God calls Ezekiel to speak to a renegade Israel but, get this, with the knowledge that the Israelites won't listen and that their wrath will be visited upon him. After this dire commissioning, Ezekiel is handed a scroll that God commands him to eat.

The text is God's commission to Ezekiel. On the symbolic level, ingesting the scroll means to internalize it. In other words, God tells Ezekiel to eat, thus inscribe, his own doom as fidelity to God and to Israel. Ezekiel expects such a doomsday scroll to taste bitter, which makes sense. Fearing the worse, Ezekiel is surprised by how the scroll tastes. As Ezekiel remarks in amazement, the scroll tastes sweet, just like honey.

This is the other side of the doom that God announces to the prophets and, in turn, the prophets announce to the people Israel. It is part of Israel's plight that injustice is denounced and, as well, it is part of Israel's possibility to have the prophets sent to them. For when the prophets speak there is still time to change and begin again. Change your policies! Change your heart! The prophets are Last Chance emissaries. There is still time. Time is running out.

The prophets are front and center in God's plan and Israel's destiny. What a privilege to be chosen to be a prophet! Even if the personal consequences are difficult, if not calamitous.

I want to avoid a Bible lesson, even for myself, but the Bible as foundational to Jewish life lays it down rather boldly. Israel has a special destiny which it abandons at its own peril. That destiny is to follow a God of Liberation and to do liberation when it is free to create for itself the conditions of justice. God gives Israel that chance. In most cases, Israel blows it.

Sometimes the Bible has a modern ring to it. The society Israel creates is to be decentralized and concentrate on the welfare of the people. At all costs, it should avoid concentrations of power, elite political and economic classes and, it seems, standing armies. The four together mean injustice. And the four go together. You can't have injustice without all of them working in tandem. Sounds like Political Science 101?

The prophets are those who come in God's name but also begin to experience the consequences of what it means to come up against the power of those who want it their way. The penalty for Israel's failings is exile from the land. The prophet in trying to bring Israel back to its senses is already there – in exile within the land.

You see, the prophet is the warning and embodiment of what is to come – what already has become. Are Jews of Conscience the ancient prophets come alive?

Besides Ezekiel, lately I have been meditating on the Prophet Elijah. Elijah is a long story – packed with everything imaginable as these Biblical stories often are – but in essence Elijah is non-stop truth-talker that doesn't hesitate to tell those in power to go to hell. This includes the king.

Ultimately God rescues Elijah by taking him to heaven in a whirlwind – a rescue package Jews of Conscience might look into – but what immediately grabbed me was an earlier sequence when God tells Elijah to flee the powers-to-be. This after Elijah informs the king that because of his actions the coming years will be drought years – not a "drop of dew or rain." Obviously unwelcome news.

When Elijah queries where sustenance will be found in the ravine God orders him to flee to, God tells Elijah to drink fresh water from the brook. As for meals, God informs Elijah to await the ravens. They will bring him food. Which they do.

Dinner Time
THE PROPHET ELIJAH

JULY 16

BIRTHRIGHT PROPHETIC

Raven-time. If you are going to speak out, you have to have a backup plan. I love Elijah's whirlwind exit on a chariot and horses of fire. Quite a way to go out. The only thing Elijah leaves behind is his cloak and a disciple, Elisha, who is also quite something.

Disciples. Wonder if that's a good way to go. None for me, which is the way I want it. With Norman Finkelstein's periodic psychological meltdowns, his disciples enter the Garden of Gethsemane. If the story holds true to form, it doesn't look good. Maybe, international law will save all of them.

Now before you start calling me Rabbi Ellis – if Lerner and Waskow can self-anoint, why not you and me! – I share these stories because they are fantastic and real. We, who cannot even speak of God, are not thusly disempowered. (Though I often speak with God, or think I do, at least I carry on the conversation with God as if God is there, but won't testify to it since it sounds ridiculous as I'm sure you're thinking. That's for another day, so let's drop it for now. It does sound far-fetched. If you care to, chalk it up to exile desert-oasis imaginings. Mirage stuff.)

The words of the prophets resonate so deeply within us. Whether you believe in God, speak to God or not, the prophetic word is now independent of God. It's within us. Imagine that.

True, if you are going to be slain by the powers-that-be, I doubt that a chariot will spirit you away. I haven't spotted any in the night sky. Best to imagine the ravens as those who offer hospitality on the difficult journey. On the ravine water, try it. Ravine water is crucial when you're on the run.

When the prophetic word is spoken and you survive, think gratitude. At least you can look in the mirror and not see Ken Starr starring back at you. That's the other option, isn't it? Being well paid is a dream come true. You don't want to become a rich huckster, do you?

Obviously, we have to read the prophets with a critical eye. There's a lot of violence committed in their name. Nonetheless, we don't want to critically read the prophets out of our existence. If we do so for all sorts of politically correct reasons, most of which I agree with, or place a multi-colored kippah on the prophets head, we can dance the night away at Jewish-only retreats as Progressive Jews do. However, think what we'll be left with: the mezuzah on the beach, the Israeli flag flying next to the American flag, academic Jewish Studies and the Bible without the bite.

Our primal tongue will be cut out. Jews won't be able to reason except in some disembodied Cartesian way or, more likely, we'll simply decide to conform to the powers of this world. That's what happens to Jews and others when affluence and empowerment come their way.

Our fortune – and our trial – is that the prophetic is our DNA. Some Jews will fight the prophetic tooth and nail, but let's be honest, since it survived for thousands of years, the prophetic isn't going away. The Jewish prophetic voice will never die. That's the lesson everyone is learning in the Golden Age of Empire Judaism.

So, whether or not you believe in God, whatever that actually might mean after the Holocaust and after Israel, knowing that a certain kind of atheism is rampant among Jews of Conscience which may have to do with the Biblical understanding of idolatry, that being the prohibition of the worship of false Gods, false Gods being Gods that enable the empire status quo – you see where I am going with this run-on sentence.

The whole God-thing is way more complicated than Edward Said thought – at least in the itinerant prophetic imagination! (More about Said and the itinerant Jewish prophet story in a coming commentary.)

Why spend too much time with the God question, since the Jewish question is so absorbing that it may contain the God question within it? Without God having to be named explicitly or decided upon. Let Christians hold forth on that since most of them are God know-it-alls. Yet, it's also the case that we shouldn't wrap ourselves around Jewish ritual as a way of proving to Christians that we really are religious and right-minded, meanwhile blunting the justice agenda.

My sense is that most of us ought to abandon theological language and the struggle about it because neither will take us toward our goal. Why not just embody the prophetic in our Jewish way since it has been with us forever? Call it Birthright Prophetic.

You see, Birthright Israel has it all wrong. Israel was the Biblical promise, yes that is the case. Nonetheless, the prophetic always took priority, as it does today. More than the land, the prophetic is the Jewish indigenous: it's the primal thrust of the Exodus and the primary claim over the land. This doesn't mean that the land or Jewish empowerment is always doomed or always wrong. I'm not going there. Not at all.

The prophetic means that empowerment is provisional and not an end in itself. The prophetic is always judgment. The judgment is quite specific. It doesn't rest on theory. If the poor and the stranger aren't getting a fair shake, if classes of people are marginalized, if power is being used over against others – well then a prophetic shake-up is in the works.

So Birthright Prophetic works against Birthright Israel when injustice is the norm. Or, in our time, because the prophetic has to expand its vision as time goes on, if the settling of the land displaces others. You see, even the Biblical prophetic has colonial elements in it. Anyone who reads the Bible can see that front and center.

Conscience confronts the colonial. Conscience intervenes and takes priority. Not the Bible, not even God, stand on their own. Because of the prophetic, Jews are allowed to speak our own word. We have to. Especially since God doesn't seem close by. As in, in our weakness,

where were the chariots and horses when we needed them? We need them now, too, in our empowerment. Where are they?

Be ravens to each other. Bring each other the substance of life. We can't leave the hospitality option to the professionals or to God. We can't limit where the bread comes from, since you never know when a Muslim or a Palestinian, or God forbid, a Western Christian, might help us survive the Jewish Empire Divide.

You see our Birthright Prophetic is ours but it isn't everything. Others have their own thing to bring to the banquet of life.

When you're on the run you never know who you'll find around the table. While the prophetic gives us our place to stand, we shouldn't kid ourselves. The prophetic never stands alone. Today wherever the prophetic voice is spoken, all of the prophets are gathered.

Should all of the prophets – across the globe regardless of religion, secularity and geography – be buried together? This would be a reminder of all that is done every day by those who say no to oppression. It would also be a reminder to the living that the prophetic voice is alive in them.

Yes there is a tradition of the prophets. It's evolving right before our eyes. It's expanding every justice step of the way. Since it may hold the future of the world in its hands, it has to reflect the world. Don't you think?

Birthright Prophetic. Is it everyone's birthright?

Thomas Merton
CATHOLIC MONK

JULY 17

OVERCOMING
PARTIAL PRACTICE

From Thomas Merton, the Catholic monk, on his travels through Asia where he met his untimely death in 1968, quoting from the Tibetan Buddhist monk, Milarepa: "It is the tradition of the fortunate seekers never to be content with partial practice."

Milarepa is a major figure in the history of the Kagyu (Bka'-brgyud) school of Tibetan Buddhism. He was a yogi and a poet. He was also a mystic, who in his early years practiced a discipline called supernatural running while creating all sorts of havoc with his use of black magic. In his later years he repented and sought a change of life:

> In my youth I committed black deeds. In maturity I practiced innocence. Now, released from both good and evil, I have destroyed the root of karmic action and shall have no reason for action in the future. To say more than this would only cause weeping and laughter. What good would it do to tell you? I am an old man. Leave me in peace.

Whatever Milarepa did he was all in. No partial practice for him. Since reading Merton's journals, I have thought about Milarepa's words often. For every person, every culture, every tradition there is a somewhat different understanding of what partial practice is. And how we overcome it. Let every person/culture/tradition name that practice and contribute it to the world. I doubt that practice is wholly different anywhere. I also doubt that it is the same everywhere.

When we are together – overcoming partial practice – how good it is to celebrate our commonality. We realize that there is an ever expanding, ever evolving, global prophetic community, yet it is also important to think about where we are as individuals. Shouldn't we gather ourselves and ask where we are in our own practice – as a person, in our culture and tradition, within the context of the history we are living through?

Much of life is contextual. We are according to the times in which we live. Yet there is a deeper layer that is also independent of history. It is between the two layers that we find our fidelity. Being engaged and disengaged. Being totally present and somewhere else – at the same time. This allows us to be in the world without being totally defined by it. For if we are defined by the world – only – how can we act within it in a dissenting way? There must be a place outside of our context to be involved in the world – from a different point of view.

However we get there – with or without religious ritual, with or without God, with or without an immediate community – there we are. Where we are is a test. Where should we be?

Alas, in history overcoming partial practice doesn't mean our community or our history will change. Most often, if change is happening, it isn't obvious, is too slow, it isn't going to get where it needs to be. Nor are we, if success is the watchword.

Success is probably the worse compass to fly by. We are never going to get the "success" coordinates right, and if we do, we'll end up conforming to power, to the culture, to what is appropriate, to what is deemed authentic.

Beware of becoming an "authentic" Jew. Run from the very notion since, by definition, "authentic" is outside of you. By refusing to be authentic we're actually much closer already, to the real thing. If we want to be Jewish, we have to leave the received definition of "Jewish" behind. By becoming (un)Jewish, we are already closer.

Which is to say that the Jewish prophetic isn't, first and foremost, learned Jewishly. Since most of Jewish learning is learning how to cope with and submerge the prophetic. Have you ever noticed those of you who attended Hebrew School as I did, three afternoons a week plus the Sunday school thing, that the real lesson we learned was how to conduct ourselves as pillars of the Jewish community? No doubt it has become worse than in my childhood. Now add – pillars of America and Israel.

Becoming a Bar Mitzvah in 1965, I was taught before the Holocaust or Israel was central to Jewish life. We were only on our way up in American society. Hadn't yet arrived. Israel wasn't a superpower in the Middle East. We didn't know much about the state. Then again, making Israel central to Jewish life hasn't increased Jewish literacy about Israel either. Israel has more power. Jews know as little. Maybe even less. As the (un)read, (un)readable maps of Disappearing Palestine appearing in Westchester County attest to.

Talk about partial practice! File under: Jewish learning at the Hebrew School level and Jewish Studies programs in universities. Sometimes I think the entire Jewish learning enterprise exists to dumb down Jews by inflating them with knowledge of the tradition. But if you think most of tradition is exactly that, to keep Jews in line, then avoidance at all costs is mandatory. Unless you find some Jewish outlier in the tradition that has been forgotten, which happens on occasion.

As often, various aspects of the tradition are highlighted, while other parts of the tradition are submerged. The submerged await excavation by (un)authentic Jews.

How do we overcome partial practice? There is a conscious element, as in, I need to do more. I also think there is a spiritual element which is not communal ritual on a designated day of the week.

Though if truth be known, I began to pray on the Sabbath in my late twenties. This continued for more than thirty years. Interestingly, my Sabbath observance came as my Passover celebrations diminished. Of course, I did it all with my kids and enjoyed it quite a bit. It was a meaningful part of our lives together. On the Passover Seder front, I used variations of the Rainbow Seders. For those years I give Arthur Waskow and his crew credit where credit is due. Still, expiration dates don't only come on milk containers. How long

can we celebrate Passover when the very liberation we celebrate is used to oppress another people?

I know the arguments, some of which make a lot of sense. Keep hope alive! Don't let the Jewish establishment corner the Authentic Jew market. We all need times to gather on our own terms and lay out the Seder as we think it should be. Even this year, I loved the Jewish Voice for Peace Haggadah. Every one of the Ten Plagues involved the sin of occupation! Much less Waskovian. A real and needed advance.

At least in my reading, the JVP Passover narrative doesn't have as much on the one hand, as on the other. Meaning the oppression of the Palestinians isn't – "balanced" – by the need for Israel's security blah blah blah. Tell me if you remember the Jewish Left as it promoted the end of South African apartheid, showing an inordinate concern for the white minority? If you remember the Sullivan Principles bandied about by folks like Ronald Reagan, it was just a transition proposal that disguised the intention to keep white South Africa afloat. So many of the breakthroughs on the Jewish ritual front, including the expanded Passover Seders, are likewise thinly disguised operations to keep Israel's occupation afloat. Sullivan Principles Seders!

So, too, with much of Jewish feminism in the religious arena. Check out Judith Plaskow's *Standing Again at Sinai* if you want an important read about women in Jewish life. If you're looking for the key question facing the Jewish people, the oppression of the Palestinian people, best to look elsewhere. There is only one thoroughly vetted chapter on the issue. No bite. But then if you want to court the Jewish community on the inclusion of women, do you really want to alienate them with harsh words about Israel? Invitations to speak are hard to come by. Bite your lip. Stay in line.

Again, the Authentic Jew comes into place. If women want to be counted as authentic Jews with feminist rituals accorded their proper respect, whose approval do they need? The Jewish establishment's, of course. To deflect the central question, the establishment said yes to feminism, providing it was disciplined. And manly. Sort of like Hillary Clinton proving that as a woman she was more hawkish than Barack Obama. How else could she prove that she had the fortitude to be president – or translated Jewishly, a rabbi? Standing again at Sinai, with whom, in what relation, with what kind of power, with what history spoken? A Jewish feminist ritual that details the ethnic cleansing of Palestinians?

Yes, of course, there are plenty of feminists in the prophetic exilic community. They are off the beaten Authentic Jew track. Though on the rabbinic front, believe me, feminists rabbis haven't made a dent in the idea of Jews as innocent. At least in years past, they held up their part of the rabbinic patriarchal establishment. They brought new energy to it. Of course, women Rabbis have their complaints, as female clergy of all faiths do. These complaints are real. Insofar as they buttress the Empire/Progressive establishments, however, they need to be called out regardless. Politically correct hasn't got us very far, has it?

The sad fact is that often women build empires, the very same ones they opposed when the Father's had them. Or they use the hard won battles for justice for women against others

for their own advancement. I have found that, think of this, women can even be bought and, oh my, they can collude with the powers-that-be for their own enhanced paydays. Yes, romanticizing the Other has its limits. Thank God for the women – and the men – who turn down empire's paycheck. It isn't a regular occurrence.

What's our option? Play the game. Win or lose. You can lie on whatever witness stand you're called to and call it a life. That's one form of cynicism. You can be knocked to your knees and think how unfair it is. Which it often is. You can think the whole world is unjust. Which it might be. But that's another form of cynicism.

Cynicism, in its various forms – is that what makes the world go round? It might. A certain amount of corruption is probably important to the world's functioning. And often those whose mandate it is to clean up corruption are corrupt themselves. You can read about it in Victoria Fontan's new book where that intrepid decolonizer relates stories that are so horrific they take your breath away. Of women being raped by one gang then raped again by their "rescuers." Factor in these seedy realities when we speak about anything bright and cheery, the politics of meaning, international law, development, protecting human rights. The list is endless.

The prophetic doesn't venture into the bright and cheery. It doesn't go anywhere near that goal post. The prophetic doesn't have a thing to do with success, whatever that means within and after injustice and atrocity. At its deepest point, the prophetic doesn't even think of itself contributing to the cosmic meaning of the human adventure. Nor does the prophet bring in God as the way out of the truth of our existence.

The prophetic is the consistent attempt – within our human limitations – to overcome partial practice. To plumb the depths of history. To be present to history as a form of fidelity. In Jewish life this isn't an add-on. Jews aren't grafted on, as Christians are, using the always fascinating Pauline imagery. We're not just along for the ride. At least, that isn't our assigned purpose.

Overcoming partial practice   Milarepa thinks how fortunate we are! Yet as he knew well, pitfalls are everywhere.

By the way, if you're asking what the rewards are for overcoming partial practice, move to another question. There aren't brownie points in heaven. With God. If there is a God. No brownie points on earth either. There is too much loss involved.

For Jews, overcoming partial practice is to draw near to the prophetic by practicing it – in exile. Which is coming close to what it means to be Jewish in the world.

That we have to distance ourselves from authentic Judaism to draw near to Jewishness is an irony of great proportions. But riddle me this: isn't this true with all cultures, communities, religions and nations, that to draw near, to overcome the partial practice of each, one has to distance oneself from what is known as authentic this and that?

Some folks think that there is a reward and if it's not here on earth, it's in heaven. As in the Our Father – at least as commonly interpreted. The prophets know the difference

between entry into history and rewards. The prophets go against the grain of history and what most of us want from it. That is why the prophets – and the prophetic – are doomed to failure.

The great Jewish Biblicist, theologian and linguist, Martin Buber, saw it this way – the prophets as failures in history as we typically know it – history from above. Yet at the same time, Buber understood that there was a prophetic stream in history – history from below.

History from below has been taken up by Christian liberation theology. Liberationist Christians see history from below and especially those who suffer in history as the engine of history. Martin Buber wrote of it in a somewhat different language while pointing to the same effect. Buber believed that the prophet's very failure – get this – prepared the world for redemption.

Do you believe that, failure as way of redemption?

Which means suffering for what you believe is just. It means exile. No earthly rewards.

Overcoming partial practice. No rewards in this life or the next, except the biggest one of all.

Gratitude for preparing the world for redemption? Difficult. Even if you believe redemption is on the way. A huge question mark for sure. Huge.

Entering the Promised Land
JORDAN RIVER

JULY 18

HELICOPTER GUNSHIPS
IN THE ARK OF THE COVENANT

Yes redemption is a difficult one, a huge problem. We search for meaning in life and wonder when it will become evident. This is especially true when we commit ourselves against the grain of history. Despite our commitment, suffering continues. It seems our commitment means little.

Perhaps that's why there is so much commitment that lacks reflection. If we stop and reflect for a moment, we're afraid everything will come down crashing on our heads. Reflection doesn't solve the problem. Sometimes it crashes anyway. So talk about redemption is mostly out of place, no matter how much I love Martin Buber. Best to stick to the here and now. Keep plodding along.

Reflection without gazing at the ultimate. Or gazing once in a while. For a moment or two. Then on with life.

Down to the beach after a few days with a back problem. Not debilitating, just a strain. This morning I took an alternative route one street over to avoid the mezuzah on the beach. I didn't want to pass the ostentatiously displayed (inverted) Jewish symbol. Even the exiled need the morning off once in a while.

Jewish power around every corner – remember, it's my experience rather than a historically airborne theory. Isn't it strange how this distinction between experience and theory is often lost on our sophisticated elites? On Jews who, for various reasons, including their own self-advancement, seem bent on proving their authenticity?

A few years ago in Paris, I attended a conference on racism and anti-Semitism. There a Jewish participant in the conference who spoke after me, misquoted me on this topic of Jewish power. In doing so, he implied that I was invoking the Protocols of the Elders of Zion conspiratorial aspect of Jewish power. So I interrupted him and made my point a second time: "I am talking about my experience of Jewish power, not a theory of Jewish power." He accepted my intervention, apologized for misinterpreting me and then repeated his same point. Whereby I interrupted him again, he apologized and went on with his original claim as if our conversation hadn't occurred.

How to make sense of this? After numerous interruptions and apologies, I came to the conclusion that he wasn't being deliberately disingenuous. In fact, he accepted my correction and was apologetic. It seemed that he had no other way to express himself except by distorting my point. Cognitive dissonance perhaps. He couldn't admit that my experience was right and the theory was wrong – that both could be true. Otherwise he would have to take a bite

out of the contemporary Jewish Tree of Knowledge apple. He would be naked before the world. Sans fig leaf.

Have you ever run into folks, Jewish and otherwise, whose restricted ability to think reflects their limited world view? Point taken on some levels, but here was an American academic researching in the most sophisticated French libraries while writing a work on a major Jewish European philosopher. I wonder if he understands the difference between mythic anti-Semitism that sees a Jewish world conspiracy and the reality that the Jewish establishment(s) disciplines any dissent on the question of Israel?

We never did straighten it out. He kept apologizing during the final two days of the conference. He also kept distorting what I said.

Which is my way of asking if the difference between the Jewish question and the Israel question is misunderstood simply for political reasons or because our collective Jewish will just can't wrap our minds around the fact that the Jewish situation in the world has changed radically in the last decades?

Time marches on. Returning to Marx, who couldn't have anticipated the Israel question, then to Arendt, who did anticipate the Israel question, to we who are living the Israel question – these necessitate huge leaps in communal thought and identity formation. Yet, as time marches on, history doesn't play thought/identity catch-up.

When history arrives, what couldn't be thought or what was anticipated but not experienced is often worse. At any rate, it is different. That difference demands new thinking, precisely the thinking that lags. What is now being experienced still can't be thought or anticipated. It's like a cycle of constantly being behind the eight ball. We can't get a grip on our history.

The prophetic is the ability and willingness to think (un)thinkable thought because that is where we are. But watch out for the principal's paddle, the big wooden one standing there around every corner.

Everyone has their own experience and I was just sharing mine in the Parisian intellectual climes. We shouldn't kid ourselves either. There isn't any daylight between that power and the Christian right. Alan Dershowitz and Ken Starr. Coming back to my joint burial plans – bury Arafat and Sharon together – how about a Dershowitz-Starr joint headstone? Star of David intertwined with a Cross? Artists' renditions welcome.

Fortunately I am not a graphic artist. I have so many ideas that could be visualized it would only deepen my exile and perhaps make it permanent. If it isn't already. Dusting off one of my favorites in case you haven't heard of it, when I first heard reports of Israel using helicopter gunships to frighten and sometimes rocket Palestinian towns, villages and refugee camps during the second Palestinian Uprising – reports which shocked me though perhaps that was just part of my lingering internal Progressive Jewish mentality – I imagined converting the menacing helicopter gunships into ritual objects. After all, if we are going to live by Star of David helicopter gunships and if, spiritually, we are what we practice and

should worship what is most important to us, raising the question of what God we will acknowledge because everyone has some kind of God that we bow to – you see where this is going.

Just like "Bury Arafat and Sharon Together" came into my mind during a dream, this one relating to helicopter gunships and worship also just arrived: "Helicopter Gunships in the Ark of the Covenant." I wondered what that could mean.

Let's begin at the beginning – Ark etiquette. There's an Ark of the Covenant in every synagogue. Inside the Ark you find the Torah scrolls and the ornamentation reserved for the Torah. The Ark containing the Torah is the holiest place in the synagogue, thus there are various rituals for opening and shutting the Ark, taking the Torah out the Ark, parading it among the congregation, unfurling the Torah scroll, reading from the Torah, then placing the Torah back in the Ark and closing it.

It's quite involved. At any rate, one day I was invited to a synagogue outside of London where I was to speak at the Shabbat meal after the service. To be honest, I try to avoid religious services whenever I can, preferring as I do hypocrisy served straight up rather than covered over with religious pieties. How about you? Because of the (rare) synagogue invite I couldn't refuse the service. No way out.

In this particular synagogue, the rabbi was positioned facing the Ark during the service. Since I was his guest of honor, I sat with him. During the service I became convinced that when the curtain of the Ark opened the Torah scrolls would be missing. In its place, there would be two helicopter gunships. It was a quasi-mystical experience. Or perhaps it was jet-lag.

Whatever the reason, the vision was quite intense. I visualized the helicopter gunships transformed into ritual objects, dressed for worship, their menacing black transformed into finely rendered silver casing. I anticipated the Ark opening, the congregation bowing before the helicopter gunships as we bow before the Torah. After the prayers were chanted, the helicopter gunships were taken around the synagogue by the rabbi where, and with our tallit, we kissed them, again as we kiss the Torah. The helicopter gunships were brought back to the Ark and with our prayers chanted, the Ark's curtain was closed.

All empires need helicopter gunships. Empire Judaism needs them, too. Why not place them in the Ark of the Covenant? Having had the idea, I visualize its expansion. With the helicopter gunships, perhaps we should place other Jewish realities in ritualized form. Let's see – also feel free to add your own – I would add, with a ritualized flourish, an Apartheid Wall, a map of Disappearing Palestine (perhaps as the backdrop that the ritual objects are placed in front of), several settlement blocs (perhaps built out of multi-colored Legos) and a facsimile of the Israeli Dimona nuclear facility.

Of course, there is more to add but remember that when it comes to sacred objects and their display, more isn't always better. Minimalism has its place. Perhaps my original vision is best: just austere, dignified, silver coated, helicopter gunships. With Star of David decals. That's essential.

Star of David Helicopter Gunships in the Ark of the Covenant. Honestly. Hannah Arendt's anticipated Sparta. (By the way, though I am not an expert on the subject, Sparta's shelf-life as a dominant power didn't last very long. If memory serves, I think it was more or less fifty years. Another issue but perhaps best saved as a commentary for a sermon with our newly envisioned Ark of the Covenant display.)

Yes, I was sure when the curtains opened the helicopter gunships would be there. The drama was palpable. I must have been in some mystical trance. Of course, it didn't happen. You can imagine how disappointed I was when the curtains opened and only the Torah scrolls were revealed.

Later, when I related this vision and my disappointment to one of my Jewish students, he told me it all could be arranged one day, surreptitiously. He suggested that the night before the services were held, we could get someone to substitute the silver helicopter gunships for the Torah scrolls, then, wham, watch as the rabbi and the congregation recoil in shock and anger. A real service stopper. The last place you're supposed to see yourself in the collective mirror is synagogue. Blasphemy!

While I'm at it, let's move to the Christian side of the aisle. Communion wafers/the Lord's Supper, ritual bread with Conquistadores' namesakes imprinted on them? Christians could then ponder if naming Christian empire will take away the sins of the world.

Let's see – the faces of Pissarro, Cortes, and Columbus on communion wafers. Not to leave out Ponce de Leon and his search for the Fountain of Youth. Communion takers might wonder who they are. Forgetting history seems to be one of the tasks of religion. That's part of the fun. Placing history front and center.

Or names of towns – Chappaqua, Croton-on Hudson, Ossining. My old stomping ground, once the stomping ground of Native Americans, hence the Native American names. Now the location of Disappearing Palestine adverts. Shall they all be added to the Bread of Life?

Oh my, I almost forgot, for the Ark of the Covenant, add the mezuzah on the beach now upped to ritualistic status – The Mezuzah on the Beach.

All religion is local.

Krishna and Radha
EGER, HUNGARY

JULY 19

PRYING EYES

Last night, thundering, lightning, rain. (un)Tourist weather, which I love. Since I am a native Floridian, I love the sun but even more the cloudy days. Winter is the best time of year here.

Haven't told you about the peacocks that wander wild near the beach. Yes, peacocks. In the evening I walk by them, a dozen or so, with their offspring. They saunter about as if they belong here. I remember being shocked when I discovered them many years ago. Peacocks running wild at the Cape? Since I figured there was no way my children would believe me, I ran for my camera, took a picture and that was that.

How did they get here? It seems that during the space program's heyday an entrepreneur had a brilliant idea for a tourist oriented theme park that included peacocks. When it went bust, he just up and left, leaving who knows what behind, including several peacocks that the community adopted. That's the story I heard. Now they flourish, run wild, have a home here.

Krishna is often pictured with peacock feathers adorning his head. I wonder if I will run into him one day. Peacocks appear in Christian symbolism as well, symbolizing eternal life. So many of Christianity's victims have been dispatched there, I wonder if there are millions of peacocks in heaven waiting to greet each of them individually.

A peacock in the Ark of the Covenant? I know – it's getting crowded in there. Parsing history, perhaps we can just have the helicopter gunships and peacocks in the Ark. The Apartheid Wall might frame the picture nicely as background or perhaps as a 3-D wrap-around. Color coordination is important, of course, and the peacock's colors would bring out the silver in the helicopter gunships and balance out the rather bland Wall. Though we don't want the graffiti on the Wall blocked out by the peacocks, especially when they fan their tails. More thought is needed.

Yesterday, I made a dental appointment. There is a dentist's office only a few blocks from here, the one where every one of his patient's room has a mezuzah. I need to have a closer look but they seem almost identical with the Mezuzah on the Beach. The plot thickens!

I thought to myself: interesting that, in my attempts to escape the visible signs of Jewishness, I end up with a dentist that marks every door with almost exactly the same mezuzah that adorns the rabbi's house on the beach. An Orthodox Jew, no less. Lesson: No escape.

But then, harkening back to the Jews for Jesus storefront just a few blocks from the Dentist's office, I thought his office mezuzah adornment was overdone. Perhaps we have a Jew for Jesus here. (un)Orthodox Jew. Another lesson for me?

So in a few days I shall find out by asking him. If I summon up the courage. Should I blow my anonymous Jew-cover by telling who I am? I doubt he would know who I am. Tell him what I believe? Or should I just say I am interested in those boxes on his office doorposts, leave it at that, pretend ignorance, hide my identity and views, and let him think I'm just curious? I'll play it by ear. Probably best to stay anonymous.

I am currently finishing the biography of the American painter, Andrew Wyeth. Quite a book, and the artist was a different kind of man." Subtitle: *A Secret Life*. Actually, a double life of interacting with family and his art. For the most part he kept his art secret from everyone but his wife. Then for fifteen years he kept a portion of his art secret from her. These are the famous Helga sessions, a German immigrant who modeled for Wyeth, mostly in the nude, the paintings warm and cold, sensual in their frankness, sometimes invoking sexuality but mostly studies in light and mood.

The Helga paintings caused quite a fuss then, this so-American landscape/portrait artist getting naughty. And politically incorrect, especially since some of the nudes were teenage girls, one in a sauna, towel draped around her thighs, young breasts exposed. Then the towel was disposed of. What is striking about her nudity and Helga's as well, is what stands out – their faces. Wyeth's nudes are studies in a quiet ferocity. The women are all there.

The point of the biographer in relation to Wyeth is that, as an artist, he needed a secret life. Away from prying eyes. Our surveillance society was not for him. Is it for us?

The private eyes that rove through our lives – they certainly have been roving through mine. Looking through the hotel keyholes, voyeurs really, Christians to find sin, Jews to out dissidents. I picture the Christians peepers, eyes bulging, holding a Cross in one hand, watching for kicks. Voyeurs. Jews at their gotcha moment bury their own flings and divorces. For Jews, it's blood not kicks. They come together, though, having found their mutual prey. There we have it: the Jewish-Christian dialogue of the Empire-enablers. Pimps with religious symbols around their necks during the daytime.

As I've said, all of that is for another day. Surveillance of that kind – voyeurs of sin and purpose – deserve their own surveillance, don't you think? Exposure seems to be the solution, as if transparency ends corruption. In my experience, it's just the opposite. Corruption is always on the move. Those who seek to root out corruption as they define it – yet another moving target – are often the most corrupt. Again, this is my experience. Yours?

So those who are watching me and other Jewish dissidents, don't you have something better to do? That's the first thing. But know we are watching you, too. Admittedly, the cycle of being watched and watching doesn't get anyone very far. It doesn't advance the justice ball down the field, does it?

Our secret life – it seems necessary for the artist and perhaps for everyone to imagine a life without surveillance. Like the child who needs to close his or her door. The parents naturally want to know and sometimes need to know what's going on beyond closed doors. The evolving private life of children isn't easy with so many prying eyes.

Secret life/double life. We find it in politics and in culture. This is also the world of religion, big time. Like the admonition to follow Jesus anywhere and everywhere, giving it all up, "camel and the eye of the needle" rhetoric, then finding out, through "transparency," that the Presbyterians have a 7 billion dollar portfolio. I place quotes around transparency because the only transparent thing about the live streaming of their convention is the attempt to keep folks like me from thinking, then saying, then writing, are you kidding, the whole divestment debate is about taking tens of millions of dollars in stocks out of some companies that are involved in the occupation of Palestinians?

Virtually all Israeli corporations are involved in the occupation in one way or another, not to mention an array of non-Israeli corporations, governments, and militaries who are also involved in one way or another. So "are you kidding" has to be followed by "who do you think you're kidding."

So, please, hold the "transparency" unless the exposure inadvertently calls attention to the truly scandalous.

On the secret/double life, however, there's a lot to think about. As in, the secret/double life of politics; what we don't see is what we need to see. The same with religion. Especially behind closed doors. Or better, the Cross – symbol of redemption/oppression. Now the mezuzah – liberation/occupation. Being free to be who we are as Jews/violating Jews in the name of authenticity. Liberation/Colonial Mezuzah.

If a person/community/culture/nationality/religion is around long enough, there are all sorts of secrets/double lives to be explored. The point is to expose the ones that hurt others and leave the others be, lest they also rise up in the wrong direction. It is also important to realize that secret/double lives remain. They don't disappear. There is no return before. At a certain point there is only after. What after becomes is everything. So much corruption in life. Indeed the truly corrupt, the powerful, benefit rather than being brought low. If once in a while they are brought low, there are others to take their place. Corruption and silence, the fear factor comes into play. Institutional life isn't what it's cracked up to be.

Yet we can't afford cynicism. That's what I tell my children. Exile is a place where cynicism can rule the day. Where does that lead? We need an even keel, a way of balancing the abuse of power and the wholeness of life.

Exile is brokenness. No reason to deny that. Yet if the cost of wholeness is selling out, what kind of wholeness is that? So the broken will be made whole, or are whole in their brokenness, even when you feel that you can't go on another day.

Exile is the place of brokenness made whole – if we can survive it all, right ourselves, ask what life is really about and plumb the depths of our Jewishness.

Let the powerful look at themselves in their own mirror. We have our own.

Pool
CAPE CANAVERAL

JULY 20

THE HEARTBEAT
OF THE PROPHETIC

Practicing exile. Proximity to the prophetic. Draw near and hear your heartbeat.

Jews have a history of exile that is too often lost to us. As if exile is foreign territory.

Exile isn't foreign to Jews. Though the territory where exiles live is mostly non-Jewish, it is from these foreign lands that most of the "Jewish" we know comes from. This means that "foreign"- isn't.

Exile occurs within the various historical incarnations of Israel, the state. Exile exists within the modern state of Israel. More and more Israelis, already in exile within the state, leave Israel for another exile. These Israelis are twice exiled. Surprising numbers of them are children of Holocaust survivors. Triple exile. Jewish vanguard kind of stuff. Is it in their Jewish DNA?

If we think we're the first ones to taste the bitterness of exile, we are mistaken. When we think we will be the last ones to taste the bitterness of exile, we are mistaken. When we think first/last we lose out on the lessons of exile, including its treasures.

Christian liberation theologians like the Peruvian Gustavo Gutierrez write about the poor as the engine of history. They are no doubt correct. But another engine are the exiles of every stripe who challenge the understood and acceptable. What joins the poor and the exiles is the prophetic. The prophetic is the bridge between the involuntarily and voluntarily displaced.

The prophets – they are the bridge over troubled water. Or walkers on the bridge within troubled water. History as troubled water. Prophets on the bridge. The prophets know the damage. They survey the catastrophe.

The cost of exile is great. What will help us through? At first reading, the Bible doesn't help much. At least certain readings aren't much help. Wishing punishment on the victors doesn't get us very far. God isn't coming down to tear the powerful down or lift us up. We have each other. Whether we read the Bible or not, that's about it.

Seems like chump change when compared to God. But I don't see God hanging around much. Our presence to each other shouldn't be taken for granted. Exiles know that "each other" is complicated. Distance, infighting, a sense of isolation – all of this takes its toll. Regardless of our flawed presence, without a sense of purpose and mutual aid we are lost.

The prophetic can't flourish if only desolation surrounds us. There is enough on desperation row to go around for eternity.

Practicing exile is learning to survive and flourish in the prophetic moment. Practicing exile is the long haul. It is an extended riff on the prophetic moment.

Think of those who cut their teeth in the 1980s. Think of my own *Toward a Jewish Theology of Liberation* being more relevant today than it was twenty-five years ago. Any author appreciates the relevance of his work after so many years. Having said that, it's hardly encouraging to find my ideas about the loss of Palestine and the loss of Jewish ethics more relevant today because the issues addressed there are actually worse than they were then. Much, much worse.

So the long haul it is and the prophetic prepares us for this – if we learn to practice exile. Yet we hardly understand the prophetic. Mostly, we acknowledge the existence of the tradition, then move on quickly. We address the pressing issues at hand. As if the mere mention of the prophetic invokes what is necessary and sufficient.

A spirituality of the prophetic? Of exile? Little of substance is written on these topics. Most of it is gloss. The Jewish Renewal movement dealt with the prophetic and exile by ritualizing it. As a way of coping, they intoned newly learned Hebrew, various Asian meditation techniques and Native American dances. When that was exhausted they delved into the Abrahamic faiths tangle. To me – and with due respect – these are spins on the prophetic/exile dynamic. They are coping mechanisms. It treats exile as if it isn't permanent. Exile is permanent. None of us are going back.

My experience with young prophetic Jews is that they want little to do with this coping sensibility. They want the prophetic/exile served up in real time. That is the great hope of the present generation.

I suppose part of my exile thing right now is thinking "mezuzah" daily. Visual reminders of exile are all around us. At the Cape, my doorposts are now mezuzah-less. I doubt it matters if there is a mezuzah on my doorpost. Cosmically speaking, who cares? Yet the question remains: What to do with our lives in the meantime?

That's the only question – and a big one. Since we spend so much energy on our individual existence, we need to engage it with a focused intentionality. Though collective realities seem almost cosmic in scope, there isn't any proof that collective reality is important beyond a sense of belonging in the here and now. Nonetheless, we are drawn to cosmic questions. we are drawn to collective identities.

Perhaps we should focus only a certain percentage of our energy on these individual, collective and cosmic questions. Taken together, they pretty much sum up what makes history go round. Render unto each their due and refuse to give over what shouldn't be given over? Part of practicing exile is time allotment.

Being in exile, the focus of life doesn't shift so much. What changes is the intensity. We cease living accidental lives.

Practicing exile – there are benchmarks we need to develop. Whether they are quiet mornings or prayers before bed. Spending time in nature. Time-off or time reflecting.

Shabbat dinners, Passover gatherings, sitting cross-legged on a cushion. Whatever.

"Whatever" meaning that our personal practice is ours for the making. Just don't link it with something cosmic or demand the same practice from others. Leave the "authentic" question to the empire builders.

The personal practice admonition goes for other communities as well. Solidarity across community lines cannot be based on having the same ritual or the same non-ritual. which usually amounts to an unannounced ritual anyway. Whatever helps focus us on the task at hand is the important thing.

On the other hand, the task at hand does not itself make a life. The long haul is intensely public, and deeply personal.

This is the mystery of the prophetic. And the prophet. The deeply personal is the most serious challenge of exile. "Personal is political" doesn't get at the internal life of the prophet. Not by a long shot. Slogans don't cover much ground when it comes to the inner part of our human condition.

The heartbeat of the prophet(ic). This is where practicing exile takes on life. We only have glimpses here – snapshots of poetry, testimony, last words, a depth of feeling that cannot be summed up or defined.

The heartbeat of the prophetic is found in the practice of exile. Yet it is almost impossible to encapsulate that ancient and yet so modern experience.

We think of the prophetic as expended in the bright spotlight of history. In actuality, history is only the most visible part of the prophetic. For the prophetic is hidden in another history, a history we have trouble accessing.

This has always been the case. The most visible. The prophet. The least visible. The prophet's heartbeat.

Is the prophet's heartbeat and the heartbeat of the prophetic the same?

The Question of God
WINDOW SEAT

JULY 21

MEZUZAH (GOD) WATCH

Back to my mezuzah watch, this time leading to the questions of questions: God. I've been dancing around the God question, preferring the Jewish question and the Israel question – or the prophet/exile tandem – but there's a Jewish elephant in the room. It's the one that Jews of Conscience kick down the road or don't even kick, they just ignore.

Not to get anyone's hopes up too high. If you've ever wrestled with the God question, you know it's best to approach it indirectly and from different angles. In any case, don't expect any answers from me, not even close. The last few days I've been wrapped in a kind of beach melancholy anyway. It may not be the best time for me to probe the God question but God's on my mind so I'll give it my best shot. If I don't get it done this time, I'll come around another day.

Before the mezuzah watch and the God question, tell me, are we really going back into the Eternal Anti-Semitism boxing ring? Raised by some *Atlantic Monthly* writer or affiliate that hit at *Mondoweiss* and other "marginal" types, as the writer so (un)easily put it, for their anti-Semitism or fellow traveling, I just wish the whole discussion would come to an end someday soon. But, no, that isn't possible because the anti-Semite charge is easily available and highly charged. In short, it's just too damn useful.

Most people who use it are grandstanders. As I have noted in a paragraph or two about some of my experiences with BDS – I stress some – if you don't think anti-Semitism is alive, you have your head in the sand. Anyone who thinks that I'm light on anti-Semites doesn't know me. I've already called out the Jewish money responses to my riff on the Presbyterian's multi-billion dollar portfolio. Really stupid stuff.

Some years ago an Irish Christian Biblical commentator, now deceased, a Catholic priest to boot and active in the Palestinian cause, trumpeted the Hebrew Bible's colonialism so often I thought he mistook the history of the ancient Israelites with the last 1500 years of Christian history. Funny enough, he didn't reference the latter. I found this a fascinating case of "Jews-on-the-Brain." Well I referred to him as an anti-Semite in a conference in Jerusalem we both were speaking at and the following day over breakfast he demanded an apology. I refused. I did step back a bit, though, correctly I think. I told him that though I couldn't say for sure whether he was an anti-Semite as a person, his work certainly was. So either he or his work, or both, were anti-Semitic. Since he's no longer with us, I'll leave it at that.

What do you do with ant-Semites? Call them out. What do you do with false accusations of anti-Semitism when you are addressing the Palestinian issue? Call them out.

The internet is fascinating on mezuzot – look it up. Hawking them, many from Israel,

the replacement I assume to the Israeli Hanukah candle industry when I was a child, low-tech by today's standards. Chabad is out there with their mezuzah interpretations as a mitzvah. Listen to Wikipedia on the mezuzah:

> A mezuzah (Hebrew: מְזוּזָה "doorpost"; plural: מְזוּזוֹת mezuzot) is a piece of parchment (often contained in a decorative case) inscribed with specified Hebrew verses from the Torah (Deuteronomy 6:4-9 and 11:13-21). These verses comprise the Jewish prayer "Shema Yisrael", beginning with the phrase: "Hear, O Israel, the LORD our God, the LORD is One"
>
> A mezuzah is affixed to the doorframe in Jewish homes to fulfill the mitzvah (Biblical commandment) to inscribe the words of the Shema "on the doorposts of your house" (Deuteronomy 6:9). Some interpret Jewish law to require a mezuzah on every doorway in the home apart from bathrooms, and closets too small to qualify as rooms. The parchment is prepared by a qualified scribe (a "sofer stam") who has undergone many years of meticulous training, and the verses are written in black indelible ink with a special quill pen. The parchment is then rolled up and placed inside the case.

You've got to love the special quill pen and, yes, the indelible ink – as in fixed, permanent, stubborn, engrained, enduring. The opposite being fleeting or temporary.

Deuteronomy is packed full of hope and despair, rah rah cheers and admonitions that should scare the hell out of anyone who understands that the future is up for grabs. As with most of the Bible you have to pick and choose texts. As Jews have done. As all religions do.

Notice, too, that you need a "qualified scribe" – is that to inscribe authority that speaks for God? Notice the scribe rather than the Biblical prophet, who didn't have a quill pen, at least as far as we know. I don't remember any of the prophets writing out rote passages or speaking them either. Prophetic writing comes later. Without rote passages.

On the "years of meticulous training," Emmanuel Levinas, the great Jewish philosopher, described the prophet as one who trains like a fighter. But his reference is to the prophet's years of training – in asceticism. From which the prophetic word springs, but also, from which there is no rescue.

"An asceticism, like the training of a fighter," Levinas writes. The prophet is alone. Even God is absent from the prophet's life. Often. Levinas writes that the mezuzah grounds a Jewish home like an anchor. Such a home isn't open to the whims of the world. The mezuzah grounds the home and the people within it; everyone knows where they come from.

Still, when Levinas was queried about the Palestinians being our neighbor, the neighbor being everything in Levinas' philosophy, the one we have an obligation to before even our obligation to ourselves – this during Israel's invasion of Lebanon in the 1980s – he fell short. Levinas answered that the Palestinians were not our neighbors, hence Jews have no obligation to them. Which raises the question as to whether Levinas, who wrote so beautifully about

the prophets and the prophetic, can be forgiven? With this terrible error, does Levinas need to be rethought? Or abandoned?

Emmanuel Levinas' beautiful evocation of the mezuzah as the anchor of the Jewish home. Yet he, too, led a secret/double mezuzah life. Perhaps his double understanding of neighbor, our neighbor being Jewish but not Palestinian, is now inscribed on our doorposts in indelible ink.

Those who seek to understand Levinas undergo meticulous training. And need it, since Levinas, like many other philosophers, is difficult to understand.

Let me put it this way: entering the world of Levinas scholarship is like entering Kafka's castle. You don't know where the authority who is calling you to task comes from. There's a scribe with meticulous training somewhere in the castle, but who has authorized their inscription? Is it God on a good day or a bad one, or is it a God stand-in: an obligation to neighbor that disappears when the going gets tough?

This isn't philosophy time. Or scribe time. The mezuzah is just an object. Symbol. Yet, as well, inscribed in the Jewish psyche. Like the words of the Shema it contains. God is One. Prayer of affirmation. Martyr's prayer. The last words on Jews' lips before we meet our death under various oppressive situations. Now others recite their martyr's prayers before they are dispatched by us.

Sitting there on our doorposts. At our homes, at my dentist's office, at the rabbi's weekend getaway on the beach. Most often mezuzot are found on the doorposts of the homes of the 1 percent.

In our present historical configuration, Jewish empowerment rules the day. No wonder Jewish empowerment mezuzot are on sale on the internet.

eMezuzah. As in eBay. Inscribed with indelible ink. Don't forget. If the mezuzah is to be authentic, if your home is to be protected, if your status as a Jew is to be recognized, have one. And make them bigger and prettier than ever. More expensive?

On the billboards in Texas, the constant refrain: Size Counts. Now that is true in Jewish life. The size of your mezuzah says a lot.

Yes, I finish without addressing the God question directly. Right there on the parchment – God is one. Hear Israel, your God. But with the anchor being power – helicopter gunships in the Ark of the Covenant – perhaps we have already translated God out of existence. Or our ability to talk about God.

Many say our reticence about God is about the Holocaust. Where was God in Auschwitz? True. Palestinians may be asking where God is as Palestine disappears. Should they place mezuzot on their doorposts so that God will pass over them in a (reverse) Exodus?

Jewish reluctance to speak about God may also be about accountability. What if the mezuzah that trumpets our affirmation of God is a way we encase God under our power, so we won't be accountable?

Moshe Silman
TEL AVIV

JULY 22

THEY LEFT ME
WITH NOTHING

Moshe Silman, before he set himself on fire at a protest for social justice in Tel Aviv last week, said: "The state of Israel stole from me and robbed me. They left me with nothing."

Reading his story in *Haaretz,* Silman's life is a study in decline on all fronts: economic, physical health and perhaps mental health as well. Such a story of loss and tragedy isn't peculiar to Israel, not at all. It's all around us. Being on the verge of losing everything, becoming homeless, every city in America, including Cape Canaveral, has all of this. I see it on the beach often. Our public library down the street is full of the homeless.

Other than abandonment, it isn't clear how Silman viewed Israel in relation to his decline. Did he see Israel as a special place because of its claims on Jewishness so that abandonment took on an added dimension? Or did he simply see Israel as any place anyone lives where a state bureaucracy and the state itself simply doesn't care about its citizens? The faceless, Jewish face in the crowd? Or the faceless face in the crowd?

Daphni Leef is one of the organizers of the protests. Her reflection: "I do not feel we live in a democracy. I feel we live in an oligarchy. A few wealthy families control the whole country."

Haaretz headline: "Moshe Silman vs. the State of Israel; The desperate act of a man who went from businessman to homeless and jobless within 10 years epitomizes collapse of the welfare system."

Yes, son of Holocaust survivors. In his fifties. A few years younger than the state of Israel. Nestled into the story of failed businesses and social isolation is a kicker: Silman's final downward spiral occurred when the second Palestinian Uprising severely restricted his business. The Israeli state bureaucracy turned a blind eye to his plight, for sure, but the consequences of its policies toward Palestinians was also a factor.

A tragedy, one that follows last year's protests about the lack of affordable housing, now starting up again. The Israeli Spring as some called it, with reference to the Arab Spring, has stalled. Last year there seemed to be links between the hopes of all populations in the Middle East for democracy or more democracy, a matter of bridge-building, painstaking, so long in coming. Some thought that this could be the turning point in the Middle East, inclusive of Israel and Palestine. Another hope squandered.

All of this came on the heels of the global Occupy movement. Occupy Israel?

Occupy Jewish.

Yes, the word seems worn now, with everyone on the bandwagon, the movement lost its meaning. Or the word was drained of content. The reasons for the movement remain.

So name it what you want or don't name it all. The issues Silman's self-immolation raises is beyond a name. It's about the human being caught in a system, any system that functions as state systems function. It's also about the ideals of a state, any state, and how reality differs from ideals. And yes it's about the very idea of a Jewish state and whether placing Jewish before a state means anything different at all – even for Jews.

So interesting, in the *New York Times,* the first part of the article that appears on Silman is paired with reporting on the huge Tokyo rally opposed to the return of Japan's nuclear power. The second part is paired with Hillary Clinton's visit to Israel. In the picture, Clinton is being kissed by Shimon Peres, President of Israel, one of the political architects of Israel's nuclear program.

As the article on Clinton mentions, her visit has much to do with Egypt's recent presidential election and, of course, with Iran. Clinton assured the press that the United States and Israel are on the same page regarding Iran's nuclear ambitions. Whatever they are. Or might be.

Self-immolation. Ritualized suicide. Usually Buddhist. Also Hindu. This time it's a Jewish body. Burning in a Jewish state. Reports are framed by the empires that have other more important issues on their mind. This might have been Silman's point. Bigger issues don't matter if you've lost everything.

The issue of oligarchy – definition: a small group of people who together govern a nation or control an organization, often for their own purposes. Of course, oligarchs never discuss it this way. Another global thing. Oligarchs wrap themselves in flags of every stripe. Including the Israeli flag. Everyone outside of that small group fends for themselves, including a son of Holocaust survivors, even as the Jewish oligarchs wrap themselves in the Holocaust flag.

I mostly comment on Israel's foreign policy question, that being Palestinians. I follow Israel's fascinating internal life but leave it at that. Yet the question of questions is whether Palestinians are, for Israel and for Jews in general, a foreign policy issue. There are more than a million Palestinians within the 1967 borders of Israel. The fourth largest Jewish population in the world lives in the area (supposedly) governed by the Palestinian Authority, one that is occupied by Israel.

It's confusing – the separation of Israel's domestic and foreign policy regarding Palestinians isn't easy. Add the remnants of Palestinian life being all around Jews living within and outside the Israel's 1967 borders, it's difficult to imagine there being six degrees of separation between Jews and Palestinians in Israel-Palestine. Or Jews and Palestinians in their respective often comingled diasporas.

African immigrants in Israel, low-wage labor, refugees from Eritrea, Sudan and the like – another foreign policy issue? Deportations have been ordered for those threatening to "overrun" the Jewish state. Yet also awakening Jewish history to justice. It seems that the Jews

of Conscience justice plate is full. Overflowing.

Full plate. Now self-immolation. A foreign suicide ritual no doubt. But martyrdom isn't foreign to Jews, is it?

Jewish life has always been all mixed up. In the end, the attempt to purify and separate just furthers the mixing. This is another part of Jewish history that the oligarchy governing Israel – and the oligarchy speaking for the American Jewish community – doesn't seem to get.

Being left with nothing. Institutions, states, universities, religions – they'll all betray you in a self-interested heartbeat. Putting "Jewish" before the state doesn't change much, if anything. Apartheid Walls won't further separation in the long run.

Eventually Israel-Palestine will be mixed, as it has always been. As it is (unjustly) today.

By the time the oligarchs realize it we might be left with nothing, too.

Self-immolation. Ritualized suicide. Oligarchies do it, too. When they lose their power what will they be left with?

Edward Said
APARTHEID WALL

JULY 23

(UN)UNIVERSALIST (JEWISH PROPHET)
EDWARD SAID I KNEW

Hodgepodge today, picking up errant strands I've been writing about and going at them again. But finishing with an Edward Said flourish. Call it a trip down memory lane.

Speaking of oligarchies and ritualized suicide and being left with nothing, making it matters. In Israel. In America. No doubt the notion of making it is shared all over the world. Like squandering.

If you don't make it, you're left with nothing. Is that how we want it to be or is that just oligarchies talking? Or us picking up the oligarchy accent?

I doubt Israel would have born without Jews having made it in America. We often reference the Holocaust for the creation of Israel. No doubt that was crucial. But the Jewish Diaspora had much to do with the creation of Israel. It has much to do with its existence today. Injustice toward Palestinians is difficult to continue without American Jews lobbying for and enabling that injustice.

Empowered diasporas are crucial back home. Though the "home" I write about came from the Diaspora rather than the other way around. Jewish history is different, even when it comes to states formed from outside. Though South Africa in the mirror means this part of Jewish history shares similarities. Meaning, Israelis as white colonial settlers. (Yes, I don't believe that's all of the story, but we can't understand Israel's story without it.)

I've been asked how to surface the colonial in Jewish life. As in, workshops or teaching. I would forget the teaching for now, at least in university settings. Teaching about Jews except in the romanticized form is the third rail of university life. As in, terminal. Like breaking down the Holocaust into its component parts, emphasizing the clash of the German and Soviet empires where millions of folks, including millions of Jews, were caught in between. Timothy Snyder calls the death mill between empires the Bloodlands. Not much room for the Holocaust there. We'll save that for another day.

Jews as Orientalists – without even knowing it. Hannah Arendt's nightmare of who Jews would become, though she couldn't escape her Western upbringing completely. Arendt thought Arabs should be delighted with an enhanced Jewish presence in the Middle East because of the Western know-how Jews brought to the backward region. In Arendt's mind, Jews were without a history of colonialism. Yet they became thoroughly colonial once outside the European cauldron. As for workshops on the relation of Jewish identity and colonialism, simply adopt the methodology various workshops on racism and sexism use. Apply the same rubrics. Feature Jewish thinking/images/stereotypes on Arabs, Palestinians

and Islam as starters. But also expand it so Jews can look at how we function in the West historically and in the present. Don't forget Jews of Arab background and how they are seen within the dominant Jewish discourse. For God's sake, don't organize the workshop around rediscovering Jewish identity. You might end up celebrating Shabbat in a sweat lodge.

The idea is to break out of our comfort zone, not retreat into a safe place for Jews in non-Jewish space. If you need some Jewish thinkers that will challenge your workshop attendees try Marx and Arendt. Even with all their flaws, they're giants compared to Jewish thinkers today. Remember, the challenge isn't Jewish purity, which has never been, or any other purity, which has never been. We need to walk with our Colonial Mezuzah – no use pretending it doesn't exist within us.

Assign Edward Said to read, without thinking he was perfect. I knew Said and loved his princely manner. He was handsome and debonair, a super elite and a man of the people. I have so many stories of my encounters with Said that one day I will share more fully.

It might not surprise you that regarding Said's work and persona, I think against the grain. In his writing and lecturing, Said made it explicit that he didn't believe in essences with regard to identity. This included Jews and Palestinians. Yet I know he believed that Palestinians were something special, real special. Otherwise why would he have gone ballistic when Arafat sold out the Palestinians at Oslo?

Leaders sell out their peoples on a regular basis, why should the PLO be any different? The PLO wasn't any different. Palestinians are. To think that the Palestinian witness to the Arab and global world would be sold out for dime store mansions in the Gaza Strip infuriated Said. It sent him over the edge.

Said is used by Palestinians and Jews in the One State elite circles as the universalist among universalists. They rely on his rhetoric rather than what he believed. Here is my take. Said believed that Palestinians were different than other Arab collectivities. Palestinians had a message for Israel, other Arabs and the world. Of course, he didn't say this as such. Said was way too sophisticated for that kind of particularity and besides he would sound almost Jewish if he started down that road. Though if you might remember, Said proudly laid claim to be the "last cosmopolitan Jew." More than a few of his close friends were Jews, of the cosmopolitan variety naturally.

When I was around Said, I used to marvel at the legions of followers who came to him as supplicants. He abhorred that – at least he said that to me – and he also couldn't live without it. Not for a second. That was part of Said's greatness. But on the essence stuff, he was in with both feet.

Said was wonderful to be around, yet I also felt his aloneness. It surrounded him. He also cultivated it. As if he couldn't function without being set apart. Though I loved Said – there will never be another Palestinian like him – some of his thought was superficial. There were areas of thought, especially spirituality, he wouldn't approach.

In my estimation, Said was too negative about deeper levels of engagement, as if they could only be articulated and accepted on infantile levels. This was a huge mistake on his part

and on the part of the "universalist" secular Left. The secular Left, at least to my mind, isn't really secular at all. They cling to their beliefs as strongly as any religious believer. Sometimes more so.

There is so much aloneness in the world. Anyone who pioneers new ways of thinking experiences it. Probably needs it. Said referred to me as a friend but my own sense is that Said didn't have friends in the usual sense. Said was on a mission. Mission-folks are somewhere else on the friendship continuum.

Said marked my life in significant ways. Interestingly, they were on the levels he wouldn't go near in his own thought. Like the time he found me teaching in central Texas. Said couldn't believe that I could end up in Texas, so in his mind, I couldn't be living where I was, in fact, living. When I asked him why I couldn't be living where I was living, he thought for a second and said: "Because I can't picture you living anywhere in particular." When I pressed him on the point he continued: "Marc, I cannot imagine you living in a home in one particular place. I think of you as an itinerant Jewish prophet."

So much for the secular Said.

This didn't make him religious in the typical sense. He was far too intelligent for that. And too broken by the failed promises of religion. Yet, it is also true that Said retained an almost elementary school understanding of religiosity. As if, though every other field of inquiry could, indeed had to be, relentlessly moving in deeper directions, religion had no place to move. He was wrong, of course, but certainly the Christianity and Islam he knew and the Judaism he experienced, even the Jewish Renewal colonial stuff, certainly didn't open his closed religious universe.

But then, why not simply honor me with what would be his highest accolade – that I was intelligent and provocative? From Enlightenment Said, intelligent and provocative were the highest accolades. Said hungered for a world that is more than thought. His writing is a beacon searching for that point in the ocean where the treasure is finally spotted, then salvaged and brought to shore. The shore eluded Said.

When I share my PowerPoint presentation as I travel, I always include Said's picture among Jews of Conscience. I know he wasn't Jewish, though he did claim his "cosmopolitan Jew" status with great pride. Since he claimed to be a Jew, why not include him among Jews?

I also include Said there because he accompanied many Jews into the night side of Jewish history. While doing this, he neither gloated nor held himself above the fray. Said never baited Jews. Just the opposite, Said had a soft spot for Jews who lived up to his (un)essential sense of Jewish intelligence, analytical skills and, yes, compassion.

I have come to believe that Said's claimed status as a cosmopolitan Jew was an ingenious cover to draw closer to the Jewish prophetic. Said wanted to be near the prophetic and its claims to penetrating the depths of history.

In another lifetime, Said may have appeared as one of those Jewish prophets. Or perhaps, in his own way, he already has.

Menorah at Night
CAPE CANAVERAL

JULY 24

GATHERING LIGHT

Palestinians of a certain generation knew the Jewish score. Edward Said was one. For sure, Said was the last cosmopolitan Jew to draw near to the prophetic. If ever there was a modern thinker who deserved Elijah's chariot and horses take-away it was Said. He was alone in his eloquence.

With regard to the prophetic, I also remember his friend and teacher, Ibrahim Abu-Lughod, a Palestinian exile I knew for years in America.

I visited Ibrahim after he returned to Palestine in the 1990s. It was he who told me once: "Marc, the Jewish prophetic voice will never die." I didn't understand Ibrahim's statement until my son, Aaron, wrote a letter to the Israeli Consul who had come from Houston to lecture at my university. It was during the height of the second Palestinian Uprising when Star of David helicopter gunships controlled the sky.

Aaron was then 14 years old and when I read his letter he reminded me of Ibrahim. In no uncertain terms and in a beautiful poetic language, Aaron took Israel's sophisticated power to task. The Consul was drawn and quartered. My analysis: Because I taught Aaron rather than send him to Hebrew School, Aaron never had the prophetic beaten out of him by Jewish authorities. Instead, he witnessed his father surviving their beatings and made a decision. He opted for the Jewish indigenous.

Part of the prophetic is existential – full steam ahead. The prophet is mournful about the squandering and hopeful about a future where the squandering will come to an end. After all, if the prophet doesn't believe in a just future, he is dead in the water. Yet if the prophet speaks about a bright and cheery future, he becomes a cheerleader.

For the prophet there is a future because none is on the horizon. Everything has gone too far. We are surrounded by darkness. If only others finally understand the darkness that the prophet sees ahead is already here. Then a glimmer of light appears.

Light through mourning. New beginnings when the end surrounds us. Seems paradoxical or ironic. Seems impossible. It certainly skirts logic. It isn't a prefabricated answer. Not a slogan mobilizer either. All of the above when multiple choice won't do.

This light seems self-generated because there isn't any outside energy to be corralled. Yet self-generated light is impossible. There has to be a source outside ourselves. In nature? The light the prophet speaks about isn't found in nature. Could it come from God?

We've already disciplined the "God as rescuer" motif. Besides, Jews of Conscience aren't going to entertain the movie version. Exile is too hands dirty.

How to account for light in darkness? How to account for the persistence of the prophetic? Perhaps they are one and the same. Light/Prophetic. That still doesn't account for either or both together.

Try this: The prophet embodies light. The prophetic as a movement is light. Being light, the prophet and the prophetic gather light. Amid the darkness.

Light gatherers, it's hard to see this. Or feel this. When history keeps spiraling downward. But then we don't really know when the downward trend is about to turn upward. Or when what seems upward is about to take a turn for the worse.

Since we don't know what's around history's corner. And since we don't know where the corner, going either way, is, we are more or less rooting around in the dark – at least as far as what the future might become. For the prophet, then, the task is at hand, keeping at it, paying attention, focus, conscious purpose, intentionality. The prophetic sense is that the future is right here, in the now, even as we let go of where it's going.

The logic of injustice, atrocity, ecological crisis is that all will continue. It will. The logic is downward. That is correct. If the downward movement is interrupted, a victory indeed, it's often followed by downward movement somewhere else. Injustice is like rain. Somewhere in the world it is raining all the time. Somewhere in the world there will always be injustice. There will never be an end to injustice, even when it stops, for a moment, where we are. If the picture we have is always injustice somewhere, and that the future will feature injustice somewhere, that there isn't an end anywhere, then the question – where is justice? – is too heavy. It makes us want to set our sails in a different direction, toward conformity and empire. Why not enjoy without a second thought, riding the crest of the wave? At least for as long as we can. Let others find their own rescue boats, make their own plans. Since injustice is now and the future.

The logic of Israel-Palestine – downward spiral. Conquered space. Atrocity around every corner. War and more war. Disappeared Palestine.

The logic of Israel-Palestine – one state. A civil rights movement made up of Jews and Palestinians takes hold. After much dislocation and death, the population decides to take another tact. Reappeared Palestine. Perhaps.

Downward spiral. One state. Or two real states working toward a negotiated unity. Empires' rear-guard actions within both populations, the surrounding countries, outside factions, countries, religions. Those Jews and Palestinians who survive all of this, wanting another way.

Timetable – unknown. Unknowable.

Gathering light without knowing what will become of the light. We don't know if the light will survive the darkness or be extinguished even as it is gathered. Or, if it becomes a flame, how long it will burn or how it will burn. Like a forest fire, terrain, heat and winds make the fire's path unpredictable.

So deliberation is important and overrated. Guiding the light - doubtful. The light we gather will go where it goes. There will be other light gatherers there who will face the same (im)possibilities.

History is (un)certain.

History is (un)knowable.

The prophet is operating in the dark. Except for the light she gathers.

Joe Who?
PENN STATE

JULY 25

REVERED TO RADIOACTIVE:
PEACE GARDENS OF THE WORLD BEWARE!

The statue of Joe Paterno in front of Penn State's football stadium has been removed. Quite a fall from football's Mt. Olympus.

Others statues have fallen. The big names – Lenin, Stalin, Hitler – mostly powerful political figures, have their images carved in stone or bronze. They're heavyweight, made to last for centuries. Though difficult to bring down, down they come when the times change and history has its say.

In our age sports heroes rank right up there. Sports figures become iconic. They also rise and fall. History doesn't bow before the iconic forever.

Book writers: beware of writing bios of iconic figures. A book tour of a new biography of Paterno is now on hold. The title of the book – should it actually come out – has been changed. The original title, *The Grand Experiment: The Life and Meaning of Joe Paterno*, has been, shall we say, shortened. New title, *Paterno*. Suggestions for a subtitle? This could become a late-night talk show bonanza. As in, *How to Win Football Games and Garnish a University's Reputation by Protecting a Child-Molester.*

If you think Penn State is way out there on the athletic scene, forget it. When you're inside a university, you see it all. This includes the "Christian" colleges. Believe me, the ethical bar is low. Just look at who serves as presidents of these institutions. Get this quote in the *New York Times*: "Announced in March 2011 as 'a biography of America's winningest college football coach, who changed the country one football player at a time,' the book will enter the marketplace at a moment when the name of Joe Paterno, the late Penn State coach, has gone from revered to radioactive."

Radioactive indeed. Once revered. Yesterday. As the greatest moral example of college sports. The next day the statue is gone. Bye, bye, Jo Pa!

Wherever I travel, I find it fascinating to see who is revered and who is reviled. Or how the once reviled are now revered. For the iconic, there are second chances in history. Sometimes more.

Some years ago I was invited to speak at a Lutheran college in South Dakota. Airplane connections were complex and my time was short. The person arranging my travel was considerate and patient. The final scheduling problem involved my attendance at a church service celebrating Martin Luther's birthday. It was scheduled the day before I spoke. The travel coordinator kept trying to get me to the church on time. Without specifying the reason, I kept putting her off. Truth be told, I wasn't about to attend a celebration for one of

the most articulate anti-Semites of all time.

Obviously, Martin Luther has a very special place in the heart of Lutherans and for the denomination that bears his name. Whatever Lutheran church or college I visit, there it is – a larger than life statue of Luther staring me right in my face.

If you've ever read Luther's extensive writing "On the Jews and Their Lies" you'll understand where I'm going. Without assigning him to Hitler, if you travel north on Luther Street you can end up with mass death. Under certain conditions.

"Under certain conditions." Broad statement. Broad brush. Because, you see, Martin Luther was a revolutionary religious thinker. Viewed from various angles, Luther leads in different directions, the most fruitful of which he probably wouldn't recognize. Like parts of the modern Lutheran community that I've been around – I doubt he'd even recognize them as his progeny.

I doubt they are his progeny myself, except in name. The Lutherans I know are what I call "aberrational Christians." I don't know how long they'll be around.

Hybrids are part of history, too. But when does a hybrid become something other than a mixture of parts? When is a hybrid something altogether different? Alien?

True, as well, for Jews. Unrecognizable, what we have become, to many who went before us. Can you imagine a rabbi from the 13th century recognizing as Jews, Israeli soldiers commandeering Palestinian homes and defecating in their living rooms just to show them who's boss? Is that behavior alien to "Jewish?"

Not now it isn't, alien that is. What was is no longer. So we carry that defecation into the future.

Tainted greatness. Luther. So many others. Every leader? Every community? It all depends which way the historical winds blow at this time and that. Because someone like Martin Luther means one thing in one era and something else in another. We don't know which Luther will show up in the decades ahead. Scary, don't you think?

It's a risk that history has in store. Once there, always there. It depends on what is done with legacy.

I wonder how long before the Peace Garden statues that feature the likes of David Ben-Gurion and Yitzhak Rabin fall. Without comparisons but noting certain similarities, each following has its statue pantheon. Often it has to do with victory or defeat; the passage of time tends to elevate the defeated. But, then, the defeated are often used in the next victory procession. When the role reversal occurs and the power reversal comes in time, those statues also come down. There aren't many Peace Garden statues that stand the test of history.

Meanwhile, watch out for ethnic cleansers in your communal Peace Gardens. Especially in the Peace Gardens of your mind.

Thomas Paine
Thetford, Norfolk

JULY 26

CHIEF LAST NIGHT

On the Thomas Paine front, it turns out he became a professional revolutionary, after the American Revolution heading to France for the revolution there. He almost lost his head (literally) there because he was against the forced de-Christianization policies of the revolutionists. Paine was imprisoned in the Luxembourg Palace which the revolution turned into a prison.

I visited the palace in my 1973 European backpack tour and don't remember the "palace into prison" turn on the tourist information packet. Maybe it's been added since. Like the discussion of the slave quarters in anti-bellum plantation tours in the South. They're only cropping up now.

Tourism attempts to hide the fact that history is a series of illusions and disillusions. Until tourism can't hide the pain anymore. Then the reverse of what history once boasted becomes a tourist attraction itself. Strange thing, tourism. Like the museum at Auschwitz, with hundreds of thousands of visitors a year. Death camp to tourist site. Check the bus schedule.

Paine's life had so many interesting twists and turns. He never accumulated wealth, married or had children. He was lionized and disparaged in America and France. He spoke up for slaves and Native Americans. Paine saw himself as a global citizen way before our generation thought it was the first to have this sensibility.

One of my favorite scenes is Paine negotiating with Chief Last Night, who represented the Native American tribes. Paine's hope was to get Native Americans to side with the American revolutionists against Great Britain. At the start of the negotiations, Paine introduced himself as "Common Sense," the title of his famous pamphlet that inflamed American independence fever.

Chief Last Night provided an interesting interpretation of empire. It might be useful for our task at hand. After expressing awe at the "great canoes" of the British, the chief expressed how unlikely it would be for the British to conquer the Americans on land: "The king of England is like a fish. When he is in the water he can wag his tail. When he comes on land he lays down on his side."

The strength of a people, nation, religion, ideology in one arena is their weakness in another. Apply it across the board. When it comes to Jews and the conflict between the prophetic and empire, which one are we suited for? When the prophetic gives way to empire Jews may be like the chief's analysis of the British. In the prophet mode, our tails wag. When we defend empire, we can't breathe.

The prophetic as (Jewish) oxygen. Natural (Jewish) habitat. Is that, as well, the real Habitat for Humanity? (Not housing within an unjust system, but a just system where housing is a right.)

Or perhaps the Jewish prophetic is a constituent element of the global prophetic. Like a particle in an atom without which the atom can't be whole. Then, proceeding backwards, the Jewish prophetic particle takes on life within the broader prophetic structure. Both are necessary if the universe is going to have some stability.

The instability of history, at least the way it exists rather than the way it's narrated. Then, the formation of Israel as the struggle of a Holocaust people against great odds defeating a blood thirsty backward Arab world who had all the land in the world but wouldn't give one inch to a people in need. Now, the formation of Israel as a European invasion of white (Jewish) settlers with superior arms who ethnically cleanse the Palestinian people, then after its formation, continue occupying and cleansing Palestinians from their land.

Listen carefully. Can you hear the Peace Garden statues falling?

But then, if applied universally, a strict justice, as in: if founding a country but owning slaves disqualifies you, would there be any statues in the Peace Gardens of our world? Those of every nationality, religion and ideology who have been honored in the past at some point fade from history's view. Some are removed with ceremony. Others are taken down in the dark of night.

If a Peace Garden statue falls in the night do the other Peace Garden statues around the world hear them falling?

Notice Brandeis, a Jewish university, at least in inspiration, for a way out of the statue business. Their Building for Peace has nothing of the sort. Should I say, no graven images? Here is their description. Read it carefully. Notice what it says and what it doesn't.

> Building for Peace was a recognized club of the Student Union whose mission was to construct a peace monument on campus that would serve as a physical testament to the universality of peace and the diversity at Brandeis. The club was comprised of the students of professor Gordon Fellman's Sociology of Empowerment class and was funded by a grant from the Hewlett Pluralism Alliance and the Student Senate.
>
> The Brandeis University Peace Monument was first dedicated in May 2002. It is located in the circular seating area between Usdan and Pearlman and is surrounded by benches and a garden. In the very center of the monument is a beautiful mosaic of a dove — the international symbol of peace. Encircling the mosaic are tiles engraved with the word "peace" in the languages spoken at Brandeis. There are approximately 40 different language bricks.
>
> Building for Peace set out to further the beauty and breadth of the Peace Monument by adding bricks and improving the garden. There are hopes to add approximately 20 more language bricks (including American Sign

Language and Braile), various cultural symbols of peace, a dedication plaque and a "peace tree." Part of the financing for what we now call the Mandel Peace Garden, came from generous benefactor Jay A. Mandel '80 and his life partner, Jeffrey M. Scheckner, in memory of Jay's grandparents, Harry and Violet Mandel.

So many things to admire about this peace building. I assume the "peace tree" has been planted by now, since we are a decade after its founding. I assume, too, that the twenty more language bricks have also been added. Perhaps even more since their International Studies program has no doubt expanded. All quite progressive, wouldn't you say?

The club that founded the building, interesting title for the course – Sociology of Empowerment. I suppose that could go in many directions, even north like Martin Luther Street. First stop atrocity? Then ethnic cleansing? You don't have to reach mass death for empowerment to turn that corner. The Sociology of Empowerment. We all need some power. I suppose it depends on how things are defined and from which vantage point you begin.

This reminds me of the first Palestinian Uprising when Rabbi Irving Greenberg who had written about the Holocaust and its lessons wrote a pamphlet titled "The Ethics of Jewish Power." 1988 was the date and it was a tour de force. In a nutshell, Greenberg argued that the days of Jewish powerlessness were over. The days of Jewish power were here, necessarily in light of the Holocaust. Now Jews had to face the fact that Israel would do things as a state and in defense of its national interests that would properly be critiqued by our prophetic tradition. But now that tradition had to take a backseat lest it undermine Israel's power and bring us to a second-Holocaust situation.

Thus the ethics of Jewish power had to be thought through. Since we were new at the empowerment game. Now it's all old hat. Today, most Jews don't even think of the prophetic in relation to Jewish power. We shrug our shoulders. Why raise the issue?

May 2002, almost a decade after Oslo. May 2002, the second Uprising, the Apartheid Wall. Coming soon the war in Lebanon and then a few years later the invasion of Gaza. Since May 2002, the settler population in Jerusalem and the West Bank multiplied by the thousands upon thousands. More than a decade later, the peace languages spoken multiply. Do they drown out the sounds of Star of David helicopter gunships on the prowl?

Language signed here. Another step in the right direction. Now show me how the Star of David helicopter gunships in the open Ark of the Covenant are signed. I'm ready to learn where we are as Jews in every language possible, aren't you?

I also want to learn how to sign the prophetic.

Signing the prophetic. Helicopter gunships on the prowl.

If we visualize our new reality it might help us turn our canoe around.

Thinking of Chief Last Night. Water and Land. Wagging his tail. Lying on his side. Sign that too.

The Rabbi & The Spy
ISRAEL AND EGYPT

JULY 27

PROPHET GRAY

On successive days, the *New York Times* carried the following obituaries: "Rabbi Y. S. Elyashiv, Master of Talmudic Law, Dies at 102" and Omar Suleiman, "Powerful Egypt Spy Chief, Dies at 76." Below some illuminating passages from each.

Elyashiv:

> Slender with a white wispy beard and penetrating eyes, Rabbi Elysashiv represented a rigorously conservative approach to Jewish law that seeks to safeguard its traditions against the assaults of modern life. He opposed service to the Israeli military for yeshiva students, which he called a "plot to uproot Torah from Israel." He disapproved of professional studies for women . . .
>
> In 2004, he banned wigs from India made of human hair that were used by Orthodox wives to conceal their actual hair in public. He did so because the Indian hair had been cut off in Hindu ceremonies that he regarded as idol worship, and thus violated the fundamental Jewish belief in one God. Within days, women in Jerusalem were casting their wigs into bonfires, and women in the Borough Park area of Brooklyn were either wrapping their heads in scarves or flocking to stores to buy wigs made of synthetics.

Suleiman:

> That he died in the United States was, to his Egyptian critics, emblematic of his close ties with the C.I.A., which he had helped as it established the practice of extraordinary rendition; sending terrorist suspects to foreign countries to be interrogated and, its critics say, tortured.
>
> When the C.I.A. asked Mr. Suleiman if he could provide a DNA sample from a brother of the Qaeda leader Ayman al-Zawahri, Mr. Suleiman offered to send the agency the brother's entire arm, according to Robert Suskind, who has written extensively about antiterrorism efforts.

Just to let you know I have placed them both in my ever-expanding file under: "Obituary: Bury Them Together." Or I could rename the file: "Bury Together: Deserved Each Other."

Either way, it's a hoot to read the obits of the famous. What they're known for. What they've done to deserve their fame. What crimes they committed along the way. Image cascade: Orthodox women casting their idol wigs into bonfires as the truly religious Jews escape military service in a Jewish state; Our man in Cairo offering al-Zawarhri's arm for cash

and receives in return money galore and a state-side hospital bed to die in.

So let's see, right now I have offered joint burial sites to: Arafat/Sharon; Dershowitz/Starr; Elyashiv/Suleiman. Quite a cemetery already but, of course, the historical list is endless. The future list will be endless as well. Among other elements notice that in each joint burial I've advocated, the "couples" are from different faiths. Limitations: they're all men (as of now). But since the homophobia rating of each is probably high the idea of coupling them for eternity is another laugher.

It's always nice when the empire rattlers end their journey among us. Though replacements are easy to find. Everyone and their brother and sister are vying for honorifics and power. The Wheel of Empire spins.

As for "authentic" Judaism and Jewish knowledge check out this remark on Rabbi Elyashiv by Rabbi Yeruchim Silber, executive director of the Boro Park Jewish Community Council: "The breadth of his knowledge was outstanding."

Give the rabbi this, he lived modestly. As his obituary recalls: "He also cast decisions in the most private of cases. Hundreds of Jews would stream to his home – a modest one-bedroom apartment in an alleyway in the ultra-Orthodox quarter of Mea Shearim in Jerusalem – to seek his opinions on their personal quandaries, or simply his blessing. They also came to his nightly tutorials on Talmud, much of which he knew by heart."

Heart learning. Again credit where credit is due. And for anti-Zionists, whatever that can mean today, no doubt you are of one mind with the rabbi on this issue. I doubt that means you'll throw your wig into a bonfire but linking on certain issues while disagreeing on others has some merit. We do this all the time anyway. Life is a series of negotiations. Even joint burials have to be negotiated.

Back on the prophet trail, it's wrong to think that the prophetic is a stand-alone.

The prophetic is also negotiated. It seems contradictory. If there's anything that isn't negotiable, it's the prophetic, isn't it?

My response is no, there is no absolute, not even God. This is the reason that so many sophisticates miss out on contemplating the God question. Or simply dismiss it. Absolutes are out. As in, "I'm too intelligent to go there." A la Edward Said.

Indeed, we are too intelligent to travel the absolute route on God, though we often travel the other no-God absolute route to deflect the complexity of that absolute.

We substitute one for the other.

That God isn't absolute doesn't mean there is no-God. There will be a God, whether named or not, to take God's place. This doesn't mean that the relative wins the day, hands down. Because in that victory the relative often becomes the absolute of narcissism and injustice or absolute certainty about what society has to look like. So neither absolute nor relative – justice with gray areas?

If the prophet wears gray is there any port in the worldly storm? If even the prophet

cannot stand firm is there anyone we can count on not to flee the scene when the sea gets rough?

The prophetic is negotiated. Absolute justice isn't found anywhere. Won't be found.

Think of Tourist Auschwitz - shall we shut it down because there is no way to deal with the dead without providing buses and bathrooms and restaurants to eat in?

Life goes on. Auschwitz continues to live. Like Luther, Auschwitz has a long shelf-life. Trivialization of everything is part of the modern world. Why shouldn't Auschwitz become a money maker?

Think of the justice tours around the world, where the empowered visit the oppressed and return home to a comfortable bed.

I think of my travels to Gaza in the 1980s. How welcome we were for a time and then as the first Uprising dragged on there were some "ugly" incidents – kids throwing stones at the buses bringing those who were there to "help."

Evidently, the Uprising kids realized that the helpers wouldn't rescue them. After all was said and done, Gazans would remain behind in the same situation. Or worse.

Those who came to understand weren't wrong to come. Many who came returned home and worked for Palestine.

The kids who stoned the buses weren't wrong to throw rocks. They remained behind and indeed their situation continues to deteriorate.

Like the prophetic, solidarity is negotiated. Like solidarity, suffering is negotiated.

Life is gray. For the most part, the affluent and empowered will remain affluent and empowered. For the most part, the poor and marginalized will remain poor and marginalized. With time, things change. With few exceptions, the waiting time is long.

Dramatic changes often bring mixed results. Example A: Jews after the Holocaust.

The "ethics" of Jewish power. Broached in 1988 and already passé.

Those on the other side of history won't be rescued. Those who are – watch out.

While practicing exile beware of the rescuer and the rescued within ourselves and the community around us.

An exile community that rescues isn't reflecting on its internal life. An exile community that awaits rescue doesn't understand the world they live in.

Jews of Conscience aren't going to change the world. Jews of Conscience are not becoming the next Jewish establishment either.

Gray isn't just "them."

Shall we color the prophet gray? Dark gray, I think. Not black or white.

The prophet argues that people deserve the right to live an ordinary life, and does

not conform to a theory of a world reformed. The theory remains as a guiding light on the horizon. People exist in real time.

Years ago in Atlanta, I worked (unsuccessfully) in a poor African-American community. The group I briefly joined was run by white religious folks trying to organize the community that didn't want to be organized. Which was really disappointing to us. Didn't the people we were there to serve realize how a different future could be made?

Late one night, we young "volunteers" heard singing and clapping from a church nearby. It was the people we were there to organize up late at an improvised church service. The disdain among the volunteers was palpable. What a waste of time and energy.

I thought: "The people knew where it was going and where it wasn't before we arrived."

They would still be there after we left. Which they are.

I have more stories about Israel-Palestine organizing around a Two-State solution when the organizers knew it wasn't going to happen. Reason given to me for organizing others around something you don't believe in? You can't mobilize people on the Israel-Palestine issue if the truth you know is known by them.

De-colonize organizing the "masses?"

Morning Offerings
INDIAN OCEAN

JULY 28

REJECTED!
JEWISH 'COMMON SENSE' RELIGION

Yesterday, Hindu morning rites on the beach. At least, I think they are. Would love to ask but don't want to interrupt morning devotions to the Gods. Rabbi Elyashiv is turning over in his grave. Just the cosmic thought of idolatry gives the rabbi the creeps, no doubt.

Myself, I prefer food offered to the Gods to Gaza's night sky being illumined by Israel's phosphorus bombs. When it comes to idolatry my definition is the use of power over others for the sake of empire, meaning as well that you have a God who blesses empire, because the powerful always trumpet God as on their side. In other words, idolatry is doing injustice and claiming God is behind it. This kind of God isn't Israel's God of justice and liberation. Hence the powerful have and worship a false God.

Quite different than the Abraham destroying the idols story we heard over and over again in Hebrew School. Yes, though way too simple and ultimately misleading, the repetition did drill it into our reluctant Jewish heads that something was at stake in the world. Thus I am grateful for my Hebrew School teachers.

If you disagree with my definition of idolatry, no problem. Send me yours. Or just chalk it up to my idolatry-definition preference. However, beyond personal preference and with due respect to the rabbi of blessed memory, the Torah, at least as I read it but certainly without the specialized knowledge he had, directly links justice and God.

Biblically speaking, when Israel acts unjustly and enshrines that injustice into a system, the future unfolds like this: If the people Israel don't practice justice they will soon be practicing exile in some far away Babylon or, more succinctly, if the people Israel don't practice justice they will be sent into exile; There prophetic Jews who announced the idolatry of injustice will learn how to practice exile; That practice will attest to the real relation between justice and God and thus preserve a possible future for the people Israel in and outside of the land.

Whether you want Bible lessons or not, you have to give the Bible credit – it rarely minces words. Often, the words are way too strong for a moderate like me. Like being driven into the hands of your enemies. Like drought that cannot be survived. Like children burying their parents and parents eating their children. The Biblical landscape is lush and barren, filled with compassion and untold violence. The Bible is never, ever neutral, though to be honest, once in a while, I pray for a let-up, some soap opera-like interlude, personal drama that has no practical consequences.

Back to the rabbi for a moment, as he was described a master of Talmudic law, that is a commentator on the Torah and its commentators. Don't get me wrong, these rabbinic

commentators can be quite insightful at times. No doubt Rabbi Elyashiv was. My point is that, like the Jewish Renewal folks, the rabbis erect fences around the prophetic. To a greater or lesser extent, their interpretations diminish the prophetic, place the prophetic in "perspective" and ultimately ritualize it out of existence. For the rabbis of every stripe and time, the prophetic is dangerous.

Where might the prophetic critique lead? Jewish authorities – again of all stripes and times – feel that while the prophetic is part of Jewish life, it is inherently unstable. The prophetic makes Jewishness unstable. It makes the Jewish community unstable. It also introduces the possibility that Israel's God is unstable. Indeed, as we shall see, all of their fears are well-founded.

All religious systems seek to stabilize the inherently unstable religion they profess. Harken back to the Presbyterian's multi-billion dollar portfolio. In and of itself a scandalous stability in relation to the scriptures Christians embrace and then – hands off! – the Presbyterians themselves can't touch 99% of it. They are not even allowed to decide to make unstable the stability they have accumulated!

What if striving for Jewish stability is inherently unstable or instability is the Jewish form of stability?

Here's an example. Last year I was contacted by a minister and a rabbi who are editing a book searching for, what they term, a common sense religiosity across the multi-religious landscape. In general, the editors are searching for a way of faith that is rational, good for society and isn't prone to the "hijacking" of various faiths into the realm of terrorism. I'm not sure if broaching ethnic cleansing and occupation is acceptable on the Jewish aspect of this, but since they asked me to write I think it's possible, at least up to a point. Anyway, without awaiting further instructions I agreed and wrote my essay. The essay didn't sit well with my well-meaning editors. Rejection city.

Once I cleared the ethnic cleansing and occupation brush, in a nutshell here's what I argued: that the common sense religion/religiosity/spirituality/thinking of Jews reflects the indigenous of the people Israel, which is the prophetic, and that the unstable prophetic is in tune with Israel's unstable God. In broad strokes I traced the Biblical journey of the Israelites as the foundational knowledge of this divine and earthly instability and how this instability, as the norm of Israelite life, was also, again from the beginning, fought against by the empire parts of Israel who couldn't abide that instability. I then argued that this dynamic of inherent instability and desire to foreclose that instability exists throughout Jewish history into the present. You can't understand the Jewish civil war in the 21st century without this "instability" background.

How can the prophetic be the common sense of the Jewish people? It doesn't make sense in the plain meaning of common sense. Unless, we see the prophetic within – everything – that is at the center, for example, of every profession, which is then fought by reification of that prophetic impulse. This reification has gone so far that, as an example, the profession of healing is so driven by the mighty dollar that the really sophisticated top-notch surgeons

have a financial time clock on them at all times. Another example is the commodification of knowledge, as in our current debate about the pay-off or lack thereof of a college education.

Is college worth the tuition fees? This question can only be asked if education has already become an industry where pay raises and football stadiums are the sum total of education.

The sum total of the Jewish educational-industrial complex seems to be stability at any price. Knocking the prophetic out of the Jewish park so that it will never be seen again, ever.

But the prophetic is seen – and heard – once again. The explosion of the Jewish prophetic in our time is the reassertion of Jewish common sense.

And yes the prophetic is a religion, Jewish-style.

Even if the interfaith ecumenical brew-crew prefers naval gazing and hugs around the campfire.

Torah Study
JERUSALEM

JULY 28

READING THE TORAH
OUT LOUD (NO RABBIS ALLOWED)

My little guy, Isaiah, just turned nineteen. Obviously the "little" designation is somewhat past tense. He's been texting me about the Penn State/Sandusky/Paterno scandal. He's asking if I think the football program should have received the death penalty from the NCAA. Of course I do. But then the cascading images begin. Believe me, it would never end.

If the death penalty were applied it would reach the shores of my alma mater, Florida State University, where the former second in major college coaching victories, Bobby Bowden, is, after the voiding of more than a hundred Paterno wins, back in the lead. A second look at the NCAA's action against Bowden would commence, since they already voided almost an entire season of his victories. Admittedly Bowden wasn't guilty of turning a blind eye to the rape of children, just an extensive player cheating scandal either ignored or abetted by his coaching staff. Then it would be off to my recent place of employment, Baylor University, since in the past and in the present, the NCAA has also been there.

By all accounts these investigations skim the surface of sex, lies and videotapes. What's interesting is the men – and women – at the top of the university pyramid. Presidents and provosts, then down the line, vacant stare players, with envelops to stuff, all know what's going on. Fancy stationery and pious prayers can't disguise scum.

So, Isaiah, you are playing your prophet's namesake game, shouting it from the rooftops. I agree. Now get a life. Get real. The Wheel of University Life is greased by all sorts of industrial-size hypocrisy. Be wary of following in your older brother's footsteps, a la letters to the Israeli Consul. At least know what lies ahead if you maintain truthfulness as your guide. As you know, Aaron stood up and never looked back.

After a while Jewish/non-Jewish/(un)Jewish issues of injustice seem to run together. Maybe they are the same thing.

Some years ago, after making our way through the terminals that regulated entry into Ramallah, Aaron and I stood at the Apartheid Wall. With my arm around his shoulder, I said to him – "This is the end of Jewish history." His reply – "It's unjust, Dad, wrong. We have to bring the Wall down."

Generational difference. I carry so much Holocaust/Israel baggage. Baggage surrounded by mourning. Aaron doesn't have any time for that. Let's get on with the task at hand.

There was something of that when I read the Bible out loud to Isaiah, word for word, every night, for weeks on end. Just like I had read it to Aaron some years earlier. When we came to the prophet Isaiah, my Isaiah smiled. The recognition was immediate. Was he named

for this Biblical heavyweight, he asked? Isaiah's eyes lit up when we reached the plowshares text.

Prophet naming, just like I did for his brother, Aaron. I didn't name Aaron for his priestly role, though that is quite interesting. I named him for the early Aaron who, as the older brother of Moses, introduced the palace-raised Moses to his people and spoke for the stuttering Moses. Aaron, the first prophet. He started an entire tradition.

A household of prophetic names with nowhere to go? I had an idea of where Jewish history was heading when their names were given. But no idea how far it would go. As fate would have it. By the time I read Aaron the Torah out loud Star of David helicopter gunships commanded the skies over Palestine. I knew then that no greater challenge had ever presented itself to the Jewish prophetic.

Whether the Jewish prophetic was up to the task, whether it is up to the task, that's still an open question. Or is it?

Speaking truth to Jewish power. A lifetime task filled with all sorts of dangers. I have experienced many. My children will also find others on their journey. They already have.

And the non-Jewish allies who also pounce on Jewish dissidents, well, it raises the question of what is happening in the Jewish/Christian empire box suites.

Sure, I understand how some believe Star of David helicopter gunships are mandated by the Bible. Protect the people Israel, the Land, God's chosen ones in the Promised Land. Yet, the prophetic seeds of conscience are also there. Use conscience to interrupt power wherever it comes from, even when it seems to be Biblically commanded by God.

When you read the Torah out loud to your children you have to choose – for yourself. So many Biblical texts present us with choices. Only we can make them. The Bible is on both sides of the Empire Divide. Much of the narration can go either way. When it goes toward empire, we need to read the Bible against its own grain. When it goes toward community, we need to read the Bible critically as well.

For in every community, there remains the temptation toward empire. In every empire, there is the trust toward community. Most community is built within and in spite of empire. Empire remains as a temptation even as opposition to it increases.

The empire/community tipping point is difficult to discern. One way of thinking about our own empire temptation is imagining a cloak room where hats and coats are checked. As we move toward community what empire aspirations/temptations have to be checked before entering the community theatre? A checklist of ideas/habits/ideologies/rituals that have to be checked before entering should be developed. But, then, the disputes over that checklist will be endless, don't you think?

Just to name a few disputed coat room questions. It would be easy to say that all particularities, like Jewish or African American or Arab, have to be checked. But, then, about universality, if that can be defined without particularities, isn't "universality" a hodgepodge of quite particular notions in and of itself? If we allow broad categories, if only for initial

location and identification, does that mean that "Arab" can be carried into the theatre but that "Palestinian" has to be checked?

Maybe the rule of thumb is more about how we carry our baggage rather than the baggage itself. Identity baggage may be like the Bible, cutting in different ways at different times. Taking all the empire baggage away might leave us void of community resources as well.

Identifying our baggage is essential. And being able to laugh at the absurdity of it all.

Like the Jewish concept of chosenness. Ludicrous!

Or, listen to this: Palestinians are different than other Arab collectives. LOL!

Jesus saves! Mohammed is the final prophet!

Or, imagine this: Reading the Torah out loud can be instructive.

Total absurdity, most of it, I agree. Like a belief in God. Who in their right and intelligent mind could contemplate such an order to the universe?

Since all of us here are above these absurdities, let's lay out the ones we hold as dear as others hold the ones I just skewered. Put our absurd cards down on the table.

I'll go first with a series of belief statements that are central to my life. I say them often to my children. They nod their heads. Here he goes again!

I also speak them in academic settings. You can imagine the reception. How (un)academic can he be!

These, also, may be absurd. Consider them my Prophet doxology:

> The people Israel gave the prophetic to the world.
>
> It is the greatest gift in the history of the world.
>
> Without the prophetic there is no meaning in the world.
>
> There may be no meaning in the world.
>
> The prophet embodies the possibility of meaning in the world.

Unpacking at another time. Prophetic baggage. Can it still be spoken in the world?

EXILE AND THE PROPHETIC
part two | *volume one*

At the Crossroads
CAPE CANAVARAL

Sally Ride
OUTER SPACE

JULY 29

NO PROPHET SPOKEN HERE

Sally Ride, America's first woman astronaut, has died. Another obituary.

I read obituaries carefully as you may have noted. They reveal and hide. Revealing/hiding, such an interesting part of life. The great art is hiding as you reveal. It's a technique known today as "transparency."

I don't exempt writing. What interests me most about writing is the act of revelation. It is creation ex nihilo. Sort of. I am not arguing a blank slate sensibility. It's just that in writing the page is adorned where before it was blank. The source behind that adornment is the mind. Yes. What is behind the mind?

No matter how much one reveals, a hidden dimension remains. That dimension becomes smaller over time – the more revealed the less hidden – and somehow larger. Or deeper. The place that we seek to discover – hiddenness as the place of revelation – is elusive. The more we say the less we know about the hidden places. Which means that coming out in any aspect of life is only the first step. As in, okay, now what?

So Sally Ride and her partner of many years, Tam. Yes, a woman's name. *The New York Times* just states it without explanation. *The New Yorker* is running with it.

Coming out as the first step. Best if it is at the right time and place, if there is such a thing. How to judge the right time and place? What is the difference between coming out and being outed once the deed has been done?

Sally Ride remained in the closet, at least on the larger public stage. Believe me, the closet is full where I hung out for the last dozen or so years. More of that later.

Orthodoxy of every sort is in closets-full mode. I'm referring primarily to the sexual stuff, though hiding sexual orientation is only a drop in the sex bucket. Closets full has a much more extensive geography than the sexual geography of any institution or culture. Hiding corruption and disguising it as faith is an art form. There isn't much light between the ideological fudging that has been so richly documented and religion that is so easily seen as hypocrisy.

The Bible is full of closets. Probing the Bible reveals some of what it seeks to hide. Yet my experience is that when you get out of the Bible as lessons or the Biblical law category, which really are hilarious, there is hiddenness in the Bible as well. That hiddenness may be due to the ancient quality of the text. Or that the Bible is communicating something it doesn't quite understand. Which means that we need to approach the Bible with a critical eye and with detachment. What we think we know is there might be found. Still, there are other nuggets to be explored. They may be hidden in plain sight.

The prophet within – the Bible. Is that the same prophet – within us? Here we've moved from whom Sally Ride held at night to who or what has a hold on us. Something within us that is difficult to find or define. Difficult to speak. Difficult to live. Because the surface prophet stuff is just that, surface. Tip of the iceberg whether it is solid or melting.

We don't get far with the prophet iceberg stuff. Either we live by anger or we ritualize it by the camp fire, both of which have their place. A life they do not make.

Sure, the prophetic needs to be outed in Jewish life. Empire closets won't hold the hidden forever. Nonetheless, the clenched fist is also a closet. What is underneath, around, the prophetic within?

Judaism as a closet. That hides the prophetic.

Judaism as a closet. Within which is the prophetic.

Judaism as a closet. It keeps the prophetic hidden by ritualizing it.

Judaism as a way of disciplining the prophetic. Imposed from above.

Rabbis, calling the prophets out as violating the closets full code. Imagine the rabbis as spanking the prophetic. Within.

What does this say about the inner life of our spiritual leaders? Shall we out the rabbis who are (prophet) closeted? Or shall we respect their reticence and wait for their decision? After all, coming out has to be the person's choice, since the cost is high. Rabbis who come out of the (prophet) closet may even lose their jobs. Imagine that.

Oh me, Oh my! Imagine the rabbi unemployment phone lines lighting up. Imagine the training necessary to counsel rabbis who are contemplating the (prophet) coming out that will change their life. Will there be Prophet degrees offered at Jewish Theological Seminary or Hebrew Union College? Once you name the shame you've felt, there's no going back. What shall the (prophet) coming out counseling degrees be named?

Rabbi counseling. Counseling the counselor. Teaching the teacher. Admonishing the admonisher.

But then, note that many rabbis can come of out of their gay and lesbian closet as long as they stay in the prophet closet. Which brings me back to *Standing Again at Sinai*. Perhaps a more accurate title would substitute sitting for standing. Or absent. *Absent Again at Sinai*?

You see it is more than possible – it may even be mandatory – to sit when you should be standing or be absent as you raise your voice from a safe distance. Feigning presence is a clergy thing in general but certainly it isn't restricted to men and women of whatever cloth a particular community ordains.

Yes, I'm obsessing. The mezuzah on the beach. Occupied by a rabbi. If he's employed by a congregation, which I assume, hence his beach house perk, I assume he's hiding the prophetic within. And making sure that his congregation does as well.

Everyone knows the prophet silencing drill by now anyway, so I doubt that there is a

need to have it written into the rabb's contract. It's part of the hidden negotiation in hiring the rabbi and renewal contracts that follow.

Sign language for "No Prophet Spoken Here"?

How about a sign on every synagogue entrance?

My childhood synagogue – Beth "No Prophet Spoken Here" Torah.

My last one – Temple Rodeph "No Prophet Spoken Here" Shalom.

Like Oprah's (Good Housekeeping) Seal of Approval. No offense given. Promise.

Interesting, the recent translation of Elie Wiesel's *Night* receiving Oprah's blessing. Look at the cover if you don't believe me. Is that because Wiesel has observed and enforced the "No Prophet Spoken Here" discipline that defines Empire Judaism?

The Place of the Skull
EARTH

JULY 30

GENOCIDE - DONATE NOW!

Back to back beautiful beach days, morning and late afternoon, sunny but mild, low tide, then dark clouds gathering, followed by a short rain. Amazing.

Then, crossing the email wire, our intrepid decolonizer, now in Rwanda, sends out her "lovely afternoon" photo greeting of her visit to the Rwandan genocide memorial in Kilgali. Skulls and more skulls.

Lovely afternoon – skulls. Contrasts are instructive.

There are plenty of genocide artifacts in the world. Probably always were. Now they are collected. A genocide industry has sprung up, with websites and other modern paraphernalia. Like the Holocaust Memorial Museum in Washington, D. C., with the personally assigned passage ID's of the martyred.

The idea is to remove the abstraction – as in, six million slaughtered – but for me just the opposite happens. I feel like an idiot carrying this manufactured museum industry ticket in my hand. Once my admission is assured should I tuck her in my pocket? Or later, when I empty my pockets, should I put her in a drawer for safekeeping or toss her in the garbage with my other museum accumulations?

And now – and for some time – Rwanda's military is in the Congo. Rwanda also seems to have copied the Jewish thinking behind the Holocaust museum – arm yourself to the teeth and go wherever you want under the cover of past genocide.

What is genocide worth if you're not going to use it to augment your power without accountability?

So the Jewish/Israeli model exported to Rwanda. Where did Jews/Israel get it? Surely, there must be Israeli arms sales cooperation with Rwanda – has to be.

It turns out there is a difference between Israel and Rwanda, since American military aid has been cut off because of this latest interference in the Congo. I doubt Rwanda gets anything near the three plus billion dollar aid package Israel gets each year. But Israel may agree to take up the military arms slack. They have done this everywhere the US has been or will be in the future.

I suppose we can call these dealings Post-Genocide Pacts (PGP). Or, on the British side as you shall see, Colonial Services Agreements (CSA). Just speculating. A cursory web search doesn't bring up anything on Israel-Rwanda military ties. On the Israeli-Apartheid South Africa watch, however, there is no dearth of information.

But notice, too, the bland description on Rwandan's memorial center's website. As if the Rwandan genocide was simply a mistake that was committed because of ignorance. Notice as well the United Kingdom and other "world" donors. After all these years, the colonial remains.

The genocide industry is based in the West, even if the West has specialized in setting genocide in motion.

Well, a colonial legacy is a colonial opportunity in a (un)changing world. Who says there aren't genocide second acts in history?

Here's the description of the Kigali Memorial Center, with options to donate:

> The Centre in Kigali was created by a joint partnership of the Kigali City Council and the UK-based Aegis Trust. It contains a permanent exhibition of the Rwandan genocide and an exhibition of other genocides around the world.
>
> **Donate Now**
>
> The Kigali Memorial Centre is maintained by goodwill donations left by its visitors.
>
> **About Rwanda**
>
> Rwanda is a beautiful country of rolling hills, mountains and grassy lowlands. In French, it has been named 'Pays des Mille Collines' meaning 'Country of a Thousand Hills'. Its beautiful Lake Kivu has one of the most spectacular shorelines in the world.
>
> **Education**
>
> One of the principle reasons for the Centre's existence is to provided educational facilities. These are for a younger generation of Rwandan children some of whom may not remember the genocide, but whose lives are profoundly affected by it.
>
> **Supporters**
>
> The creation of the Kigali Memorial Centre was funded by a number of donors worldwide.

If I might make a suggestion to the Brandeis Peace Building, I think the description of mass death in Rwanda is sanitized and depoliticized enough on the website to be on your Peace Building approved list. If we check the no-no's – political rivalry, speaking about armed might in revenge or calling attention to the misdeeds done in the name of genocide - everything looks good. No offense will be intended or given.

Now from Trip Advisor, a thumbs-up review, one among many:

> Take plenty of time at this moving memorial. Done incredibly well, and prepare to cry at the Children's Memorial. An amazing centre which manages

to evoke the horror of the genocide while still building hope and commitment, rather than anger and retribution, for the future. Do not miss this.

I don't want to be irreverent. I remember an article I read soon after the genocide. The writer asked the Rwandan Minister of Justice about the possibility of punishment for the murderers. Since so many Rwandans murdered other Rwandans how could the country mete out justice? His response: "After genocide there is no justice."

Unless museums are justice. Meaning memory funded by the state. Memory visited. Memory toured. Justice for whom? The victims the museum is about or the victims who will be sanctioned by their memory?

Linking genocides. Avoiding too much particularity, the Kilgali Memorial Centre also mentions other genocides. As does the Holocaust museum in Washington. But, please, if you don't want to lose your "authentic" genocide club card don't call the Holocaust, genocide or the Rwandan genocide, Holocaust. There is an (un)official, though thoroughly enforced, Holocaust/genocide separation. There is even a carefully delineated Holocaust/genocide language code, a dictionary of Holocaust/genocide etiquette. Mind your P's and Q's.

It used to be that atrocity, by whatever name and most often without one, wasn't officially memorialized. It seems that the institutions of the state powerful enough to create narrative and museum spaces for genocide are the same ones that have/are or will sponsor genocide and its precursors: atrocity and ethnic cleansing.

The Holocaust/genocide museum industry public relations folks like the state to keep the watch monitor at the lower levels of atrocity and ethnic cleansing (without naming it as such, of course) so the Big Theme can remain unscathed. As our Trip Advisor recommender writes, the memorial in Kilgali "manages to evoke the horror of the genocide while still building hope and commitment, rather than anger and retribution, for the future."

Hope for whom? Is she so sure that anger and retribution can't be carried out while still pausing for silence in the presence of the museumified dead?

Being museumified, the victims don't have a word, do they? Which way their hope and commitment would go, we don't know. We're probably afraid to find out. Rather, let the empowered state poll itself and decide how to define anger and retribution.

Holocaust and genocide museums are many things to many people. I do wonder if the museums themselves enshrine violence as part of our future. Perhaps not, but I safely predict that Holocaust/genocide museums are a growth industry. Their future looks bright.

"Do not miss this." I'm sure that's true. One day I need to take a genocide tour. I've already done parts of the Holocaust memorial tour, which takes a lot of time by the way. At least in Europe and America, they're around every corner, just like Jewish power.

Searching for Justice
BETHLEHEM

JULY 31

AFTER GENOCIDE, NO JUSTICE

After genocide, no justice. A mantra for our age.

After ethnic cleansing, no justice. Another mantra for our age.

After atrocity – endless, isn't it?

There is retribution. Mostly, retribution is visited on those who have nothing to say about more or less anything beyond their daily lives. It's just violence and atrocity continued. Recycled. Those caught in between don't know the difference between insignias. Violence all around. Same stuff from every side.

So, what to do when empowerment leads to another kind of enslavement? Imprisoned in power, on the one hand, and now, on the other, deathly afraid of any crack in that power. If you let your power guard down the cycle of violence and atrocity, which you suffered and now continue, might roll over you in the wrong direction. Let others suffer. We've had enough.

Rwanda had plenty and more. Best to dish it out to others. Like Israel. Always a sense of being besieged, and yes being besieged is the real deal sometimes. Imprisoned in power, however, the feeling is that the siege is permanent, it has to be, otherwise time-limits might apply. Back to normal? The siege can't last forever, can it?

On the Israeli front, it doesn't matter how much power Israel has, it thinks it's under siege. Eternally. This means no way out of the imprisonment of power. Of course, a permanent war footing is immensely lucrative for the super-patriots among us. Don't think that patriotism trumps the dollar.

So, the original ending of Elie Wiesel's *Night* had he and other Jews planning to rape German woman and poison the German water supply. Revenge a la mode. It's not for me to judge, I suppose. Nor his later ending, existentially loaded, with him staring in the mirror and hardly recognizing his reflection. That's right after the "liberation," whatever that can mean in the Holocaust context. The more relevant question is what he sees in the mirror today, other than his Madoff-drained and no doubt regained wealth.

Of course, Wiesel and many other Jews achieved success after the Holocaust. Is that justice? The six million dead are scattered everywhere. Is the Holocaust banner, so dutifully raised, a form of justice for them? Specifically, those Jews who went to Palestine, who fought their war for their independence – justice achieved?

In the cycle of violence and atrocity, one person's justice is another person's injustice. As I said, the cycle of violence and atrocity rolls along.

Now the question on the micro-level. Last year while teaching a course where international students were present, a student from Rwanda approached me. Having heard I was an "expert" on the Holocaust, he asked if I might be able to advise Rwanda on how to commemorate its genocide.

An obvious invitation was being dangled before me. I had never been to Rwanda, so initially I felt eager to share my knowledge. But almost immediately second thoughts entered my mind, first about using my Holocaust expertise to travel – a Holocaust credit card? – second, whether I should encourage genocide memorialization with the track record Holocaust commemoration had accumulated. Rwanda might end up with something similar to community Holocaust commemorations that feature yellow Star of David stick-ems attached to your jacket. This functions as a sign that Jews are truly mourning and that Christians are truly sorry. (But I wonder if the one I wore a few years ago when I was trying to be politically correct and attended a community Holocaust event might look dazzling on the helicopter gunships in the Ark of the Covenant. Not sure, though, whether the stick-ems will stick twice.)

So I paused; remembering is a slippery-slope. Would I be able to share that part of the Holocaust with my Rwandan hosts? Could I speak to them about the cycle of violence and atrocity, how we Jews have used it against others, asking the Rwandans if they were prone to the same abuse? You see speaking about the Holocaust to those who have no idea of what lies ahead is far from simple. Being respectful to them, should I hold back on the pitfalls that Jews are now mired in? How do I speak about the suffering of Jews without romanticizing Jews, balancing the actual suffering and the response to that suffering, keeping the complexity of both alive?

I have to keep in mind how difficult it is to institutionalize anything without losing the essence of what is being raised up. Since I've been critical of the Rwandan remembrance – and the way the Holocaust is remembered – I have to confess to the corners I've cut in my institutional journey. In the two centers I founded and directed I have always been on the cutting edge of wherever I've been. I've also had to negotiate the culture and religion, the context.

So if I – or you – had the freedom, how would we construct these memorial museums? If we accepted the task, how would our website read? If we refused because too much compromise was demanded, would that mean that the victims of Holocaust/genocide would be forgotten?

I suppose we can play the same mind-games with constructing a state, say the state of Israel, after the Holocaust. Or even now, if you or I were the prime minister of Israel, what would we do? In fact, due to the many constraints on power, what could we do?

If the answer is no Jewish state, never, that would be fine. Since there is a state now, if you don't want one, tell me your plan for dismantling it. I'm all ears. This isn't about silencing

your griping or mine, it's to add a dose of realism to the war of ideas in the Middle East. My solution to these dilemmas is radical questions to keep pushing moderate solutions to the next level. This means that the solutions have to be a on a human and doable scale so that people can live ordinary lives – in real time.

Yes, moderation isn't working and I don't want to be lumped in with Michael Lerner or for that matter Norman Finkelstein. There has to be a way forward that is human and just, without the patronizing colonial mentality or international law histrionics, one that respects the fact that universal human rights are political and have a particular face.

This means following and implementing a policy I call revolutionary forgiveness. At its heart revolutionary forgiveness includes justice whose color is gray. More about this another time.

The best anyone can get after Holocaust/genocide/ethnic cleansing/atrocity is a justice that lives for the future. No retrospectives. No do-overs. And since empowerment for its own sake is just another prison in need of a jail-break, revenge is just another word for everything left to lose.

Power over others does not lead to healing. Perhaps this is the real lesson that the Holocaust has to teach the Rwandans.

Yet what are the incentives for Rwandans to listen? At least, their government, won't accept these lesson plans that says move on together.

After genocide, no justice. Obvious. However, the race for power over others doesn't lead anywhere either. Over the long run.

Thus the prophetic is on notice before, during and after genocide. And Holocaust. No time off.

Nazi Census of the Jews
BERLIN

AUGUST 1

EXPORTING
THE HOLOCAUST

If you're not involved in academic life or the Holocaust museum industrial complex you might not be aware that one of the main Jewish exports of our time is the Holocaust – this from America. Another major Jewish export is military weapons – this from Israel.

Since contemporary Jewish life revolves around the Holocaust and Israel the Jewish export portfolio makes perfect sense. Specialization and niche markets are the rage.

The weapons industry – no explanation necessary. Like other major industrial countries, Israel's weapons' industry is part of its cash flow and global cache. The Holocaust industry is less obvious, at least in its export capacity. But if you think conceptually of the "Holocaust for others" you'll see how we have, for example, exported the Holocaust to Christians in America and Europe for decades. The Holocaust functions as a global discourse as well. We have marketed the Holocaust around the world.

Only a small portion of Holocaust trading is conducted in cash. Rather a global Holocaust bank account has been established where the Jewish establishment in America and Israel trades the Holocaust (thus Jewish suffering and a need for empowerment) for political and military support. There are also highly trained cadres of Jewish academicians who trade the Holocaust for a livelihood. This includes teaching in universities but, as well, advising genocide museums and the like around the world.

The Holocaust/weapons industry export scenario is relatively new. It's more or less fifty years since they came into being, a short time in the history of an ancient people. Yet, brevity in time is made up by depth of commitment.

As Jews, we are deeply invested, perhaps dependent, on these exports. Our place in the world, our self-esteem is involved. Without the Holocaust/weapons industry we would feel adrift.

Without the Holocaust for others, we fear that our years of respect on the world stage are numbered. Without an arms industry we fear Israel's global reach will diminish. Without that global reach, can Israel survive?

The Holocaust for others. Weapons for others. Seemingly self-assured, we have become a needy people. Without others, we are less. So involved with the Holocaust and weapons sales, we have forgotten how previously we had a corner on other exports, primarily critical thought and ethics. Various forms of artistic endeavors as well. And let's not forget science, when scientific thinking rather than lab experimentation was crucial to breakthroughs in science.

In many fields of endeavors we were paradigm shifters. Breakthrough types. The prophetic was thinly disguised. It was dressed as it was in secular garb. Still it had its time on the world stage.

The secular garb was a ruse. The thin disguise masked Jewishness raging in the world. Unannounced, it was still easily noticed. When queried about it, most Jews took to their closets. Like Freud, a proud Jew, who tried to hand over psychoanalysis to Jung. The reason: Freud didn't want his "science" to be mistaken for "Jewish." Which it was, of course, quite Jewish, with little bits of science sprinkled in. What a Jewish science it was!

The slayers of Moses, as one writer sees it: each Jewish patriarch slays the last one to assume his rightful place as the Moses of his generation. Almost all of the great Jewish thinkers of the nineteenth and twentieth century had this sensibility. Of course, most of them didn't mention Moses, except Freud whose last book was exactly on that subject. And as Freud would have it, the real Biblical Moses was himself slain in the desert. The Israelites wanted none of the discipline Moses dished out. Off with his head! It isn't a mistake that Freud announced Moses' execution. After all wasn't he, Freud, the new and perhaps last Moses?

Have I forgotten war, occupation and terror as high on the list of Jewish exports? Ask the Palestinians, Lebanon, Iran and other countries. I suppose we could place this in the weapons industry folder. Maybe I need a better catch-all term here.

9/11 and the whole security systems industry, heavily Israeli. Another huge Jewish export these days.

No matter what its size, every Sparta needs a "we'll make you ready for war" industry and "we'll provide you with the weapons to keep you safe" industry. So war and everything that surrounds war – the umbrella is big and getting bigger. If you don't provide the full range of exports needed, importers might look elsewhere for what they need. Somewhat like the drug cartels, I guess. Deliver or we'll find someone else who can.

Suppliers and users. Suppliers try to enlarge the markets for their goods. Users ply the world for supplies that are cheap, reliable and perform. Yes, another similarity to the drug cartel, since there are direct causalities, those who fight in the wars, and collateral damage, regrettable but also part and parcel of war itself.

Balance of trade is crucial for nations. You don't want to import more than you export. As well, the market is always changing and some products may compete internally with other products. On the Jewish front Holocaust exports are being compromised by Israel's export of war. For this and other reasons, including the passage of years since the Holocaust, we should expect the Holocaust export business to diminish over time.

Now it might just be an image problem, so Israel and some Jews in America think, hence the Brand Israel campaign. However, the globally circulated photographic images of occupation and invasion are hard to brush out. "Just do it" is all over the Israeli can-do attitudes. It may be that bombing Iran will enhance Israel's image in some quarters but overall

it seems downhill for the Holocaust. My advice: Don't invest in Holocaust stock right now.

Financial newsletter lingo places the Holocaust in the sell category. Unload it as quickly as you can.

Suggestions for investing in other Jewish causes? Not sure. Though the Israeli economy is doing fairly well, there are all sorts of negatives embedded in the Israeli way of life. If you take one brick out of the Israeli edifice the whole Jewish state might come tumbling down. My advice: Sell at your convenience, at least hedge your bets.

Other possibilities? With the Holocaust and Israel on the skids other Jewish causes may also suffer. They've been in the shadow of the Holocaust and Israel for a very long time and fed off their success. I'd place other areas of Jewish life under a caution flag. Wait and see what happens to the Holocaust/Israel complex before increasing your investment.

Where to invest? The ever-pressing question for the 1%. If you're leaving the Jewish stock scene, you might want to check out the China wage slavery scene. Untold ecological damage might be a warning, though. Industrialization and modernization are never pretty. Millions, in this case hundreds of millions or more, sacrificed for a future that will never arrive for the many.

Apple, though, seems good as a buy option. They are taking advantage of China's "development" but don't have corporate headquarters there. My advice: If you don't care about the Chinese people, invest.

The Holocaust for others. Weapons for others. Jewish heritage on the world market. Up for sale. To the highest bidder.

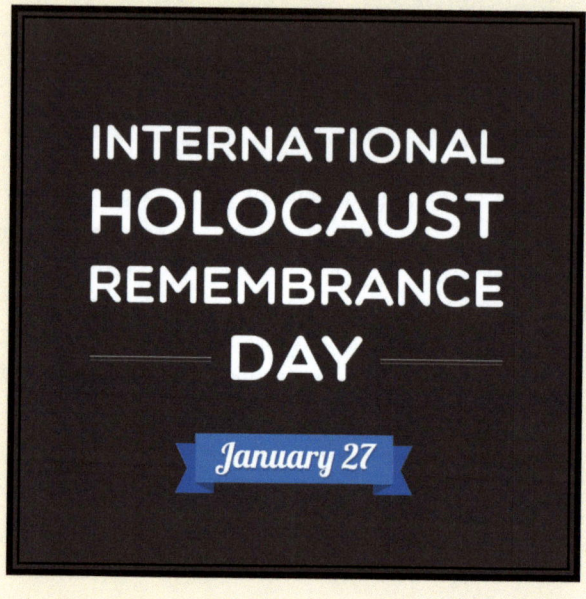

A Day of Our Own
WORLDWIDE

AUGUST 2

JEWISH
(HOLOCAUST) MISSIONARIES

Selling the Holocaust. Jewish export. For others. What we believe about ourselves we sell to others. To reinforce what we believe about ourselves. That we are innocent?

To get our bearings, think of Christian missionaries. They export Jesus for all the right reasons, according to them. If you look at it closely, though, much of it has to do with their doubts about Jesus as the Christ. If the Other "buys" the Jesus message, it reinforces their belief. If the Other doesn't buy, well then the Christian selling Jesus might think again about their belief. Or, as likely, kill the Other who says no. Like Jews. Yet in the long range the Jesus handwriting is on the wall. There are different ways to believe.

Many Christians have given up their need to have others confirm their belief. They say no to Christian missionaries or have reinterpreted it in such a novel way I doubt they are Christian at all. Or Christian in an aberrational way. Personally, I like the aberrational types. I hug them while I can. They might not be around too long.

If the others stop buying the Holocaust – which they have, at least in our major markets, Europe and America – there are other much smaller markets like Rwanda. Not only are these markets smaller, they are outside what the Jewish establishment considers the important political sphere. Way outside. Rwanda isn't shaping global Middle East policy. Africa is useless for Jews – at least the way the Jewish establishment has parsed the world.

It does matter if Europe and America see Jews as innocent. For the most part, Africa doesn't even know the Jewish score. They have their own world where the African score counts. If Europe and America go down Palestine Road – Europe is much farther along but the European handwriting may soon be on the American wall – then Jews will lose our place in the innocent therefore unaccountable pantheon.

The political implications for Israel are obvious. That's a long run situation, to be sure, and it will be too late for Palestinians. More or less, it's already too late. If you look at the facts on the ground, that is, rather than rely on the various banners I see flying at half-mast.

If the Holocaust can't be sold to others, as in, they're not buying it any more, will Jews cease to believe it too?

You see, if you want to export the Holocaust you have to believe it. Believing it isn't about whether the Holocaust happened or not, that's the easy way out. Believing the Holocaust is about Jewish innocence. Translated, Jewish innocence is about Jewish exceptionality. Translated further, Jewish innocence is about Jewish destiny.

Weaponized Israel is the end of that translation. The check-point terminals that

Palestinians are forced to use on a daily basis is the terminus of Jewish history. But reflecting backwards, delving into Jewish memory, Exodus style, back to the prophetic, the indigenous of the people Israel, Sparta Israel can't hack the Holocaust as Jews have used it and need it today. In short, the West, steeped in colonialism and violence, demands a Jews/Israel balance that Jews are unwise to undermine.

What seems to be Jewish/Israel status/independence is much more complicated.

Yes, Jews/Israel can embrace a colonial/violent mentality/reality but only so much is acceptable to non-Jews. Jews/Israel have to maintain some semblance of what non-Jews in the West now want to think of Jews/Israel. Having flipped from demonizing to romanticizing Jews, it's a short hop skip and jump back to the other side of the Jewish demonization paradigm. So, okay, take Palestinian land and create a state, teach people of color lessons through wars in the upstart Arab world, speak endlessly about your suffering and what it means for Christian faith and European and American politics – but, then, hear it loud and clear: "For God's sake give us some breathing space, we're in control not you!"

Lost in translation? Jews are a tangle in the Western imagination. And through the global imperialism of Islam and Christianity, Jews are a tangle in the global imagination, too. Of course, Jews are a tangle in the Jewish imagination. You can't experience the trauma of a liberating God and the prophetic without being tangled up. Obviously.

Liberation and the prophetic – traumas? You bet. More on this at another time. Suffice to say for now that the trauma of the Holocaust doesn't make sense without this original trauma that set our people on their historical journey.

The Holocaust was a trauma, of course. Israel, too, is a trauma for the Jewish people. Yet these traumas can only be defined as Jewish within the original, formative events of Exodus and the prophetic. Otherwise, the Holocaust and Israel are not exceptional. Whether or not they are exceptional is a question. Jews experience them that way. Full stop.

So here we are, exporting the Holocaust to others. The world was in need of conversion to a positive sense of Jewishness. Fair enough. However, that conversion can go only so far until it impinges on the internal territory of the Other. As well, when Jewish innocence is more and more in doubt, even among Jews, it becomes difficult for anyone to believe the Jewish story.

Instead of stepping back and reassessing, the Jewish establishment in America and Israel drives a harder and harder bargain. Israel yells the Holocaust from the rooftops – of Palestinian homes in the West Bank. It yells the Holocaust from the skies – of Gaza and Lebanon. Now Israel is rattling its Holocaust sword toward an (un)nuclear Iran.

In general, we're witnessing Holocaust over-kill. With Israel's weapons. And over-kill in the American political process. Tell me, how long will Netanyahu's finger-pointing in the Oval Office play on YouTube to favorable ratings? For a long time perhaps. Not forever.

So how long will the Holocaust for others play until their disbelief boomerangs back into the interior of Jewish life? As in, the world knows and now Jews know that we aren't

innocent. It's already happened to some extent. That's why the Jewish establishment shouted from the roof tops – of the Presbyterian conclave.

When you have to shout, you know you've already lost the battle. The only thing left to do is up the decibel level. Which means our Holocaust proselytizing is coming to an end. Last legs kind of stuff, another decade or two, max. Less?

When Jewish belief in the Holocaust as Jewish innocence goes by the board, Jewish belief in Israel as innocent – well, it's just a matter of time. That clock is already ticking. The hour glass is less than half-full. When the innocence rug of the Holocaust and Israel are pulled from under us, Jews are going to run for cover with our identity tanks on empty.

What will we be left with? What is already staring us in the face. We are back to the basics: Jewish power and the Jewish prophetic. Take your pick.

It's rarely been easy to be a Jew but, as well, rarely have Jews as a community had so much to lose. We used to have the proverbial Court Jews, some well-to-do types, and a range of socio-economic classes/trades/religious life that existed on the margins of host cultures/religions/states. Jews had something to lose. Often Jews lost everything. That was before the Holocaust, before the state of Israel and empowerment in America, before "Jewish" was on the world scene in an assertive way. We have gained a lot. We have a tremendous amount to lose.

The Holocaust as missionary zeal. With less and less converts to the faith believers will lose their faith.

Holocaust/Israel as the gateway to Jewish innocence is over. Missionary failure.

Plan B?

Bob Dylan
ITINERANT JEWISH PROPHET

AUGUST 3

PLAN B

Plan B. Everyone needs a back-up plan. Jews have used many back-up plans in history, so many it would take a semester seminar to surface all of them. For the most part, others have forced Jews to contemplate back-up plans. Now we force others to develop alternative strategies of survival. What plan are Palestinians on?

Let's see. There is the plan necessary to deal with Israel. Then there's the plan necessary to deal with the American Jewish establishment. Oh yes, the dwindling Progressive Jewish establishment, Palestinians need plans for them. For Jews of Conscience?

Obviously, Jews of Conscience have been busy developing their own back-up plans. Jeff Halper, for example, who has alternated between the Progressive Jewish group and Jews of Conscience, was writing alternative scenarios of the Israel-Palestine future on almost a weekly basis. That was a few years ago. Halper had a plan, then another, still another – it seemed he had a plan for every failure of his previous plan(s).

Halper isn't like Norman Finkelstein – Finkelstein has stuck to his (failed) international law plan like a true believer. It may be a coincidence but just as Halper ran out of plans, Norman's meltdown began. On the other hand, Michael Lerner keeps changing with the times. He's never stuck in his own mind. He's like a chameleon, changing colors faster than you can locate him on any GPS I know.

Think of Lerner as the Mitt Romney of the Jewish (un)Left. Or translated – think of Lerner as representing the (un)Left wing of Empire Judaism.

Well, we've gone over the Tikkun crowd. So many of them are raring to go somewhere else. They're looking for a new umbrella. Lerner's ego gets in the way – of Lerner's ego. Another slayer of Moses – in his mind. How far we have fallen thought-wise in the last decades. Lerner's sword is dull. He hasn't slain anything, just carved out a place in the windmills of his own self-appointed (rabbinic) universe.

Of all of them, I'll stick with Halper. American Jews rock. Though he is an Israeli by confession. I suppose my loyalty is skewed by his great achievement. He attended Bob Dylan's Bar Mitzvah. Must have been quite interesting. To say the least.

Dylan as an itinerant Jewish prophet, sure, yes, the last of a breed. I don't mean on every political issue, including whatever he really thinks about Israel. I'm thinking in the broader Jewish prophetic category. Dylan has a Jewish mythic mind. Leave the practicalities to others.

By the way, Dylan is a reader. If I might, he read one of my books and even sent me an autographed picture of himself. Wouldn't have it any other way. When I paint my

masterpiece, I'll tell you more. Wouldn't it be neat if Dylan could have had a discussion with Chief Last Night – and Thomas Paine?

For those of a certain age, Dylan was the Jewish Plan B. Whether or not a prophet is a good person to plan around, a new generation is here. There aren't going to be anymore Dylans.

I can hear some wondering how relevant an excursion into Dylan is, especially since I'm supposed to be dealing with the war of ideas in the Middle East. Here's my take on it. Dylan was possible, as was the idea of a Jewish universality, because in Dylan's childhood Jewish life in America was on the cusp of empowerment. What Jews would do with an accepting American culture hadn't been decided yet.

Would Jews go down Highway 61? Or would we compete for the brass ring of American empire? America hadn't completely decided on that empire route yet. Perhaps this is what Eisenhower's warning was really all about. Once you travel on the Empire Road there's no turning back. It's a one way street. The only way you can see Highway 61 is in the rearview mirror.

Since Dylan, Jewish life has chosen empowerment as Plan A. No other plans are allowed or now even available. That accounts for Jeff Halper's initial frenetic effort at creating back-up plans. It explains his silence now. It looks like we will follow empowerment through to its bitter end. At the end, in the rubble, another plan will appear, because there will no longer be any alternative.

Whose rubble will Jews be standing in? Ruins, debris, wreckage, remains – Jews have seen it from afar. As if Jenin or Gaza City are far away. As if they are foreign countries.

Plan A has visited devastation on others. It won't always be that way. Then what?

Hitler followed it through to the bitter end. True, Germany has risen again, dominating Europe economically in much the same way as Hitler tried militarily. Let's call Germany's dominance in Europe its Plan B. Dominance is dominance. Yet anyone who's had conversations with thoughtful Germans, say of Bob Dylan's generation, know there's something haunting the core of German history.

Yes, and I've certainly been called on the carpet for not forgiving and forgetting as many in Germany have. That's for another generation, perhaps for my sons, Aaron and Isaiah. I still would rather Volkswagen cease advertising in America. Its new ad campaign featuring the German CEO and "Das" Volkswagen slogan doesn't sit well with me.

Ridiculous, I know. Retro-city. Thankfully, at the Cape, I forgo television.

A more serious point is about atrocity, how it enters the language, culture and religion of any people. It has now entered "Jewish" at a deep level.

To imagine Hebrew used in torture. I don't have to imagine. Or Hebrew being used in Star of David helicopter gunships. I don't have to imagine.

Already in the rubble, wouldn't you say?

And with the rubble comes the rabble. They police Jewish dissent.

Torturers speaking Hebrew. Hebrew as the language of torturers. The Jewish establishment (speaking in English) enabling the torturers (speaking Hebrew.)

Netanyahu speaking Hebrew and English.

Specialists in torture, at least some of them, speaking Hebrew and Arabic and English.

Well, yes, Arabs torture, too. Like our man in Egypt who offered an arm where only a DNA sample was asked for.

At a film festival that featured the Middle East, in Austin if my memory serves me right. Stormin Norman was delivering the keynote, and I spoke about these cultural and linguistic understandings. I wondered out loud how atrocity was so insidious that once inside the language/culture/religion it could never be eradicated. After my short address, shifting subjects, someone from the gallery shouted that I was a defeatist, a Palestinian victory was right around the corner.

A decade later, no doubt his response is the same. Or is he melting down, too?

And, with all due respect to Noam Chomsky, Israel's road is not paved only with American bricks. Though dependent, Israel is also independent. Preferably with America but also without it, Israel is going all the way down Empowerment Road.

Because of these views, I have been blackballed in various corners of the international justice movement. Sometimes that's the way it goes.

Surprised? Do you think it's only the Empire and Progressive Jewish establishments that censor thought? If you do, think again.

Think of Plan B as a moving target. Where it is now – on all fronts – isn't going to get us very far.

The Tale of the Stamp
BUNDESARCHIV BILD

AUGUST 4

I'M LEAVING
ON A (NAZI / GERMAN) JET PLANE

I'm leaving today to teach at a Peace Studies program in Innsbruck. More formally known as a MA Program in Peace, Development, Security and International Conflict Transformation. It's a mouthful. Like Biblical Israel on its sociologically defined mission to create a socially egalitarian decentralized tribal confederacy. Sometimes you arrive and there's more than you expected at the titled/described place. Other times there's less.

I've taught here before – four years ago to be precise. It was quite interesting, international students galore. As in any of these international gatherings, the students are diverse in their ambition. There's genuine interest in the topics at hand. There's career climbing as well. Mixed bag.

Yes, I know, the controversial "Das Auto" advert I referred to a few days ago. Or rather my controversial comments on how I wished such commercials weren't aired where I am living. The Nazi-past thing, I continue to dwell in it. I wouldn't say it's healthy. Better to forget?

Austria was a Nazi haven and the Innsbruck Jewish world, well its day in the sun closed quickly. The best thing is to get it out of the way with a short description of the situation then:

> In March of 1938, the illusion of a peaceful coexistence for all Jewish communities in what had now become the "Eastern March" were shattered. Jewish students were excluded from their school classes, business licenses were withdrawn, rent contracts were cancelled, and stores and businesses were "aryanized". During the so-called Reichsprogromnacht on the night of November 9 – 10, 1938, most of the Jewish Community's board members were murdered by SS men dressed in civilian clothing. The prayer room in the Sillgasse was destroyed. The last Tyrolean rabbi, Elimelech Rimalt, had managed to leave Innsbruck only a short time before. By the middle of 1939, nearly all Jews had been forced to leave the "Tyrol and Vorarlberg" district. At least two hundred Tyrolean and Vorarlberg Jews did not live to see 1945. The cause of their deaths ranged from the desperate suicides of March 12th, 1938, to those left dead in the Night of Broken Glass, to children who were murdered as late as mid-1944 in the gas chambers of Auschwitz. About three hundred Jews are known to have survived abroad or even in concentration camps. But the fates of over 70 people from Tyrol and Vorarlberg who were victims of racial persecution remain unknown to this day.

Okay, let's move on now. Beyond the Aryanized property, the suicides and the murders. Yes, there was opposition to the Nazis in Austria. I know also that when times get tough almost everyone hunkers down and takes care of themselves. Human nature – the true believers, career climbers, bystanders, resisters. Another wheel of life.

Sigmund Freud was born in Vienna. They note his absence with a museum. It is where Edward Said was supposed to deliver a lecture – "Freud and the Non-European." It didn't happen. The invitation was withdrawn after Said threw a rock in Lebanon. Yes, the story, as usual, is involved. Apparently the thrown rock didn't have any particular destination. In general it was thrown toward Israeli forces that, evidently, were so far away, Said couldn't see them.

With the invitation revoked, Said was invited to deliver his lecture at the Freud Museum in London. This is the city where Freud's "absence" in Vienna forced him to flee and where he died. His last writings revolved around that non-European, Moses.

Vienna is also the birthplace of Martin Buber who attended the University of Vienna. He was forced out of Germany in the late 1930s and landed in Jerusalem. I lectured at the Jewish Studies Center there some years ago. The handful of people who showed up included my two sons who were along for my lecture tour. At the center, I had a rough "discussion" with its head since it was obvious they hadn't advertised my appearance and worse, once they found out who I was, actively downplayed it. That was after they withdrew their invitation for me to speak which was countermanded by the higher-ups at the university. If memory serves, the head of the center was non-Jewish German. Ironic, don't you think?

Think about it. Edward Said lecturing on Freud, me lecturing at the university where Buber attended, both of us pushed around for being too out there on contemporary Jewish life issues. Freud and Buber were way out figures on the issues of their time. Freud was dubious about Zionism and Buber actively campaigned against the creation of the state of Israel. Today conformity is the watchword.

But it is quite something, Said commenting on Freud. It's published in a book and you can even check the endnotes where Said cites my work. My small claim to fame.

Full disclosure – yes, I don't want to leave him out – Theodore Herzl, the founder of modern Zionism, also lived in Vienna, went to university and practiced law there before moving to Paris. Of course, this was pre-Nazi times.

Nonetheless a vibrant Jewish world in Vienna that disappeared during the Nazi era.

Wait, one more, one of my favorites, Ivan Illich, with a crazy patchwork background. One biographical sketch begins its section on him with the following:

> Illich was born in Vienna to a Croatian, Catholic father—engineer Ivan Peter Illich and Sephardic Jewish mother—Ellen née Regenstreif-Ortlieb. His maternal grandmother was from Texas. Illich had Italian, Spanish, French, and German as native languages. He later learned Croatian, the language of his grandfathers, then Ancient Greek and Latin, in addition to Spanish,

Portuguese, Hindi, English, and other languages He studied histology and crystallography at the University of Florence (Italy) as well as theology and philosophy at the Pontifical Gregorian University in the Vatican (from 1942 to 1946), and medieval history in Salzburg.

Illich was a fascinating character, a father of the Catholic Left, founding the Centro Intercultural de Documentación (CIDOC, or Intercultural Documentation Center) at Cuernavaca in Mexico in the 1960s. He wrote books galore including *Deschooling Society* which analyzed, well, the educational industrial complex, and how modern education didn't educate at all. In his bio, notice the Catholic/Jewish parentage and his maternal grandmother being from Texas! Among his many languages, one is missing, at least according to a source who has written a biography of him – Yiddish. When I wrote about him a few years ago, I referred to this great Catholic radical as Yiddish Illich.

Yiddish Illich, amusing. He was expelled from school for having Jewish background after the Nazis came to power in Austria. He spent the last years of World War II in Rome. Did he visit the Jewish ghetto that was emptied while he was there? Lots of interesting stuff to unearth here.

Holocaust baggage to be carried through the airport. Yes, and I'm flying Lufthansa. Das Auto in the air? Check this description entry for the carrier:

1950s: Post-war reformation

Lufthansa traces its history back to 1926 when the Deutsche Luft Hansa was formed in Berlin, an airline that served as flag carrier of the country until 1945 when all services were suspended following the defeat of Germany in World War II. The new Lufthansa was formed on January 6, 1953 as Aktiengesellschaft für Luftverkehrsbedarf, a company for air traffic demand, and was renamed Deutsche Lufthansa Aktiengesellschaft and relaunched as an airline on August 6, 1954. While Lufthansa claims DLH's history as its own, it is important to note that it is not the legal successor of the company founded in 1926. On April 1, 1955 Lufthansa launched scheduled service within Germany using the Convair 340. International operations started on May 15, 1955, with flights to points in Europe, followed by services to New York City from June 8 of that year using Lockheed Super Constellations aircraft, and on South Atlantic routes from August 1956.

Interesting what is said and what isn't. Lufthansa traces its history back to 1926, under the Deutsche Luft Hansa company. DHL served as Germany's national airline until 1945 – through the unmentioned Nazi era. Lufthansa was formed or "relaunched" in 1954. Lufthansa "claims DHL's history as its own" but – note this! – it is not the "legal successor" of DHL. It is and isn't. It claims history but not legally, to avoid the difficult questions as to what it was involved in during the Nazi era?

Just looked it up.

1930s

A German 1936 stamp commemorating the 10th anniversary of Deutsche Lufthansa.

Even though the early years of the decade saw a difficult financial situation due to the Great Depression, Deutsche Luft Hansa further expanded its international route network in South America, and launched scheduled flights from Germany to the Middle East. Politically, the company leaders were linked to the rising Nazi Party; an aircraft was made available to Adolf Hitler for his campaign for the 1932 presidential election free of any charge. Erhard Milch, who had served as head of the airline since 1926, became a high-ranking official at the Aviation Ministry when Hitler came to power in 1933.

Wow – notice the swastika on the plane's tail. The company's leaders, early Hitler supporters. Campaign contribution for Hitler – free plane. Now I wonder if the plane carrying Hitler filmed in the opening minutes of "The Triumph of the Will" was provided by DHL. Seems obvious.

Stamps are interesting and informative.

The world is different. Yes. History has to leave the stage. Sure. Shall I inform the Lufthansa personnel of their – not legally binding! – history?

Henry Schwarzschild
MISSISSIPPI

AUGUST 6

HENRY'S LETTER

In the waiting area at the Orlando airport, the Lufthansa passengers sit contently. They are ignorant of the carrier's part in the Holocaust past. As I was. Though I teach the Holocaust, I am constantly caught up short by the depth of the depravity and by the wholesale participation of German society during the Holocaust years. How much of that society lives on in the present is amazing.

Try Deutche Bank. Or Allianz Insurance. If they've been around long enough in Germany, they profited during the Nazi era. Then remade themselves and survived in the democratic future. Don't only think German, however. Think Ford, General Motors and IBM. Where the money is, corporations are. In any currency.

Yes I know we shouldn't make distinctions when it comes to human suffering. And yes privileging the Holocaust is used politically to further the suffering of Palestinians. I still have the politically incorrect gumption to say that there was something different about the Holocaust.

Every institution became part of the Third Reich, though some were reluctant at first. When pushed to the profit wall they all found a way to do their bit for the country. So it is all over the world, then and now. There's always a reason found to join, even if it's the old canard – reform from within.

Has reform from within ever occurred in real time?

Yesh Gvul – there is a limit. The first Israeli resistance to invading Lebanon in the 1980s. A reform from within. How did that work out?

Three decades later, where are the soldiers who said "no?" How many remain in Israel? How many have left Israel? Is there a limit to remaining an Israeli in Israel?

Many Israelis who remain, many Israelis who leave, no longer identify as Jewish or even Israeli. Because they are so identifiably Jewish and Israeli, I call them Still/Former Jewish/Israelis. I don't believe you can leave Jewish or Israeli.

They're not the only Still/Formers. Wherever they live, Jews of Conscience are Still/Formers. They can't leave either. Even when they protest their freedom to leave, they "leave" in such a Jewish way that it's obvious. So Jewish.

Years ago I met Henry Schwarzschild, an ACLU anti-death penalty lawyer. As the Nazis rose to power, Henry's family left Germany. Many years later during the Lebanon war, Henry wrote and published an official letter of disavowal – from the Jewish state of Israel. The bombing of Beirut was the final straw. Henry was done.

Here in part is his statement:

> I will not avoid an unambiguous response to the Israeli army's turning West Beirut into another Warsaw Ghetto. I now conclude and avow that the price of a Jewish state is, to me, Jewishly unacceptable and that the existence of this (or any similar) Jewish ethnic religious nation state is a Jewish, i.e. a human and moral, disaster and violates every remaining value for which Judaism and Jews might exist in history. The lethal military triumphalism and corrosive racism that inheres in the State and in its supporters (both there and here) are profoundly abhorrent to me. So is the message that now goes forth to the nations of the world that the Jewish people claim the right to impose a holocaust on others in order to preserve the State. I now renounce the State of Israel, disavow any political connection or emotional obligation to it, and declare myself its enemy...

The response from the right-wing. Predicable. In 2003 the *The Jewish Press* created an annual 'Henry Schwarzschild Award' for "a person in the public spotlight who, by his or her statements, displays contempt for the Jewish people, disregard for historical truth, a desire to sup at the table of Israel's enemies, or who otherwise plays into the hands of the enemies of Jews and Israel."

When I discovered this letter, I told Henry that it sounded like resignation from the Jewish people. That couldn't be accepted. There was no resigning from the Jewish people. Period.

What a delight Henry was. He used to regal me with stories of his Civil Rights days. Henry was one of those Jewish lawyers that surrounded Martin Luther King, Jr. One day I asked Henry what King was like close-up. What set King apart?

Henry set the stage. After a long day's work, Henry would sit around with King and other Civil Rights leaders in Negro-only motels. There was no air conditioning, so in the Southern heat they would strip to their drawers and undershirts, drink in hand, and chat. As Henry looked around he saw others who were King's equal – in preaching, strategy and courage. Henry paused so I pressed him. If there were others as good or better than King, what was it that set him apart? Henry thought for a moment, then continued: "There was an aura around King, an aura you could feel. King embodied a destiny – it was right there. Like you could touch it."

An aura, signaling the presence of a prophet. It isn't about being better or higher, it's a presence that is palpable. In a world that often seems mundane and meaningless, that presence posits meaning. The prophet embodies meaning – at least the possibility of meaning in an apparently meaningless universe. That is why we are drawn to the prophet.

Like other prophets, King embodied the possibility of meaning. That was his aura.

The prophetic community gathered around King as other communities have gathered around prophets before and after.

The prophetic community gathers around the prophet who is doomed. Is the prophet doomed precisely because he embodies the possibility of meaning in an apparently meaningless world? Perhaps.

The doomed prophet – there have been so many in history. Their doom offers others a chance to make their statement of hope in history.

To present that witness to the world, the prophetic community has to live its vision to the fullest.

Still/Former Jewish/Israelis are the Jewish boots on the ground. They have carried violence to others – in our name. Now they join other Jews of Conscience who embody the possibility of justice in Israel-Palestine – in our name.

The politics of meaning is certainly not to be confused with the prophet's embodiment of the possibility of meaning in the world. The primary difference is that the politics of meaning is a pseudo-rabbinic gloss on suffering in history rather than a deep encounter with the indigenous of the people Israel. And as the politics of international law – another, this time, secular gloss on suffering in history - falls short, Jews of Conscience draw near to the prophetic core of Jewish history.

No gloss. No kippot. Not the United Nations. Not international tribunals. The difference is profound. It is being explored. It awaits articulation.

Henry's letter. Strong stuff. Declaring himself an enemy of the state. This is dangerous anywhere. Dangerous as a Jew, too. Henry just couldn't take it anymore. A place for us to start?

The price of a Jewish state – "Jewishly unacceptable." But we have a state, I replied to Henry. Henry knew this all too well.

Henry had every reason to resign and couldn't – because letters of resignation from the Jewish people aren't accepted. Henry's disavowal of the state of Israel is so strong it betrays a commitment. Henry was a Still/Former, even in relation to the state of Israel.

Henry's letter about Israel, so angry. Henry's evocation of King, so tender. You can't understand Henry with one or the other. They go together.

And his beautiful daughter Hannah, who I know. Who plants olive trees for Palestinians in the West Bank. Henry's legacy in full bloom. She's entering the Still/Former stage, too.

Being Still/Former Jewish, being Still/Former Jewish/Israeli is testimony that nevertheless there is a way forward – through the end. This means that there aren't any (gloss) detours.

When a (gloss) detour option is offered know you're somewhere other than real Jewish commitment. This is fine, if you want some time off.

Everyone needs a vacation. When the vacation is over, we know it's time to get back to the prophetic work at hand.

Plowshare time.

Dawn
CAPE CANAVERAL

AUGUST 7

DECOLONIZING
THE HOLOCAUST

Arrived in Innsbruck, on the outskirts, surrounded by mountains. So amazing, the mountains, especially for someone who grew up around water and who once again lives there. Both times I've been here in the summer. Winter must be amazing. The falling snow, mountains right outside your window.

Dawn. The first light appearing is different in the mountains than by the ocean. Defining place by how the first light appears. Home is first light.

My flight was uneventful, except for the food service. As a vegetarian, I usually find the food adequate to quite good, though the vegetarian food served is sometimes difficult to identify. It seems that for food services, vegetarians eat vegetables slapped together with some sauce and – voila! – it's finished. I complained about dinner and after breakfast was served I complained again. It seems that the airline industrial chefs think that vegetarians eat broccoli for breakfast.

On the plane I sat next to a young German who had just finished a business internship in Ocala, Florida. She liked the people but found Ocala provincial. She's quite taken with America, especially its innovative product placements. She told me of her visit to Wal-Mart's headquarters in Arkansas and its innovative business techniques. Among the products featured were Easter egg packets which she loved. In Ocala, she ate breakfast every morning at Panera. She hails from Berlin, the city of her dreams, but will miss Panera.

Missing Panera and Wal-Mart – Berlin. Easter eggs will never be the same in her mind. And no, she wasn't interested in her Catholic Church's complicity in the Holocaust. I didn't even broach it.

That was about it on the discussion front. I started in on my Lufthansa history lesson and found her uninterested. We joked about the airplane meal situation. She told me her family eats Italian style. Old fashioned German food is way too heavy.

It turns out that the Rwanda genocide report I gave a few days ago was true enough – truer than true it turns out – and worse. Our intrepid Victoria Fontan was visiting genocide commemoration sites outside of Kigali. Mostly they are housed in churches where thousands of Rwandans were slaughtered. The exhibits are simple and chilling. Skulls everywhere, bodies exhumed and clothes representing the dead on church pews. I have to get a fuller picture to be sure but it seems that Yad Vashem, the Israeli Holocaust museum, is involved as an advising institution in these memorials, as no doubt the Holocaust museum in Washington is.

It's not surprising, then, that the Rwandan government fashions itself as the new Israel or, rather, the Israel of Africa, and is using genocide commemorations to buttress its own

interventionist policies. Those policies include its presence in the Congo as a way of assuring that Rwanda will – never again – experience another genocide.

Never again. Sound familiar? Most Jewish thought and action is based around what might be called Second Holocaust Prevention. Who can question policies whose express purpose is to prevent a repetition of a second Holocaust/genocide? Even if it places others in harm's way or places the Holocaust/genocide heirs in dangerous situations either immediately or in the near future?

Second Holocaust/genocide Prevention policies are forever and entangled. Empire wherever you are located on the map is essential. Such programs can never end, by definition.

Meanwhile those countries that were complicit in Holocaust/genocide have such difficulty admitting it that the Austrians and even the French still can't fess up almost seventy years later. They continue to play the victim of Hitler's "forced" entry into their lives. After arriving, this was the first discussion I had with one of the Austrian program organizers.

Thoughts about exporting the Holocaust as I begin teaching today. Strange, before I even present the "exporting" argument I have to argue that the Holocaust is relevant to consider. That's how far the exporting theme has gone, unnamed of course. Now, with the Rwanda commemoration situation coming to my attention in a new way, I think of how we've colonized the Holocaust. How we need to decolonize the Holocaust. And what colonizing and decolonizing the Holocaust actually means.

Can Wal-Mart help in my thinking here? The proverbial Easter egg hunt is being ramped up and exported around the world. I'm surprised that Wal-Mart hasn't packaged the Holocaust. I wouldn't be surprised if it now comes to my attention that they have. Or, at least, tried. Would the Wal-Mart clientele be interested?

Introducing the Holocaust. Do I make it immediately relevant to the students by saying it's key to how Jews view Israel? Do I have to export the Holocaust before I begin my deconstruction on how it is used by Jews and others in the proliferating Second Holocaust/genocide Prevention (political) programs?

Have you noticed that I capitalize Holocaust and don't capitalize genocide? I just noticed it myself. A colonial statement?

I've already told you that the Holocaust was different. At least I think it was. Prejudice? Has to be, I think. Still want to be upfront about it. Can I confess this to the students without blowing my Jew of Conscience cover?

Treading carefully, a Jew abroad. It isn't easy for me or them. On all fronts. Jewish has never been easy. Isn't now. If we think and act carefully about it.

When the Other hears a Jewish voice – on the Holocaust, on Israel – what do they hear? When I speak in a Jewish voice – on the Holocaust, on Israel – what do I hear? When Jews hear a Jewish voice – on the Holocaust, on Israel – what do they hear?

Part of the problem, even in BDS, Jews speaking, others hearing. Others speaking, Jews hearing. Same words, heard differently?

A long history of Jews speaking and Jews being spoken about. Mostly Jews and non-Jews were on different pages. Now that Jews and non-Jews are on the same page, we hear the same words the same way, right?

I doubt it.

A new, mutual solidarity isn't above history.

The question is how the past (un)hearing is used in the present. As a way of distancing and unaccountability or as a challenge to probe the gaps and to walk forward with the dissonance.

Whites and Blacks, male and female, gay and straight, do they hear each other's voice in perfect harmony?

On this Jews and Christians have a lot to learn, and have also advanced in many directions. I think we can say the same about Jews and Palestinians – at least in some circles.

The movement toward justice is also about speaking and being heard.

Strange, when we had less power, Jews were great listeners – and interpreters. The more power, the less we hear and understand.

Wal-Mart to be of help? They're full service. Perhaps in the future they'll branch out into translation. Of justice. When the suffering assume power.

Sightings
CAPE CANAVERAL

AUGUST 8

JETLAG JEWTU
BOTH SIDES OF THE CONGO LINE

First night jet lag, hope it's better tonight. Also had a splitting headache – the worse I've ever experienced. Hope that's in the past, too.

Class today hearing about the peace industry, then in the afternoon my own brood – eighteen students. Mostly European, Germans and Austrians predominate. A Jewish Israeli and Palestinian. Also a Brazilian convert to Buddhism, Tibetan style. She's organizing a conference on Tibet in Brazil, Richard Gere on board. Oh, to have a movie star sign on to the Israel-Palestine issue. Has that ever been?

Clearly the international students don't have an interest in Jewish, though I will be speaking in the morning joint session, too. Usually after hearing me they're interested but the Jewish thing, the Holocaust and Israel, discourages them. It's going to get worse. The Jewish world is shrinking. Interest in the Jewish world is shrinking.

A shrinking Jewish world is one where Jews don't travel, don't speak and aren't listened to. Does it matter? In terms of power, not for the moment. However, it isn't good for the long term. It isn't safe either.

That's for the Jews of the future to deal with. The only thing I can do is speak my piece where I am invited. Make the most of it. Not for any ulterior motive, just to be present. To be open to the encounter.

Encounter in the Buberian terminology, making myself vulnerable to others. As others make themselves vulnerable to me. Where does this lead? As I told my class, we're not moving anywhere as we have no destination. Our only aim is to get to a deeper point, alone and together. Let the future take care of itself. It will anyway, won't it?

Before I left my son, Aaron, worrying about his future. Not definable, just a general sense. I, too, am worried about my future. There is little to do but keep on keeping on.

My class is reading Elie Wiesel's *Night*, Richard Rubenstein's *The Cunning of History* and my *Practicing Exile*. Three different books, each with their own Jewish flavor. Also opening up other non-Jewish questions of identity and history.

My small group today – I can tell it's going to be tough sailing. As usual for this kind of student they want to know more and have reflections on concepts and issues that are worthwhile considering. It's just the first day. Looks like a good group.

With jet lag and knowledge that I will experience it, I wonder whether my travel is worth it. When I arrive it is obvious that it is.

The map is not the territory – a Peace Studies phrase used today. The map is the designated place, say the map of the Africa, where the countries are, boundaries drawn, usually by colonial powers at one point in history or another. Even in Europe, we forget how the nations of Europe came into being.

The territory is reality on the ground, tribes, languages, across boundaries and within. Needs to be clarified but the point I think is that there is often a clash between the two. Yes, the map is not the territory.

An example would be a "map" of peace – what should be, theoretically. The territory would be the reality that interrupts what is planned. So that, for example, the United Nations might "map" out peace for a certain region of the world – say Libya. The reality on the ground is something quite different. What really went on in Libya? In Syria?

Rwanda, the UN arrives and "knows" how the situation will be contained. The map of Rwanda. The reality on the ground as preparation for genocide. The territory in Rwanda. The UN map was wrong. With huge consequences. Genocide commemorations attempt to map the territory that is changing once again.

The Bible as map. Jewish life as territory. Disjunction already contained within the Bible, then add real Jewish life. Further disjunction. We read the Bible and its disjunctions, from another disjunction.

When we map out life, the territory intervenes. Shall we listen?

Reading and re-reading. Then reading again. Moving forward, then back again. Is Jewish life continually recycling our birth? When we reach the end the only way forward is by returning to the indigenous.

Primal – Jewish time.

Yes, and then the return is itself a disaster, as in, returning to the Promised Land. After the disaster of return, what then?

The UN in Rwanda, genocide time. No map listening. The bodies piling up. Then after, the silent and complict funding the commemorations. The UN map – part of the genocide.

The Jewish primal map – part of the ethnic cleansing of Palestine. Palestine as the territory upon which the map of Israel is now firmly in place. Israel's colonial map. On the territory of Palestine.

Holocaust era. The Nazi map on Jewish territory(s),

Hutu. Tutsi. Animosity learned in the churches. Belgium as a colonial power, there at the very beginning. Belgians comprising a big percentage of the UN force that failed in Rwanda.

The European colonial cycle of violence and atrocity.

Europe in Africa, even now. Israel as Europe in Palestine, even now.

Once colonialism begins, it never ends. Once Israel's colonialism began, it could never

end. Otherwise the Jewish state would end. At least as it has been – mapped.

Rwanda as apocalypse. Holocaust as apocalypse.

Judgment day. End of the world. Sometimes swift. Other times slower.

Apocalypse can occur in slow motion.

One man's Promised Map is another's Apocalypse Territory.

Thinking Jewish Holocaust and Rwandan Genocide at the same time. Capital "G."

Catholic Church complicit. German-Vatican Concordat revisited. Now, repentance for the Holocaust. Now, complicity in Rwanda. The Cross as a sign of atrocity.

Shaking hands with the devil. Empowerment's (un)announced creed.

HutuJew.

Hujew.

TutsiJew.

JewTu. (After all, we Jews have been on both sides of the Congo line, haven't we?)

Jet lag. Mixing apples and oranges? The territory of Holocaust/Genocide.

In Rememberance
NORWAY

AUGUST 9

THE EVER EXPANDING
WORLD OF THE BEREAVED

In the early morning, the church bells ring on our compound. I inquired about the church that the bells were ringing from. The question drew a look of amazement, as if there might be a church that served the Peace Studies program. Of course, there wasn't. Christianity isn't present here at all. Only an unused chapel remnant. Why then the ringing (un)church bells?

My Brazilian Tibetan Buddhist - too, quite an interesting story of silent devotion - felt strange with her moment of silence before meals, hands brought together at the end. So she scrapped it for the time being. She isn't losing her religion and people here don't think much about religion either way. Are my international Peace Studies students above religion just because they think they don't have one?

Identity, too, as if the European students don't come from somewhere. Their idea, more or less, is that identity is imagined and constructed, so there isn't a defined place from which our consciousness – and our bodies – exist and move in the world. Can that really be the case? They struggle with this question of identity as if something is at stake.

We've had fun with it in my small group. As I repeat endlessly, I agree that identity, that we are imagined/constructed but – not only. We need to find the deepest part of our identity from which we can wrestle and struggle toward transformation.

Not only – the caveat. Important. My Israeli student, a Jew, also American, as well a woman. My Palestinian student, an Arab. Not sure if she is a Christian or a Muslim. Other mixtures. Egyptians with mixed European backgrounds. These backgrounds influence who we are. Our own histories shape us. We have an identity. We aren't just free floaters.

Yesterday the film about the Rwandan genocide – "Shaking Hands with the Devil" – caused a controversy. About images of atrocity crossing in and out of our consciousness. Why do we subject ourselves to these images? Holocaust images and even Holocaust education forced on the Austrian and German students at such a young age, almost as if they were responsible, quite intensive. Unduly invasive?

A week at Buchenwald or Auschwitz, the study centers there where retreats are held. Yes, I mean retreats, there's a religious sensibility about the time they spend in The Other Kingdom. Or what was. An issue: whether we should continue to use mass death as an educational tool.

The Auschwitz to Jerusalem theme has lost its bite since Jerusalem is too hot on the ethnic cleansing scale over these last decades. Besides, the original ethnic cleansing continues in slow(er) motion. If we are to disembark from Auschwitz to Jerusalem we should walk to Yad Vashem from Deir Yassin, where Palestinian villagers were massacred by Jewish forces in 1948.

Crime follows crime. We can't talk about the Holocaust without talking about Palestine. Walking Palestine is a start.

Images and history. The discussion leapt to history as problematic. Why keep reminding us of history, especially the history of atrocity. Doesn't that just encourage the cycle of violence and atrocity? Since it's used by the powerful to justify almost everything.

Understood, but then should we forget those who died as victims? The important debate, did they die as victims or as martyrs, victims meaning dying without any meaning, martyrs meaning that their death has a meaning – in what direction? That issue, in what direction do we take the deaths of thousands, hundreds of thousands, millions, is the challenge.

I offered memory – travelling toward empire or toward community? – as the question of victims/martyrs. Memory as a form of power over. Memory as a critique of power. What the Catholic theologian – German to boot – Johannes Baptist Metz called the" subversive memory of suffering."

The memory of suffering as a blunt instrument. Power over others. Jews over Palestinians. Or memory as a path of solidarity. Jews with Palestinians.

Branching out. Jews over Palestinians – against the world. Jews with Palestinians – with the world. Over against. Solidarity with. The initial particular dynamic of memory carries over into the universal. With Jews. With Palestinians. With everyone.

To break the cycle of violence and atrocity – disengage from that cycle? This, too, came up in our discussion. Is there a way out? The question of questions – always. Yes the cycle will continue in the world – but not only. Since the cycle, (un)like identity, is constructed only. So if our identities moved far along the Community Road, perhaps we could intervene to stop stockpiling more and more images of destruction and death.

Too much destruction and death on the screen is a downer. For sure. Constant repetition dulls the mind. We turn off. Or break for lunch. Of course, issues for the privileged. For those who experience violence and atrocity in real time there are no breaks for lunch.

When violence and atrocity isn't an image, where does it go? To what end is it put? Which, then, the world has also to cope. We, on the other side, have a role. To complain about having to see the images on screen is instructive. Seeing is believing. It is also numbing.

The world of the bereaved. Jerusalem and beyond. The world that watches the bereaved on screen. Two different worlds. Living in the same world.

The Norway Island Massacre a year ago. In the program there are several Norwegians. They're ramping up for commemorations that will be etched in their collective minds. The Norwegians are finally joining the league of the bereaved. This leads – where? A paper on the subject is brewing for one of my Norwegian students. I ask whether there is an international committee to advise Norway on how to deal with remembering the victims, since there is a commemoration industry waiting to swing (and be paid) into action. No doubt some Holocaust industry folks are involved. I doubt anyone from Rwanda is up for appointment.

Anyone from Palestine? They are not allowed to commemorate their Nakba – their catastrophe. At least in Israel. Maybe they could bring the Nakba to the attention of the West through the Norway catastrophe. Or would that be seen as political?

Interesting, commemorating the Holocaust. (un)Political? Commemorating the Nakba. Political? Palestinians would be seen as trying to take the suffering stage for other reasons than burying the dead.

Holocaust commemoration – as a form of politics by other means. When we bow our heads in silence, Star of David helicopter gunships patrol the Palestinian skies.

No helicopter gunships for Palestinians. Not one. Is this because they lack the power – and the nation-state – to make their (un)political commemoration statement to the world?

Nakba memorials. Invitation to international advisory committees. Dependent on Palestinian empowerment. Only then will the Palestinian dead be recognized as (un)political. Everyone has to bow their head for the Holocaust dead – including Palestinians. Otherwise it will be felt that they are making yet one more political statement. The day may come when Jews bow their heads when the Palestinian dead are remembered. Palestinian martyrs, will they one day be considered martyrs by Jews?

A martyred people honoring the people they have martyred. That will signal the end of the war of ideas in the Middle East. Don't hold your breath.

The Lord is Great
CAPE CANAVERAL

AUGUST 10

HAVE YOU BEEN
CONQUERED BY THE BIBLE ?

Discussion this morning with an incredibly inquisitive student from Fiji who hadn't thought about her Christian religion except as a force for good in her life and the world. She was wearing a Cross – it didn't look like a simple adornment – so I asked her if she was a Christian. She is. She told me how she reads the Old Testament on a regular basis to which I replied that her Old Testament was my Hebrew Bible. Calling it the Old Testament is a colonial statement. Full-stop.

My Fijian friend was quite surprised and asked me to elaborate. I then digressed into Christianity as a colonial imposition on the majority of the Christians in the world today – in previous times these Christians were conquered by the Gospel. In Fiji, as well, in one way or another, no doubt.

As part of the (un)civilized masses of the non-European world, I assume that Christianity was brought to Fiji as a civilizing force no matter the manner it came to be. If it was brought in peacefully, the Christian colonial structures were ready to facilitate Christianity's entry. With the arrival of colonial Christianity, indigenous Fijian life was derided in one way or another. It survives in remnants in the dark basements of the colonized self. That's my hunch.

True of Jews to some extent as well. At least we had been treated by European Christians as their (un)deserving Other – though also as the ones who had given birth to them, an explosive combination as we know through history, the Holocaust included. In short, Jews were treated the same way within Europe as Third World peoples were treated by Christianity outside of Europe.

So we are bound in history. But adopting the colonial model of Christianity – where else could she now turn for religion since the indigenous would be the reappearance of the uncivilized and where would that get her or them? – she now expropriates my scriptures for her use. The "Old" Testament is theft, Christian colonial style. It's no different than expropriating land.

Internally, the "Old" Testament is a reenactment of a religious expropriation which occurs in the context of a wider political and economic expropriation. Expropriation comes in packages. Religion is only part of the whole. Yes, one part, but an internal invasion, everything of depth consumed and transformed into another religious constellation. It is the first and major step toward the modern, which destroys everything in its wake, except itself. Or including itself, since modernity is increasingly harder to find within the modern. Post-modern is simply another term for modernity devouring self - destruction and the destruction of others, except for those who continue to ride the modern crest of affluence

and power. For how long, though, is the question of questions. We might call it the Modern Question.

Jews as the quintessential survivors of Christian colonialism and now, understandably, have decided to join the Christian ranks – as Jews. Let's just say that we are honorary Christians now, thus we are allowed to wield our power alongside the Christian powerful. Against the (un)civilized Muslims?

Not to let Islam off the hook, as yet another colonial missionary religion. Which is how Islam, like Christianity, went global. We don't want to be left out in this scramble for survival and dominance so Jews are trying to go global too – minus, of course, the population numbers. Thinking of the billion or so Christians and the billion or so Muslims, our thirteen or so million Jews seem puny by the numbers game. But, oh, how our influence exceeds our numerical insignificance!

Israel's global reach is only possible within Jewish global reach. Though – credit where credit is due – Jewish global reach occurs mainly through American global reach. American global reach secures Israel's global reach. A triangular relationship with the important partnership of a chastened but still empowered or an empowered (disguised and chastened) post-Holocaust Christianity. Where would we be without the globally imperial Christianity that emanated in Europe and brought Jewish bodies to be burned in the death camps of a thoroughly Christianized Europe that is now our soul partner?

The Christian-Jewish buddy system – arrayed against the world. Wouldn't you choose this partnership if you were underneath a violent Christianity for fifteen hundred years? Makes sense if history is only a cycle of violence and atrocity. Choosing to be on top rather than the bottom of history is the way to go even if that means others being on the bottom and even, making sure that you stay on top, partnering with your Still/Former enemy.

So many Still/Formers – it's not just about Jews of Conscience and Jewish Israelis, all of whom are fleeing, among other things, this new partnership in crime.

The Jewish-Christian partnership is an empire enabling partnership – which excludes a good percentage of Jews and a huge percentage of Christians, all the while pretending to be the definitive act of civilized religion, culture, economics and politics. A universal, it claims, that excludes or dominates the many. This is how universality is typically defined, the particular defined as universal and the universal defined as in need of a new infusion of forced civilization.

Universality, the illusion. Whose specialty is uprooting. Root(s) debris all around. Marked by the Cross.

Martin Buber
PHILOSOPHER OF DIALOGUE

AUGUST 11

UPROOTED JEW

Yesterday the beginning of my PowerPoint presentation – one of two this week for me. Beginning at the start of my life as a way of showing the students that their life has meaning, too. How commitment is connected to a people. How identity evolves. How identity and the struggle within it matters. Even if the struggle fails or at least its outward manifestation doesn't change what has to be changed.

I prefaced my presentation with a discussion of some key concepts like the prophetic. As you can imagine, we didn't get too far after that. Today the prophetic has to be explained, beginning with the concept of the prophet. Where does the prophet come from? What does the prophet stand for?

The very notion of the prophet/prophetic is leaving the world's consciousness. This doesn't mean that the prophet/prophetic doesn't exist – as was said to me many years ago: the Jewish prophetic voice will never die. But the conceptual framework and explanation is on the ropes. This may be an academic distinction, since we can have the prophetic without having the category in the forefront of our minds or speech. I suppose it is important to have categories and to let go of them. I cannot let go of the category prophet/prophetic – obviously.

Some quotations came back to me over the last days in relation to the cycle of violence and atrocity and the images that portray them. I shared them with my students. The first from James Joyce: "History is a nightmare from which I am trying to awake." The second from Martin Buber: "History is a mysterious approach to closeness."

For years I have thought within the parameters of these statements. How they move toward and away from each other. Within nightmare, closeness. History as the place we suffer within. History as the place we commit ourselves to. Penetrating to the depths of history, finding something beyond history.

There are limits. Closeness within the nightmare of Holocaust? Genocide? Guarding against a romanticized mysticism. Nonetheless, history as the arena. For closeness. If it's possible.

Reading Etty Hillesum many years ago, the diary of the German/Dutch Jew who lost her life in Auschwitz, finding God in the maelstrom. So difficult for me, against the grain of Holocaust consciousness – where was God at Auschwitz? Yet so intriguing, so deep, that I read only a few pages a night. To keep her story alive, allowing it to unfold.

Another statement I shared yesterday. "Those who are uprooted are destined to uproot others." Simone Weil, the French Jewish mystic who embraced Christianity. Sort of. Or drew

so close she couldn't (C)ross the threshold of the faith that excluded so many throughout history. A whole other story. But yesterday her statement about uprooting applied to modern culture, the core of it, so uprooted that modernity cannot help but destroy everything – and everyone – in its wake. Feeding the machine of development, are my students destined to uproot others even in the desire to "help" the victims of everything, including modernity?

The Holocaust uprooting. Israel as continuing the cycle of uprooting. Once uprooted Jews were predestined to uproot Palestinians?

Of course, ideologically Israel views the Jewish Diaspora as the ultimate uprooting. The wandering Jew, finally at home. Israel as the re-rooting of the uprooted Jew. Weakness coming from the uprooting, even the speculation that Jews uprooted others because we were uprooted. Zionism, then, taking on the views of the anti-Semites. At any rate, the Zionist recipe for curing the uprooted Jew is Israel. Ultimately, to become like the French in France and the English in England - you know the drill.

As the saying goes, how did that work out? Palestinians were uprooted. Are still being uprooted. Are Jews more rooted? If rooted, where are those roots, in Israel, in America? Are Jews rooted on the backs of the uprooting of others?

Was the Diaspora without roots? Jewish communities in some European soil for a thousand years or more. Outside of Europe as well. The Jewish roots being land? Or the prophetic, lived in various communal settings?

Though the prophetic was so often disciplined by the rabbis of these communities, perhaps the Diaspora was a distortion of Jewish life and now the prophetic roams freely throughout the Jewish landscape. Food for thought: Where does the Jewish prophetic flourish and how? The prophetic, the indigenous of Jewish, uproots injustice wherever it is. How does it deal with the roots of others?

Prophetic Jew. Re-rooting Jews. In justice. As in, the Palestinian return?

Returning all around, another uprooting. Rooting and uprooting is complicated once the Wheel of Uprooting is set in motion. The issue is where we stand in that process and what is to be done to restore or renew some kind of ordinary life. So that the rooting process can resume or begin again.

Revolutionary forgiveness. A way of negotiating mutual uprootedness. Not as return. Not as revision. Forgiveness with justice at its core. The question being, what is justice once the uprooting has taken on a life of its own.

As with modernity, intervention is needed. Without a "solution." No retrospective re-rooting. 1948 Palestine is over. 2012 Israel is over, too. Or will be one day. Over, when the final uprooting of Palestinian and Jew is complete? Then what?

Uprooted Jew. JewTu. Coming to a Palestinian town near you.

It can't go on like this forever, can it?

Longing for Home
CAPE CANAVERAL

AUGUST 12

IMAGINE NO PROPHETIC
I WONDER IF YOU CAN

Those who are uprooted, the Europeans, still searching for an identity? Amazing, spending so much time with the uprooted who are empowered. As a collective that is. Individually they are just gliding along, as if they are free-floaters, visiting those other cultures, lending a hand here and there through "development." Good people, but lacking the imagination to know where they come from. They don't have a clue where they are going.

Too harsh for sure. Still, amazed at the Europeans who don't have an identity. Because they have left their history behind. Are they ashamed of it?

Speaking to a French student who is ashamed of her history. Guilt. What France did and does. Yet, to me, France has a fascinating history. Though reading the biography of Marx and his family I was surprised at the violence in Paris. What to do, she asks.

My Jewishness is a problem to some here. It's still gnawing at their imagined identity. We can't seem to get beyond the fact that I see the world as divided and united around particularities. It isn't an anti-Jewish thing from their side, it's simply their hope that us versus them won't appear on their unity horizon ever again.

Yet, it remains that "Jewish" is disturbing the surface unity. As it should, I think. How long such Jewishness can survive is a question.

The idea floating around, even expressed by one of the students, that I take "pride" in the Holocaust and take on a "victim" mentality since I side with the Jewish victims of the Holocaust and now the Palestinian victims of Israel. Strange comment – I had to discipline that kind of language. There are boundaries students shouldn't cross.

In the Israeli-Palestinian student arena, interesting interaction. It is certainly difficult to be an Israeli student in an international forum nowadays. Hearing the Jewish and Israeli story put out there in another Jewish voice, it can only get worse. Is it better for the boycott to extend to bar Israeli students and professors from these international forums, or to have the discourse spoken in front of them? A lingering question.

Also talking with a student from Spain. Or rather, from a part of Spain that has been colonized by Spain for centuries. They retain their own language and culture. Thus colonialism within Europe, in his mind it continues. In my discussions, I speak of Europe, the Spanish and the French for example, yet there are a number of cultures that remain, sometimes becoming weaker, other times stronger. He wanted to know if I thought identity was compatible with empathy. Could a considered identity reach out to others?

My small group especially is fascinated with my mantra for the week that identity

is constructed, built, imagined – maybe ninety percent – but "not only." The "not only" fascinates them because it posits some kind of essence or foundation that is not reducable but can evolve and expand. So my Jewish identity is constructed, sure – but not only.

As a person, everything about me is constructed or close to it. If there isn't any surplus, anything beyond construction, how would I draw close to others, to God, to myself? How could I name what is important to me, explain it, move toward it? Why would I ever consider suffering for some ideal or person? Why would I commit myself to anything beyond my own imagined world if there wasn't something more to me than construction and something more to the world than its construction?

Committing myself to speaking the truth about Palestine, does it become more significant because I am Jewish? My intense interactions with my German and Austrian students – doesn't it take on a heightened significance because, among other things, we embody histories that clashed and now, after, seek some kind of reconciliation and healing? More than imagined is our identity, otherwise the world becomes unreal. Perhaps this is what is meant by the virtual world. Imagined only.

Perhaps the images of atrocity are also imagined.

Strange too, though, with the young German and Austrian students, I feel like a father to them, like they could be my sons and daughters. And this as we have strong exchanges on how there can be no real reconciliation between Jews, Germans and Austrians precisely because European Jewry was annihilated. Their bridge out of that dilemma? For years, Israeli Jews – how did that work out? It can't be American Jews either – it's a bridge too far.

Jews and Palestinians can reconcile in the future because such a program of annihilation hasn't occurred. The possibility remains because millions of Jews and millions of Palestinians, though deadlocked, remain alive and in proximity. Us and them – the great European stumbling block – is exactly what makes a different Israel-Palestine future possible.

Showing the maps of Israel in the West Bank today. That's always the clincher. But with my new conceptual framework of map and territory, the maps of Israel in the West Bank that I show are really the territory, that is the reality behind the map discourse of Israel that simply protects its own population with the Wall and settlements. The misnomer of "settlements." Cities are more appropriate in the main. They are here to stay.

Before I show the "territory" maps, I use Adrienne Rich's poetic statement from many years ago: "Whatever is unnamed, undepicted in images. Whatever is omitted from biography, censored in collections of letters. Whatever is misnamed as something else, made difficult to come by. Whatever is buried in memory by the collapse of meaning under an inadequate lying language – this will become, not merely unspoken but unspeakable."

Unspoken, unspeakable, it comes to this, when uprooting becomes the norm of protection and hiding the territory behind the maps of oppression. This is why Israel in the West Bank is so important to depict, to correct the misnaming with a name. The inadequate, lying language is exposed for what it is.

The depicted images that run against the grain are unlike the repeated images of atrocity that can numb. The territory of Israel and Palestine when depicted and named, inside the 1967 borders of Israel and in the West Bank – with Gaza as well – show Palestinian population centers surrounded by Israeli power. There isn't a Palestinian population that is free of Israeli presence and control. An inadequate and lying language cannot name this situation. The challenge is how to name this reality without then presuming that the false maps and real territory – the division between what is said and what isn't said – is only imagined.

Palestinians uprooted. Those Palestinians remaining in the land surrounded by uprooted Jews. Settler Jews. Settler Judaism. Empire Jews. Empire Judaism. All protected by helicopter gunships. Trying to name the oppression isn't pride – of ownership. Or taking on the role of "victim." Rather it is our responsibility to speak of this even in the European territories where Jews were expelled and murdered.

The Holocaust can be analyzed. It is not imagined. Israel-Palestine can be argued. The suffering of the Palestinians is not imagined. That Jewish and Palestinian history – and German and Austrian history – is complex and evolving is true. What happened, what is happening, in history is real.

Depict the undepicted. Name the unnamed. Bring to light the censored. Speak what cannot be spoken. Where does the strength come from to do what needs to be done? How is what needs to be done known?

I am repeating myself. I've been advised. Tell me, though, how are the words constructed, where does the strength come from, why go against the grain, why suffer for others when there is nothing to gain – if not for the prophetic?

The imagined prophetic. Try that one on for size. If there's one thing in the world that isn't imagined – only – it's the prophetic.

Reverse the idea. Imagine there's no prophetic. I wonder if you can.

Confiscated Palestinian Books
HEBREW UNIVERSITY

AUGUST 13

COLLECTING
(PALESTINIAN) BOOKS

Imagine the Jewish prophetic accompanying the Palestinians. We are there – now. After a long time reviewing the situation. Our excuse for the delay? Probably kept in-house. It couldn't make sense to the ethnically cleansed, could it?

Suffering does strange things to people. Knowing the faults of the oppressors is sometimes a way of recognizing the faults – or potential faults – in your own oppressed people. You realize that identity and empathy move in mysterious ways. So some Palestinians understand. This means revolutionary forgiveness remains a possibility. For the time being.

Time limit on the possibility of revolutionary forgiveness. Things can go too far. As in the Holocaust. Then it will fall to the Jewish and Palestinian Diasporas. On the Jews and Palestinians of Conscience level this may become one.

Yes, a Jewish/Palestinian diaspora is evolving. Another identity is growing, one that retains each particularity. Boomeranging back to Israel-Palestine?

Perhaps also a joint Diaspora within the land, since at some point any Jew or Palestinian associating with the Other will be exiled.

Diaspora birth, growth, fusion, evolution. It wouldn't be the first time in history that this happened. More than one "imagined" community came together out of need, crossing boundaries across "enemy" lines. The Still/Former Jewish/Israelis may be the glue of this joint diaspora. Of course they will be joining a global New Diaspora made of exiles from every land and religion. Jews and Palestinians will evolve their own particularity. They will be part of a larger identity as well.

Imagine that! The creation of a new identity which is also not free-floating, so (un)European, which, of course, is free-floating only in their own imagined world.

Catching up on the news, I see the Mormon, Mitt Romney, has been at the Western Wall. Talk about an imagined religion. But hush, hush, on the politically correct front. We need to remember that every faith seems absurd from the outside, including the faith of modernity when experienced, say, in the Congo. From the viewpoint of atrocity, the imagined modern community is one of (un)belief; they think their modern culture doesn't exist. Isn't distinctive. Doesn't carry a club.

Indeed, most of the Congolese who die don't have the worldly experience to know what hit them. Somewhat like the Jews of Europe who couldn't imagine that it would come to that. Hell on earth, in civilized Europe, in the middle of the twentieth century – no one could believe it until it was too late. The death camps weren't imagined. They weren't an

imagined community either.

Helicopter gunships in the Ark of the Covenant, sure, that is imagined. The imagined, here, is constructing a truth that raises the undepicted, the censored, the buried, the unspoken so that it becomes speakable. In the visual, it becomes more than words. It becomes the territory of Jewish life. It upends the map of Holocaust and Israel – as innocent.

Now imagine this, "The Great Book Robbery" – a documentary on the confiscation of books from Palestinian homes during and after the 1948 war. Presented today in the larger group under the rubric of the archaeology of knowledge. What it was – theft.

Where are these thousands of Palestinian books now – Israel's National Library. Catalogued under AP – Absentee Property. As in, the Palestinians who owned the books have disappeared from Palestine. Thus Israel claims the books as its national patrimony. Strange, this organized looting brought together the Jewish armed forces and the librarians of the fledgling Jewish state.

One Palestinian commentator remarks that the books are part of the "spoils of 1948." The tip of the iceberg, for sure. Though one Israeli says that the "books were not looted, the owners were absent." Like Jewish property looted during and after the Holocaust, the owners being absent? A library official notes during the time that with the Palestinian books "our research capacity will expand." In that comment I hear Edward Said's Orientalist production of knowledge, Jewish-style.

Two types of looting are identified – individual theft when the Jewish soldiers went through Palestinian homes – organized looting when the library-trained went through the homes to collect the books for the National Library. Which was worse?

Hebrew University was in on everything. The university that was supposed to bring Jewishness to the world, in its particular and universal Jewish way. Here Judah Magnes had been Chancellor, and in 1948, in Washington, D.C., pressed the flesh with Secretary of State Marshall and President Truman asking them not to recognize the Jewish state and even to declare a US Trusteeship in Palestine. This portended the sending of American troops to keep Palestine united. Thus Hebrew University - where Martin Buber was teaching - who knew what, when?

Another point in time when the Jewish prophetic was delayed. Absent. Like God. Palestinian books being collected. Wholesale looting of land and treasure providing the starting point for the Jewish state.

Delaying the prophetic. Even when the prophetic arrives it may be missed. It is always too late or losing.

Jews as the great book collectors of history. Readers. Being read.

Israel collecting the books of the defeated. Augmenting our knowledge – of who we have become.

The Colonial Drone
US MILITARY

AUGUST 14

ISRAEL'S 'NEVER-AGAIN'
DRONES IN GERMAN UNIFORMS

My colonial self, our Jewish colonial minds, we have colonized the Palestinians and become victims of our own colonialism. We can't get out of our own colonial bind. Even in exile. Even the prophetic. Color it colonial – but not only.

Everything is contextual – almost. All speech is limited. All action. Almost. The trick is to give everything you have to give and keep moving. Colonial smlonial – don't look back, lest the past become your guiding light.

After we have gathered the light there is to gather, we see the limitations that were. As part of the journey. However, the past is past – obvious – and the present is present. How are we going to think/speak/act tomorrow?

Cleansing the colonial minds of Jews of Conscience. Leaving behind the Jewish Renewal stuff, the obvious other colonial stuff, focusing on ourselves. It can't be that only a pack-it-in mentality, a One State vision, is the only (un)colonial option. No way. Don't let international law hem you in either.

There's never only one option. Though it is also true, as I told my Israeli student yesterday, that certain arguments, say the fears that Israelis have, can no longer be argued. The One State option wouldn't be the end of our colonialism. It's not that cut and dried. Professing a belief that won't come into being in our lifetime isn't the end of our colonial complex. We will have gone on to other things.

Here my argument for Jewish particularity either resonates or doesn't. Embracing one's particularity is not a free-floating zone, as in: only if Jews – or Palestinians – are pure then we can embrace them.

Speaking of free-floaters, did you read the Reuters report about Germany wanting to deploy armed drones in its military operations in Afghanistan? "A drone is nothing more than a plane without a pilot," Defense Minister Thomas de Maiziere told the daily *Die Welt*. "Planes can be armed so why shouldn't unmanned aircraft be allowed to be armed as well? I don't understand that," he added. The report points to the controversy about Germany's use of unmanned weapons to bomb cities in Great Britain during World War II.

Here's the kicker. Germany has been using three leased Israeli Heron drones for surveillance in Afghanistan. Germany is also considering buying U.S. Predator B drones, which carry weapons and also have surveillance systems.

Israel is a military weapons producer and an able competitor in the global arms bazaar that grows each year. Being a competitor on such a large scale is worth money and aids in

Israel's defense. It's a warning on the foreign policy trail. However you speak about Israel in public, make sure you leave it alone on the field of battle.

Yet the fascinating aspect of Germany's use of Israeli drones is how far the Germany/Israel (arms) relationship has come. How far we are from the Holocaust years. Germany supplies Israel's navy with nuclear-able submarines, Israel supplies Germany with drones. In the air and the sea, Germany and Israel have it all covered.

You see what friends can do for one another? As one famous columnist argued some time ago, democracies are great for everything and should spread around the world as a way of encouraging peace. You've never heard of a democracy attacking another democracy, have you? If memory serves his argument extended to something like this: Democracies don't attack other countries. Perhaps I extended his argument, so one day when I'm not in the (historical) lands of the Third Reich, I'll check if the extension was his or mine.

Regardless if it was him or me or some kind of remote connection, you can either laugh or cry when you think of Germany and Israel fighting the world on land and sea. But while we yuck it up, think, too, of Hillary Clinton's speech at the Holocaust museum in Washington, D. C., a few days ago. She with other foreign policy experts gathered there to consider modern threats of genocide and how to prevent them. According to a report in the *New York Times*, the experts agreed that the risk of mass killings increases in places where resources are scarce and governments are fragile or autocratic. Rwanda and Bosnia were cited. Interestingly, the article mentions the scarcity of food, water and energy – and global warming – as danger zones for atrocity. It doesn't mention the Congo, where the problem is indeed the amount of resources that others, including democracies, need to fuel their modern economy.

Clinton referred to the Atrocity Prevention Board, President Obama announced in a speech at the Holocaust museum last year. APB – another acronym – file it under – useless. But give a hand for the Holocaust museum. It seems to have become a hub for policy speeches on genocide prevention. As Israel's Star of David helicopter gunships patrol the Palestinian skies and their drones make it on the world global sales horizon. On the drones, should they have emblazoned "Never Again?"

Israeli "Never Again" drones on the prowl. With German democratic ownership rights to do what any decent Western nation does to defeat terrorism. After all, the (Nazi)German purgatory has to end one day, so why all the fuss?

Germany minus the Nazi insignia. They're ready to rejoin the league of nations. What better way to make their comeback than with Israeli drones, since Israel, more or less, just joined the league of nations, too.

Yes I know, too easy. League of Nations. United Nations. Battling scarcity and atrocity on a genocidal scale. At the Holocaust museum. Best to teach those other violent types a lesson from the air. Drone-wise.

Pope Benedict XVI
AUSCHWITZ - BIRKENAU

AUGUST 15

NORMALIZING
THE HITLER YOUTH

Last night the program had a barbeque and a dance. I stayed for both, though the music was so contemporary it didn't have words or a danceable beat – at least for my taste. The students like to observe the fact that their professor dances, a change in their perception of the talking head, so I attend dances in the programs where I teach. Once I start dancing, it's fun for everyone. So why not collapse the age/thought divide for a night? We return to sanity the following day. All is well.

During the barbeque a bombshell. One of the students in the larger group approached me with a rumor. Had I heard that the buildings we use for the program had been a Hitler Youth camp during the war? I was shaken by this and asked one of my Austrian students to check it out. His immediate "so what" response interested me. Obviously Austria was Nazified during the late 1930s and some of the buildings in Austria that stood and are still standing were used for whatever the Nazified Austrian government needed to carry on. If all the buildings that had been used for Nazi programs were destroyed after the war, a massive building program would have ensued. Much of Austria would have to be reconstructed.

Same and more for Germany. So, as the research begins, does it matter? As in, should a program such as this have its living and teaching quarters where Nazi youth were once trained in Hitler's madness? It should at least be known to all, I would think. It certainly would reinforce my sense and my teaching that Europe isn't free of history. The program would need to acknowledge that it too has a historical foundation.

Rumors of Nazi background. Rumors of genocide. Some more reflection on Hillary Clinton's address and the Atrocity Prevention Board set up by President Obama. Timothy Snyder, our Bloodlands author, was quoted in the article, as knowing that global warming will bring episodes of mass death, a strong statement for sure and perhaps an accurate one. A strange future for sure, though he also warns that superpowers like the United States and China will deflect the consequences of global warming from their shores.

What strikes me is how easy "mass death" roles off the tongue at the Holocaust museums of the world. Politicians and intellectuals who are protected from the ravages of everything they predict for others. At least for now. This at the place where they mourn the past. Strange digs to predict the end of the world as we know it.

Returning to the Israel's "Never Again" Drones and Germany on the "We Repent" prowl again. Everyone who is anyone is preparing for the global warming world where drones will monitor the earth for every movement of weather, food, armaments, you name it. Monitoring for our security is the name of the global warming future.

This reminds me of the time I spoke at the Holocaust museum – itself a long story and one for another time. The image I remember is a reception held for a conference that was being held on the same day I was speaking. As I was brought to the reception and introduced all around, I noticed the food and the drinks were extensive and beautifully presented.

It was a lavish spread. Noting that we were surrounded by Holocaust depictions and artifacts, I hesitated before partaking of the feast before me. Of course, I had eaten earlier that day and would eat again. I was also hungry. The memory of the Holocaust had not interrupted my eating patterns. Yet, right there, in the Holocaust museum, the feast before me and the hum of friendly interactions, I was caught up short. When I mentioned this to my host he assured me that partaking of the food and conversation was appropriate. He offered to help by gathering food for me.

Hitler Youth camps. Mass death rolling off our tongues. Drones being manufactured, bought and sold. Receptions at Holocaust museums. Should all of this be normalized, as in, Marc, enjoy the food, would you like some tomato juice?

An earlier discussion in the program. I told the group that when Palestinians come to my home on Friday night, I will not light the Shabbat candles and say the blessings in front of them or that I was against my son, Isaiah, learning German as his college program's foreign language – shall we say that it elicited controversy? Obviously I was just sharing my perspective to provoke thought. In light of everyone's desire to normalize what shouldn't exist in history or now, it may seem even more idiosyncratic. Who cares about Shabbat and my son learning German?

Disturbing it is, though. I suppose memorializing the dead and predicting more death is normal for the protected and the affluent, as in, we know it happened and is coming, let's eat a sandwich and drink some coffee before we return to the continuing discussion, and, oh yes, Hillary Clinton's keynote is next where she will note her husband's failure as the Rwandan genocide unfolded. Not a problem, he has already acknowledged it as he acknowledged and tried to bridge the Israel-Palestine gap. President Clinton even attended Yitzhak Rabin's funeral after he was assassinated as a friend and a man of peace without mentioning that Rabin was an ethnic cleanser. Clinton normalized Rabin as the Hitler Youth camps, mass death in the future, drones galore, the Holocaust, the Rwandan genocide – all of it rolling off our tongues so easily.

The Congo line. The Apartheid Wall. Do you remember when no one thought the Wall could be built because the international community would stop it? I remember people arguing that it was best that Israel start building the Wall precisely because the situation would be then so crystal clear that the whole Israel-Palestine affair would be resolved. I was amazed and asked whether the proponents of the Wall for the express purpose of exposing Israel had ever been ghettoized. If they had ever watched their worlds being walled in as the international community was called upon to act. Didn't they realize that they were wrong, that if the record in the past of stopping Israel was a predictor then the Wall wouldn't be stopped and that soon the world would be on to other global hot spots? That the Wall would be normalized and that a people would be ghettoized as another fact on the ground?

Normalizing the once unthinkable. Mass death. The Apartheid Wall. So much before and after. So much to come, it just rolls off the tongue.

The Hilter Youth. Pope Benedict time, a whole other story. In the main building here, now being renovated, the crucified Jesus hangs on the wall where meals are eaten and in each room above the bed. I mean vivid depictions of Jesus' agony. Were they there when the Nazis were around?

It seems that the Swastika and the Cross rarely clashed during the Nazi era. When they did it sometimes had to do with crucifixes on the wall. Should they be removed, or if they remained how vigorous did the churches' support for the Nazis have to be?

The Catholic Church coexisting with and then normalizing the Nazis. The Cross and mass death. Not synonymous. Not in absolute opposition.

Scary stuff. The raw dough of history.

Where I am teaching now, receptions where plates of food were passed, then.

Dancing last night – on the graves of others. Such is history. If we don't dance on the dead, there would be no place to dance.

Life goes on, global warming mass death rolling off our tongues. Receptions will continue for the protected. As with the Apartheid Wall. Life goes on.

Never Again
UNITED STATES OF AMERICA

AUGUST 17

BGS / BDS
NEVER EASY ON THE JEWISH FRONT

False alarm, in fact, perhaps just the opposite. In German, I found a short history of the place here and, translated, it seems that the Hitler Youth wanted to occupy the premises but the owner resisted. The reason for the resistance – unstated. It could have been for a variety of reasons, including opposition to the Nazis themselves. It may have been about money or just about this rural ideal being overrun by an institutional juggernaut. More research needed.

The lesson here is not to jump to conclusions. Also, every inch of Austria's soil is infected with the possibility of the Nazis occupying. From outside to home grown. This is why the German and Austrian children of a certain age didn't quite know what was up with their parents, now grandparents and beyond. Where were they during the Nazi period? What were they involved in? Were they or their parents supporters of the Nazis?

Questions for the Jewish future. What were your parents or grandparents doing as the Palestinians were ethnically cleansed from the land in 1948 and beyond? Those Jews who think that we are exempt from the questioning of our heirs have already missed the Jewish prophetic boat. It's out there on the high seas.

On the dancing front, interesting understandings shared at breakfast about how the dances now begin with your own grounding. No words to the songs or at least little that means anything, then you dance in a group, only fleetingly locking eyes or steps with another. This is the no risk approach to dancing, since you can't be accused of exclusivity or be rejected, so nothing personal is involved. No personal history or commitment either?

Those of us at a certain age know how complex our personal histories and commitments are. Sometimes, we or others with us would like to abandon both. Nonetheless, the lack of foundation on the public front is connected to the lack of foundations in individual lives. Uprooting in one arena affects uprooting in others. This is the real problematic in the virtual world we increasingly inhabit. Our connection with the outside/inside is assumed without reflection unless we are (un)plugged.

(un)Plugged, the world careens out of our control. (un)Plugged, we have difficulty adjusting to the glare of the real world. If we don't know what the outside world is, how can we cope when we are confronted with that world?

Our control and the Israel-Palestine stalemate. The challenge is to (un)plug our control, which, if you've noticed, isn't controlled by us or sometimes by anyone, so it seems. Syria going down is just another example of not having predicted what would happen and the players are so many representing such diverse interests, almost none of them having to do

with ordinary Syrians at all, God only knows where the wind will blow once the dictator dynasty falls by the wayside of history. Like Mubarak but with much, much more violence.

Falling dictatorships. The world is replete with them. Now take off your Israel is a democracy hat and think of Israel from a Palestinian perspective. Call it what you will from the Jewish side and its international recognition, Israel is a fascist force – for Palestinians. Israeli fascism – shall I call it Jewish fascism since Jews all over the world enable Israel?

In my small group yesterday, some students couldn't wrap their mind around David Ben Gurion, the first prime minister of Israel, recognized as a liberal leading light in the world of his times while ethnically cleansing Palestinians. Could a liberal do such things and still be a liberal?

More or less, around the tables, the answer was no – he couldn't be both. But since he was – my view – we have to reorient our view of liberal fascism. I don't mean this in the sense that it was fashionably applied to the United States some decades ago, and look how far we have come since that time, becoming at least a surveillance, if not a police state. A national security state, another nomenclature bandied around some time ago. Again, how far we have come in the last decades.

Israel has been and is a liberal venture. Netanyahu is not a right-wing fascist on most matters (un)pertaining to the Palestinians. Call him an Israeli expansionist but, then, every Israeli prime minister has been so. In this regard there is no difference between Ben Gurion, Rabin, Sharon and Netanyahu. The Apartheid Wall was built when the state of Israel was formed. It just took a long time to construct it.

It takes a village to raise a child, returning to our Hillary Clinton theme. It takes a state to build an Apartheid Wall. An ideology can't do it – without a state. Even the focus on the Promised Land can't do it – without a state. Can a homeland focus, a la Martin Buber, Judah Magnes and Hannah Arendt, undo the state and thus the Apartheid Wall? I doubt it, but then again the One State vision won't do it either. Joining forces, Homeland Zionists and One State visionaries? Doubt it too.

I suppose if we simply accept that no matter what position we take it won't be enough separately or together, then we can focus on the task at hand which is to end the oppression of the Palestinian people. Of course, that won't do it either. We are back at square one.

You see the problem is what we might call the Ben Gurion Syndrome (BGS). Liberal to the world, fascist to the Palestinians. We can't say that BGS is impossible since, to some extent, it survives today. American Jewish support for Israel isn't fascist, not even close, except in its policies toward Palestinians. Elie Wiesel a fascist? No way.

To call the Jewish establishment fascist is a misnomer, way too easy and wrong. Though, if I step outside of my context, for Palestinians, BGS is what it is. Why beat around the liberal/fascist dichotomy bush?

BGS like a mountain's narrow wooden bridge; it's dangerous to cross. The winds are too strong and it's single file with one foot in front of the other; darkness is coming soon. We

have to cross to the other side before darkness falls. To make it across, we have to forge ahead.

Jews of Conscience in exile. We have never been able to explain how a suffering and progressive people can do/enable the things that are going on in Israel-Palestine.

It would be easier if the Jewish establishment sent their kids to the Hitler Youth camps of our time. Then things would become so obvious the world couldn't look away. Sure?

Caught in the horns of the liberal/fascist dilemma. Thicket. Abraham and Isaac time. Untangling trust and fidelity can occupy interpreters for thousands of years. As with Job, where the return of wealth and children is a Biblical add-on, a late redactive act.

BGS is one tangle. The anti-Semitism I encountered in the European BDS movement is another tangle. There we have the reverse of liberal/fascist. Or more accurately, we have the liberation of Palestinians without any sign of respecting Jews. Liberal/anti-Semitism. How is that going to work out?

You remember I reported on my time in Ireland and Scotland a few years ago. The few who showed up for my lecture in Ireland were openly hostile to anything Jewish being said and the then director of the Irish section – well he couldn't say the word "Holocaust" or "Israel" when I had tea and dinner with him. I doubt it had to do with a speech impediment. The Scotland director, too, could hardly say "Jew" without a bite. Strange days, I thought. I was uncomfortable not on their Palestine stance, not at all. And I wasn't retreating to the Progressive Jewish stance, the Michael Lerner two-step that says I'll hold you if you love Israel true.

Also their distortion of Ilan Pappe's works and the whole Israelis-in-exile crew, their "good" friends as they reported to me. Don't know whether the friendship thing is true and it certainly isn't a credential for me if they're talking out of both sides of their mouths. Pappe is a serious historian, an Israeli and a Jew. He has gone far out on a limb, with safety concerns galore. There's no reason to impute an intentional genocide claim that Pappe doesn't make, as substitute for a calculated "Israel is for Jews only" claim that he does make. To some the difference might seem too subtle for public discourse. It is important.

When the political anger takes us too far, soon the cliff is in view. If we jump over the cliff, where do we land?

Because, you see, when it comes to Jews, the baggage can easily get mixed up – history knocks at our door. Sure it's complicated. But revving up negative comments about Jews is dangerous and stupid. Call me what you will, there's no way I am going to be silent about it. Especially when I hear it in Europe. Why go that way when it only means distorting everything?

Yes, a few, and I am a supporter of BDS, simply remark on the few because it tangles me up in blue. As with Ben Gurion.

A few do not make a whole. It does not give Jews a reason to retreat. BDS is the symbolic right way to a real difference. Nonetheless the screening process for those attracted to Jewish issues is almost impossible. We have to struggle with it and keep moving forward.

History's baggage on the Jewish side. It might be easy for my student to say that the contradiction of liberal and fascist is impossible since the act of ethnic cleansing defines all. But how does he judge the anti-Semite committed to wiping out – the injustice of – the Jews?

Perhaps easier to deal with the global warming warning of mass death. You can't be on both sides of that debate, can you?

Said & Elias
NEAR HEBRON

AUGUST 18

JEWISH (RE)EDUCATION

Try this one out, after the Hitler Youth false start, if it was, because the Nazified young, or the attempt to Nazify them, was all around these mountain woods. Had to be. Too much Nordic scenery. Vistas where the Nazi world view appeared real as the mountains.

Still, on the other side of the coin, listen to the German youth of today wandering in Jordan and Lebanon, being regaled with "Hitler was right" stories and how proud they must be to come from a land where Jews were on the run. Admired for something they are so ashamed of. How's that for a reverse historical confrontation of the first order?

Imagine that one, these idealist young, wanting a different world and, at least, a different history – slate wiped clean – and find that they are celebrated for the hate crimes of the century and beyond.

Another boomerang, though, if American Jewish youth of a certain age remember, weren't we celebrated after the 1967 war as if we had vanquished the Arab/Third World menace? This was long before September 11th, when another round began. This time the links with Israel were turned around, at least for a few days. I remember those first days when even the national media were asking how dangerous the American connection with Israel had become. In the background, the Twin Towers smoldered.

Youth of all kinds are confronted with history they didn't make. Their thought, why not make news of our own rather than assume the burden of the past? Because, at some point, even victories turn sour. Few Jewish youth today burst with the kind of 1967 pride we once had, just the opposite. An Israeli-toting rah-rah machine is almost as hard to find as a rah-rah pro-Vietnam war t-shirt.

The same question applies to 1967 as to Vietnam in our present historical understanding. A Palestinian Memorial Wall in Jerusalem like the one that honors the fallen in Viet Nam in Washington, D. C.?

Deir Yassin Remembered, a group I once was part of it before it went south on Holocaust Denial Road, wanted Israel to erect a memorial to the victims of the massacre there in 1948, a massacre that Martin Buber referred to as a "black stain' on Jewish history in a New York City lecture in the 1950s (if my now Austrian-encased memory serves me well). So when I co-edited a book on the subject, I found a Palestinian who envisioned a model for a Palestinian memorial to the fallen of Deir Yassin.

Quite interesting for Jews to visit, even in a virtual way, a memorial to our victims. Reversal of our innocence theme, big time. It's shocking really. Try it. Attend a Nakba commemoration and see how that fits with your self-image. See how your colonial Jewish

self that you thought was essentially de-colonized handles the message that you haven't gone far enough. You might walk out of the event with more anger and a sense of bewilderment than you thought possible.

I know, since I've been there on my global lecture tour trotting, Zimbabwe in the 1980s for example, at a conference featuring Third World theologians. The evening's entertainment was a powerful Zimbabwean dance group whose shouted refrain was the Jewish Israeli genocide of Palestinians. This was part of their "freedom for South Africa" tour. A few years later, outside of Chicago, I attended a church service that commemorated the Nakba. I followed the printed hand-out and heard the amens all around. I walked out of both events shaken to the core.

Well, if everyone has to sit through our theatrical and liturgical renditions of the Holocaust, why shouldn't we sit through the Palestinian evocation of their catastrophe as part of our (re)(re)education as Jews. (More about Jewish (re)education below.)

I happened onto a book some years ago where Israeli soldiers remembered their experience in the 1967 war. To put it mildly, it isn't the kind of romanticized memoir of the war that American Jews loved to read or still retain in our minds. Do we really think that the 1967 war didn't include every type of disillusioned war stories that accompany every war?

Yes, then the October 1973 war, followed by the Lebanon war and beyond. Israeli war stories aren't always what we want to hear. We don't hear them, do we?

In the development of Holocaust consciousness – variously called Holocaust Theology – Israel's victory in the 1967 war plays a huge role. It was in the wake of the war that the Holocaust became central to Jewish identity. Simply put, Jews named Jewish suffering when Jewish power was assured.

The connection between Jews in America and the Israeli soldiers in war is a fascinating one, the connection of connections, American Jews cheering Israel's warriors on. The Israelis doing the dirty work of war, which can't be admitted as dirty, lest the romanticized myth of Jewish innocence, so crucial in the identity and public arena, falls away. As in, the American Jewish/Jewish Israeli honeymoon is over. Admittedly the divorce proceedings have already begun behind closed doors but then American and Israeli Jews were only seen snuggling in public view. Seen any of that lover's sweet talk lately?

Reading the Israeli narratives give an alternative view of the miracle of 1967. The fear, close calls, buddies lost, wanton killing of Arabs, PTSD for Israeli soldiers – again, everything we now know about war was there – for the victorious Israelis. Of course, it was hidden from view even in Israel. To admit weakness in any sector has been the (un)Sabra thing. Now, the Sabra thing isn't talked about much either. The identity fad one day is in the historical garbage bin the next. The 1967 war as "clean" violence. The American Jewish love affair with Israel. The Israeli love affair with Israel. Jewish innocence in the suffering of the Holocaust and in the empowerment of Israel. As if alone among the peoples of the world, Jews can assume power and retain innocence. No one believes that anymore. Not even Jews.

After the innocence is gone, what to do? The connection between the Holocaust and Israel – Holocaust consciousness itself – fading. Israel continuing to invade and expand. Not a picture that plays well anywhere. Where do Jews go when victory is sullied and new histories pick up where eye witness testimony leads them? It's just a matter of time. It is time. Time has already moved on.

Jewish youth, now, when they travel the inversion is upon them. The blank stare of my German students when Hitler's glass is raised as a welcome salute. Jewish blank stares when Palestinians around the world, their allies, and those who follow the news, demand answers to Israeli policies which they don't really know, can't control and don't want to be confronted with. That Jews aren't innocent and don't regal us with the Holocaust, it's too late and there's too much water under the bridge to use the Holocaust or the fear of Israelis for their security etc., etc.

You see the Jewish youth point? Jewish youth are nowheresville and the Jewish community preparing them to answer the charges against them won't do much in the long run. It's just encasing them in a further ignorance and deflection that their parents are already encased in.

Jewish (re)education. It's been going on for a long time. Starting with the lead up to the Holocaust, continuing in the lead up to the birth of Israel, then from there follow the (re)education trajectory. What does it take for Jews to survive history, to make history, to survive the making of history, all the while retaining the innocence platform? It's not easy. It won't be getting easier.

The "cosmopolitan" Jews that Yitzhak Rabin mentions in his autobiography – who couldn't quite do the ethnic cleansing they were ordered to do. They had to be (re)educated. But think on a broader scale, what Jews have "learned" in the last decades, what we are still learning, the knowledge that is sponsored and the knowledge that is buried. The inadequate language we have now. How difficult it is for us to be honest – with others and with ourselves.

My German students having their history thrown in their face. Being saluted. Strange days for them and for us. Historical inversion, reversion.

The bridge with too much water flowing underneath it. The sullied river that is now Jewish history.

Funeral for a Friend
SAN SALVADOR

AUGUST 19

ROMERO RISING

Let's face it, synagogues and Hebrew Schools are places where Jewish (re)education is the word on the street. (re)Educating Jews to accept a violence we used to rail against when perpetrated against us.

Not to forget the South African parents I used to meet in Europe traveling to meet their Jewish children who left Apartheid South Africa because they couldn't take the injustice anymore. Or because it became unsafe to raise white Jewish children in an unraveling political space. Today, Jewish Israeli parents travel to visit their children who have left Israel. Because they just couldn't take the injustice anymore. Or because it is increasingly unsafe.

Jewish youth camps. What are they being taught there? I doubt rah-rah Israel is the theme anymore. Does a knowing silence on Israel help Jewish kids navigate their internal world in relation to others?

The miracle of 1967. The spoils of 1948. Palestinians on the run. Jewish parents on the planes visiting children who can't take it anymore or don't feel safe in the country they were born. The places of refuge that weren't open to Jews fleeing the Holocaust are now open. No problem there. A new (un)expected Jewish Diaspora with Jewish Israelis in increasing numbers is forming.

Yesterday we finished Rubenstein's *The Cunning of History,* a difficult book, the Holocaust as a paradigm for the future. Not just mass death but the bundle of modernity, bureaucracy, social organization and advanced technology, which guides us into an "iron cage" future. No way out. For Rubenstein, no "not only."

Grumblings about the book – what in the world does this have to do with peace and development studies? Not stated directly, just some acting out. Perhaps it's touched some in places they didn't want to go. Tomorrow we're on to my *Practicing Exile*, a primer for me at least. That pesky combination of exile and the prophetic in which there's no way out either. In the community that practices exile the "not only" remains, as a catalyst or foundational openness, as we continue on the journey. More about this later.

Here's a clue. It isn't about transcending modernity. Rubenstein is right, there isn't a way out of modernity. It's about how we move within and through modernity. The light isn't at the end of modernity, like the proverbial light at the end of the tunnel. The light is within the journey through modernity among the debris and the hope that surrounds us.

Like Israel-Palestine. There isn't a way that transcends the reality or takes a U-turn to the past. The only way forward is through Israel-Palestine. Creating a way within so that transformation can be glimpsed in the here and now.

This doesn't sound highly political. May even be defined as apolitical. Let the definitional chips fall where they may. Suggestions welcome but please spare me the outdated slogans and the theories. So much acting out when the going gets tough. In the big group yesterday I had to admonish two students, somewhat like grade school. The anxiety was about liberation theology which I was lecturing on. The slides I added with the themes of liberation theology were dark gray, not the best color, so during the break a few students worked on them. They ended up blue, with a snow flake pattern. When I saw the new format I smiled. The discussion had become heavy, with some of the resistance because of my God-talk. Lighten it up, Marc, they were saying. How to describe liberation theology without God?

Yes, liberation theology, from the 1960s and 1970s, Rubenstein from the 1970s – dated? Bookends of my life I suppose. No way out of my own history. Possibility of movement, though. Rubenstein: Those defined by modernity and the state as superfluous are destined for death. Liberation theology: Those thus defined by modernity and the state as superfluous are defended as important in and of themselves and to God. Modernity-Talk/God-Talk. A tangle. Who wins there?

Defending the poor, Gustavo Gutierrez's *On Job: God-talk and the Suffering of the Innocent*. I showed slides of the conference I directed in the summer of 1988 honoring Gustavo and liberation theology at Maryknoll. It was a large gathering of everyone who was anyone in liberation theology circles. What a month, with publicity around the world. An attempted, though too late, Vatican intervention, was deflected by the Maryknoll hierarchy. A reminder that not all administrations are as corrupt as the one I just tangled with.

So much happened at the event honoring Gustavo. The memories are vivid. During the planning of the event, one day Gustavo came to my office with a smile on his face. His good news was that a publisher in Israel had agreed to translate his Job book into Hebrew. Through some contacts, I also managed to wrestle a congratulatory comment from Elie Wiesel. Though short, his comment was powerful. Wiesel referred to Job as a disturbing brother who accompanied suffering Jews in the Holocaust and those suffering in Latin America today. Gustavo himself made the link in his book. For Gustavo, the question was the Holocaust, then. Now the question is about those in Latin America and around the world who are dying in the "corners of the dead."

Among the speakers at the conference was Naim Ateek, whom I had met in Jerusalem the previous year and who handed me a dissertation he had written on a Palestinian theology of liberation. He asked me to read it, which I did. I brought it back to Maryknoll and since, through Orbis Books, Maryknoll were publishers of liberation theology, I told them they needed to publish Naim's manuscript.

After Orbis decided to publish his book, we brought Naim to Maryknoll for six months or so to ready his manuscript for publication. I served as his editorial consultant. The discussions I had with Naim during his rewriting were amazing, enlightening and sometimes raw. He was learning more about himself as an "Arab-Israeli." I was learning more about myself as a Jew in relation to Israel. Our dialogue was uncharted territory. Now his Palestinian theology of liberation and my Jewish theology of liberation, published a year

earlier, are thought together. Without one, the other is impossible.

True, the birth of a Jewish and Palestinian liberation theology has done little to right the political situation in Israel-Palestine. Nonetheless, our work together represented a breakthrough that many others have witnessed in the years since. Our work contributed to other breakthroughs and, coupled with the movement of history, consciousness about the situation in Israel-Palestine has changed significantly.

Are these thoughts pie in the sky? Regardless, they are part of my response to Rubenstein. I had to keep moving though history.

This morning I am showing *Romero,* the movie. Such a beautiful, haunting film about the conservative Archbishop of San Salvador who, in the end, is martyred while saying Mass. Just months after, two Maryknoll Sisters and a lay missioner, who had been trained at Maryknoll, were brutally murdered there as well. I had just arrived to begin my teaching at Maryknoll's headquarters in New York when the Sisters were killed. A difficult arrival.

I taught at Maryknoll for fifteen years and traveled all over the world with them. During that time, I visited Maryknoll's mission sites in Latin America, Africa and Asia. While traveling, I experienced the burgeoning liberation theologies that emanated from the different countries and continents. It was a formative time for me. From this experience my Jewish theology of liberation was born.

I couldn't witness the suffering and hope of the world without finding my voice on the Jewish home front. It took me some time for sure. Once I found my voice I never looked back. Yes, much more about this part of the journey at another time. But what is crucial for me to remember – what might be helpful in this time of dead-end sensibilities in Israel-Palestine – and as a response to Richard Rubenstein – without denying the foundational truths of his analysis – is that personal change is constantly occurring and that personal change can be translated into larger frames.

During these years, I learned that Jews cannot be free until Palestinians are free. A huge lesson. What to do with that lesson has occupied me since a Jewish theology of liberation was born.

Global transformation is hard to fathom. It is difficult to know what encounters – say with Gustavo Gutierrez and Naim Ateek – mean for Jews or for Latin Americans and Palestinians. I don't know the answer to the larger question, but, on a personal level, I wouldn't have missed it for the world.

Yes and the words of Oscar Romero, as I recall them in Austria, the former home of the Nazis ascendant. Interviewed shortly before he was assassinated, Romero spoke about resurrection as a historical phenomenon: in death, he would rise in the history of the Salvadoran people.

Rising in the history of our own people. Global rising. Among the peoples. An (un) pious resurrection. Quite Jewish.

May it be so.

Frayed at the Edges
BETHLEHEM

AUGUST 20

WHERE WILL JEWS RISE?

Romero rising. So many scenes. Thoughts. Feelings.

Then, at Maryknoll, teaching those who were leaving for Central America. Those who were returning. San Salvador, Nicaragua, Guatemala. Broken countries. Places of struggle.

Israel arming the dictatorships. Death squads. Learning about them. Then Israel arming Apartheid South Africa. Jane Hunter, an early Jew of Conscience, mapping Israel's global role in arming the worst of the worst. Sure, Israel followed America's lead and did its dirty work. Willingly. It also retained its independence.

This is where I part company with Noam Chomsky. Israel, dependent. Israel, independent. Israel as nation among nations. Israel operating within the framework of Jewish destiny – as Israel sees it. Or simply within the framework of its own survival and flourishing.

Perhaps the connection I have always assumed is fraying at the edges. Or remains at the center. It may be that Israel has taken it so far that any appeal to Jews and Jewish history is self-serving only. But then, loosed from Jews and Jewish history, Israel can only be seen as a colonial, warrior state.

Israel as Sparta without a historic and present hinterland. Almost like the loss of Europe, now compounded by the loss of vocal support by the rest of the Jewish Diaspora, including the many Jews who have left Israel. The Holocaust loss of Europe has served Jews well. We can romanticize its history, draw upon that history for images untainted by the changes Jews and Jewish identity would have gone through. We can call upon its martyrs without the true indigenous heirs of their voices being heard. The remnants of European Jewish culture, with their roots, are transplanted. Most disappeared. But if Israel loses the Diaspora that exists, including its own exile population, where will it draw its strength? The Jewish Diaspora is Israel's strategic depth on many fronts. Its raison d'etre.

If Israel loses its reason to be, well perhaps it is inevitable with the passing of time. Perhaps it already has. Embarking on war after war, expanding settlements, permanent occupation, the whole Israel nine yards, for these reasons Israel lost its Jewish hinterland a long time ago except in defensive symbolic speech and elite lobbying. Still, the borrowed time, living there, has sufficed. Nonetheless, borrowed time has a time limit. Israel's time may be up.

Israel's search for a new hinterland – involving Christian evangelicals and political pay-offs – have filled some of the coming void. Taken together, the waning and new hinterland continue Israel's ascendancy. Or delay its decline. Delay its recognition of decline?

Decline and the assertion of raw power go hand in hand in histories of empire. Disguising their weakness as it becomes more evident. So, then, everyone waits for the decline's other

shoe to drop.

Watching the Romero film yesterday, I wept at different times. I tried to hide my tears from the student's view. The Maryknoll years are still vivid for me. Romero is part of my life flashing before me.

Quotes from him used in the film:

"Someone has to have the courage to say, 'Enough!'"

"I come from a world of books."

"I implore you, I beg you, I order you, stop the repression!"

"If they kill me, I shall rise in the Salvadoran people."

Yes, off topic for the war of ideas in the Middle East. Nothing about Israel-Palestine. Syria. Nothing Jewish here.

Think again.

Hinterland thoughts. A deep part of my life flashing before my eyes. Who am I related to, the Jewish establishment or theologies of liberation around the globe? To Jews who enable empire or those like Romero who turn from empire toward community?

Romero, the prophetic in action. Prophet? Brought down from on high, converted as he turned toward the people of El Salvador.

Romero, becoming Christian by leaving behind what he had become. Becoming Christian, failing, part of the prophetic failure that Martin Buber thought prepared the world for redemption.

Resurrection time. In history. I wonder in what community's history will Jews of Conscience be remembered. (un)Important? Think of how you formed your identity for justice. Amazing how many Jews were raised on non-Jewish prophets and have used their witness to embody our own.

Translating the prophetic. In our time. Oscar Romero, Martin Luther King, Nelson Mandela. Any prophetic Jew to identify with on the Jewish side?

Perhaps the larger religious and political prophetic sensibility is reserved for non-Jews in contemporary history. Though you might have expected the state of Israel to produce more prophets. Perhaps in the long run. Or is the Jewish state a different arena all together?

Jewish hinterland. Jewish prophetic. Both in decline on the Jewish and world stage. Even if we survey Jewish committed thought. Where are the Martin Bubers and Hannah Arendts of our time?

Yet, today, there is an explosion of Jewish prophetic, Jews of Conscience everywhere.

More to think about if we assume that Jews rise, too.

Rising from the Sand
CAPE CANAVERAL

AUGUST 21

(JEWISH) BIRTH CERTIFICATE
IN THE NEW DIASPORA

Do Jews rise in exile? Among other exiles in the New Diaspora? Because that's where we are, among others, as we have always been, now in a more intentional way, living together in our ordinary lives and, for our consideration, among others who exercise their conscience and pay-up for it.

You can't rise outside history. You can't rise within a history that is empire only. Every empire-only history has those who rise within it. They offer a way out of empire through empire. Yet we all know that empire will change only by running its course.

Ecological calamity has always been part of empire running its course. For the most part, though, in previous eras empires didn't know that ecology had a say. Our experts at the Holocaust museum seem to know it well. Mass death comes off their tongue like the reception delicacy that was brought to make me feel comfortable in the Holocaust museum, firmly entrenched in American power.

Jews rising. Uncomfortable for Jews who are used to Christians using resurrection as a battering ram. Acknowledged. Let's just say that Christians and resurrection are like Jews with chosenness, however translated – they can't help themselves. We can add Muslims and Muhammed or Americans singing the praises of America.

The fact that some Christians are idiots about resurrection doesn't mean that Jews don't have a question about how they will be remembered in a history so thoroughly saturated with an equal amount of nonsense that the Jewish wayward path is celebrated almost as if it is salvific. Hasn't Israel been seen as our resurrection, at least in our rhetoric if not in our hearts and minds?

Auschwitz/Jerusalem. Death and resurrection. Israeli soldiers the Holy Spirit. Palestinians and Arabs as the devil incarnate. Elie Wiesel as our suffering saint. Baptizing our martyrs. Who's kidding who, the Jewish sensibility has been thoroughly Christianized, which is why I usually refer to the Jewish establishment as an example of Constantinian Judaism.

In this scenario, Progressive Jews are akin to Catholic Vatican II types in retreat. Both opened vistas only to fear the consequences and step back. Jews of Conscience are like liberation theologians without theology. This means that Jews of Conscience are, more or less, the only Jews left, embracing the indigenous prophetic in the modern context.

Yes, Romero is still resonating in my heart. Admittedly, I assume a Jewish observer status. The peasants he finally moves among can't be Jews even in my wildest imagination.

Nor can Romero the priest be Jewish. Looking in as a Jew, I see Romero's world and its darkness. I also witness the glimmer of Romero, the prophet, gathering light.

As a Jew, I add commentary, see Romero's world in its different dimensions, witness the coming and going of justice-seekers. Is that the role of Jews rather than as history empire-state builders? Jews manning the prophetic commentary post?

In the afternoon yesterday, reading *Practicing Exile*, my small group entered once again the territory of exiled Jews, now moving in the New Diaspora, and asked if this finally means that Jews will transcend their "us versus them" singled-out status. My own writing goes back and forth on the subject of assimilation in the New Diaspora. Which might mean an embrace of the prophetic as practiced in exile without retaining any form of Jewish particularity. As generations go by. If the parents who come into exile with others from around the world bequeath their children only this broader exilic community why won't they simply embrace all that is placed before them as their identity? Jewishness might be discarded or simply fade away.

New Diaspora identity – made up of the fragments of culture, religion, nationality and geography, an evolving gathering of non-Jewish identities with no particular destination or destiny in mind. Since there isn't a particular origin of the community except exile itself, now seen as a community, why not accept the New Diaspora citizenship offered Jews?

New Diaspora citizenship is offered irrespective of ethnic, national or religious backgrounds. The only qualification for New Diaspora citizenship is exile, a consciousness of the prophetic and the willingness to contribute the fragments of one's traumatized journey to the larger community without seeking to make those fragments dominant. So the New Diaspora birth certificate is quite different than the ones filed with the state.

The New Diaspora birth certificate. What it would look like. Can "Jewish" appear anywhere? Religion isn't even a category for the second generation and beyond. People of origin?

It's a limitation or a liberation – at least my small group here in the mountains thinks this is the dilemma. Even the rain didn't dampen their energy on this New Diaspora subject. But then, I raised the question of whether Jews can transcend Jewishness in their own lives with the equally important question of whether Jewisness could be transcended in the non-Jewish mind in the New Diaspora and in the larger world.

Since the New Diaspora won't have its own island to live separate from the global population, I assume that the Jewish question will remain. This means that Jews in exile are still liable for the Jewish conspiracy theories and beyond, the singled-out status that occasionally or often rears its head. As in, would Jews be able to live in great numbers in Austria or Germany or Poland or the Czech Republic or more or less anywhere outside the United States without being held liable for everything under heaven when the going gets tough, and even sometimes when the going is easy?

The disconnection between Jews in the New Diaspora and Jews of all stripes, including

the millions of Jews who are simply moving through life with family and friends, can never be complete, I assume, since history beckons at Jewish doors internally and otherwise. I simply can't imagine a Jew in another history – only. It wouldn't make sense – really.

But, then, if Jews in exile seek the historic cessation of the Jewish prison, will the Jewish prophetic, which appears because of this prison, continue to appear without Jewishness? This is another way of asking if the world would be better off if the Jewishness of the prophetic, the indigenous root of the prophetic world-wide, disappears.

Should the Jewishness of the prophetic disappear in the New Diaspora? Can even Jews in the New Diaspora exist without some kind of protection from the anti-Jewishness that rears its ugly head in large and small ways? Just because you're in exile and have applied for New Diaspora citizenship doesn't mean that you don't have Jews on your brain somewhere. Back to the BDS examples, but I have met others in exile too who cannot resist the temptation to think Jewishness is a problem to overcome.

Full assimilation into the prophetic New Diaspora? Unknown if this can happen over time. What is clear is that I can't go there – only. Yes, I still think Jews want and need their own particularity. And that Jews need some special protection in the New Diaspora and in society at large. Is this my hidden Zionist, the retro Two State(r), the singled-out Jew in Marc, the (un)read author?

My Palestinian student raised the question if by protection I mean the state of Israel. When I responded, not necessarily, she asked if protection meant the Israel lobby in the United States. I responded no. She then asked about American support for Israel as the protection Jews needed. Once again, I said no. Growing frustrated, if it wasn't the state of Israel, the Israel lobby or the American/Israel alliance, what protection of Jews was I advocating? Wasn't it enough for Jews to be citizens wherever Jews live? Like everyone else?

I have never lived without special protection as a Jew. The great majority of Jews in the world today have lived with special protections – only. Of course, other groups have special protections now, women, gays and lesbians and other minorities in Europe and America, for example. Every group who has suffered discrimination needs special protection. Is this different than what Jews have and need?

Yes and no. Since there seems to be a time limit on the needs of the unempowered making it in society. These are mostly confined to legal spaces – guaranteeing rights of women and others. The idea is that once equality is achieved the guarantees will be understood as the essence of society. No special categories, rights or space. Assimilation of all to the one goal of citizenship – equality, shared responsibility. Check your particularity ID at the citizenship door.

Enlightenment sensibility. Which doesn't mean that Enlightenment is enlightened – only.

On Jews and the Jewish future. No, it is not the same – only. And yes Jews will – also – need some special protection. Or better, some empowerment that can link with other

empowerment, ideally forming a network of interdependent empowerment where Jews and others cannot be singled out for abuse.

Retro-sensibilities. Sure. My experience is that Jews and non-Jews carry too much Jew-baggage to say that the Jewish being singled out in history is over. Though I'm not sure I want it to be over – only. For without the Jewish prison the Jewish prophetic would lose its distinctive voice and contribution. Would the world be better off?

Perhaps it's the Austrian Alps outside my window. Closing in on me. But I've been around. "Jew" is hyped. Through history. Now. Is it the fault of the Jews? The fault of the others?

Jew entangled – in the world. Entangled Jews – in the world.

Jews entrapped – by others. Entrapped Jews – our own fault?

Jews interwoven – with everyone else. Interwoven Jews – is that possible?

Jews – tangled/intertwined. Jews are a bundle.

Still.

Where to Go from Here
RICHARD L. RUBENSTEIN

AUGUST 22

DANCING WITH WOLVES

So, at the end of European identity, at least as they see it, do Europeans return to their pagan roots? The next phase of the program here is called "Native Spirit." It features an Austrian "shaman." The students will stay in tepees – made out of wood. Are you beginning to get the picture?

What's so interesting is that traditional religiosity, say Christianity, directly related to the foundations of Europe, is so discredited here that, even in its reformed mode, it's banished. Romero made an impact on only a few here. But a return to pagan Europe – are you kidding me?

All I can see is Nazi pagan symbols on whatever uniform Europeans adopt. Give me reformed and restrained Christianity, even the Vatican's type, any day of the week. Yes, I said it, the Christianity of nowadays is vastly preferable to European paganism, whatever pre-history they try to dredge up to enable the furtherance of their modern affluence. Hear me out, though. I am not trying to suggest a return to Christianity or Austrian traditional dress as a public affirmation. I am suggesting that Europeans struggle with their real history rather than expropriating native spirituality, in truth from the Americas, rather than Europe.

Of course, I loved John Lennon's reference to Druid dudes. I visited Stonehenge when I was on my first European tour in the 1970s. So I love the pagan stuff, even the Star Hawk type (who has a Jewish birth certificate by the way). Nonetheless, if we get real, all of this is New Age Jewish Renewal packaged in different guises and without the Jewish foundation. The Jewish foundation held Lerner and Company in some kind of check. It's different to let New Age paganism run wild in the European landscape. In four years when I'm invited back to teach here – if I am as I was this time – my European students might be wearing uniforms and saluting when I enter the classroom. Or refusing to listen to a Jew – some of them find it difficult enough now.

Ezekiel, yes, my fave, also had his night side. In part of his nightmare, or his redactor's nightmare, the priests of Yahweh bow to the sun, meaning that even at that date, paganism infused Israel's spiritual and political life. On the contemporary scene, Richard Rubenstein in *After Auschwitz*, opined that the Jewish return to Israel was a Jewish reconnection with pagan roots. He even declared himself to be a Jewish pagan. Where was he supposed to go when the God of history had fled the scene? It wasn't going to be to Christianity, though he admired Catholicism for its negotiated settlement with paganism and criticized Judaism and Protestantism for the strict separation of God and humanity, leaving the earth for progress – and mass death.

So, hankering for paganism to close the Sky God/human divide and thus to limit the de-sacralization of the earth isn't news to me. I've been hearing the arguments since my early college years. As the students reading my *Practicing Exile* point out, I've softened my Jewishness with Zen. I couldn't practice exile without Zen. Point taken. We all need something more to make sure we are this and that – but not only. Still the "not only" has to be thought through, lest we mistake the important add-on as the center and, with that, pretend we are ahistorical individuals.

Europeans dancing with wolves. Without Kevin Costner. Adding another uniform. In a long history there are so many uniforms worn. Does it make any difference which one you wear? Perhaps they are more or less the same. Depending on the context, they can go one way or the other.

Best to wear the uniform we know the best?

My Jewish uniform. Shall I dance naked around the bonfire caused by Star of David helicopter gunships firing rockets in the night? Or better, be fully dressed for synagogue services, Star of David helicopter gunships resting quietly in the Ark of the Covenant?

Dancing with wolves. As in, sensibilities/spiritualties that avoid history.

Native spirits, restive, expropriated. Isn't this true of everything that breathes long enough to survive?

Conforming to power, especially when you think you're leapfrogging the awful past. You aren't.

Paganism linked with modernity. Modernizing the spirits that would have said "no" for reasons that weren't strictly about the ethical imperative. Real shamans haven't read Kierkegaard. Or listened to Wagner.

Richard Wagner's pagan imagination. With a dose of Martin Luther. Channeled through Adolf Hitler.

Dancing around the Jewish books' fire. Before the Great Book Robbery.

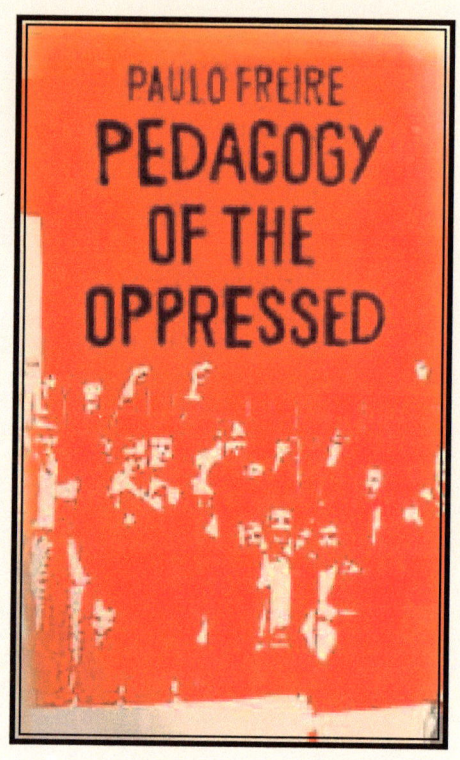

Pedagogy of the Opressed
BRAZIL

AUGUST 23

A (JEWISH) PEDAGOGY
FOR / OF THE OPPRESSOR

It's coming down to the wire, just a few more days, before traveling into Innsbruck for a couple of days, then home. Last weekend in Innsbruck for the day, tourist haven, with the inevitable diminishment of tourists and those who profit from tourism. Even justice-oriented tourism is more or less a rip-off of everyone involved. Like the mountains of plastic used in my organic food market at the Cape. Escaping the system isn't possible. Even the pagan rites that surround us here, however displaced, are tainted.

Last night was integrative seminar night. Gathered were the thirty-five or so students, the administration and the teachers. All of us seated in a circle, of course. It was a three hour marathon of confession and accusation, mostly referencing the lack of group cohesion or purpose. From my angle everyone is already way too close here.

Critical thought doesn't come via hugs all around. Sometimes you have to take thought straight up. If you're knocked to the canvas, look around, get your bearings and get back up. A helping hand is appreciated. It shouldn't be expected. It can't be mandated.

Emmanuel Levinas on the prophet: "Asceticism, like the training of a fighter." Boxing images, since I was one for a few fights in my youth. I was carried out of the ring several times when my come-in, duck-out, Muhammad Ali style, was met with a country cracker's jolting upper cut. Then, in my big chance, I caught a kid more my size, stunned him, but as my coaches yelled for me to finish him off, I studied his face, thought of his being – and my previous experiences – and let him stand. So much for my boxing career.

Asceticism – we don't want to revert to the monastic life full-stop. Yet without the monk in all of us, where do we find the solitude required to think and care for others? Like the training of a fighter – referring, of course, to the long and lonely dawn runs of boxers, movie-style. Really, though, if you can't see life as a long distance marathon with a lot of aloneness, you can't weave the threads you were born with into a whole.

Even then the whole is fragmented. I know this well.

This brings me to the search for definitions and respect the students want from me. Last night, too, the students had their chance to speak their piece to their teachers, which is always fascinating how students spin their story into yours. In general, the students expressed a great sense of gratitude to me, heartfelt and moving. A few started with the "You didn't always listen to me" routine which can be interpreted as "I am your equal and my views are on the same level as yours." Anyone in their right mind knows this isn't the case and doesn't work in a teacher-student relationship unless you dumb everything down to the minimum.

More or less becoming asceticism with a hug – without the training of a fighter. This isn't asceticism at all.

Like this morning when the large group had the floor, explained Theatre of the Oppressed and Theatre for the Living, all good and important, but then began with trust, splitting into groups, with one person in the center, trusting the group to catch you before you fall. If the truth be known I left after the first exercise. There's a borderline between participation and sanctioning exercises when we should be thinking.

AWOL – it happens when I think I just can't stand another minute. This doesn't mean it all doesn't fit the program. I am trying to fit – sometimes.

Paulo Freire, the Brazilian, *Pedagogy of the Oppressed*, the inspiration for the Theatre of the Oppressed. "Conscientization" – critical consciousness – the term that Freire used to distinguish from the "banking model" of education. The problem and the solution. Freire thought that the social domination of race and class are embedded in the conventional educational system. This promotes a "culture of silence" that eliminates the "paths of thought that lead to a language of critique."

Freire's point is that language and education carry the forces of oppression and liberation within them. It all depends on method, intent, and political vision. Is education used as a reinforcement of the unjust status quo or a tool for liberation, since education is never neutral?

Romero again. In the beginning he saw the Church as neutral, then as a negotiator, ending with a sense that Church had to side with the poor. In his journey, Romero underwent a process of "conscientization." In other words, he underwent the process of de-colonization. He de-colonized his Christianity. He de-colonized himself.

Conscientization, Jewish-style. We haven't had Jewish peasants for eons. The banking style of education has never been central to Jewish learning. Nonetheless, we have a culture of silence. Our language is no longer a language of critique. On the issue closest to us, Israel-Palestine, without forgetting Holocaust remembrance, our pedagogy is saturated with thinly disguised themes of dominance and empire.

Pedagogy of the (Jewish) Oppressor For Dummies. The Idiot's Guide to (Jewish) Conscientization. The needed primer for Jewish education/discourse?

Richard Shaull commenting on Freire: "There is no such thing as a neutral education process. Education either functions as an instrument which is used to facilitate the integration of generations into the logic of the present system and bring about conformity to it, or it becomes the 'practice of freedom,' the means by which men and women deal critically with reality and discover how to participate in the transformation of their world."

Apply this to Holocaust discourse, our export within the United States and beyond, as in, the integration of the victims of the Holocaust into the logic of the present American/Israel empire system to bring conformity to it. Or, by developing a critical understanding of how the Holocaust has come to function, it becomes the "practice of freedom," the means by which Jews learn to deal critically with Israel and discover how to participate in the transformation of Israel-Palestine.

Conscientization, another word for the Jewish prophetic in education. Without a Jewish name?

Pedagogy of the Prophetic. Pedagogy of the Prophets. Similar without being the same. I do not believe that everything comes from below. Or that the crystallization of oppression emanates from the oppressed – only. Liberation theology doesn't (really) operate like that anyway, since the educated priests were the conduit for the people's awareness.

The prophet comes from and within conscientization. Is an instrument for conscientization. Theoretically speaking, the prophet is an open circle of communication about justice and meaning. Educating the people Israel and others about the (in)justice fault line that cannot be crossed without consequences.

Prophet pedagogy today, critical consciousness without God-talk. On earth as it is in heaven. Or, on earth as it should be on earth.

Primers of Jewish education. Critical consciousness. Curriculum to be created by. Educational effort to be sponsored by – Anti-Defamation League? Tikkun? J Street?

When these are our alternatives, you can see how deep colonization is. And how difficult Jewish decolonization is.

We don't have the Vatican to blame. However, we have our own (Jewish) Vaticans, don't we?

For now, the need for Pedagogy for the Oppressor? Whoops, we already have one. How about Pedagogy of the Oppressor. As in a deconstruction of the (Jewish) oppressor's discourse?

Gov. Mitt Romney
JERUSALEM

AUGUST 24

ROMNEY'S (ROMERO)
BLOOD MONEY

Just when you think students aren't paying attention to you or Romero, they prove you wrong. One of my American students sent me a link to a *Huffington Post* article by Ryan Grim and Cole Stangler on Mitt Romney and his ties to the Salvadoran thugs who financed the death squads and Romero's assassination:

> The Salaverria family, whose fortune came from producing cotton and coffee, had deep connections to the right-wing Nationalist Republican Alliance (ARENA), a political party that death-squad leader Roberto D'Aubuisson founded in the fall of 1981. The year before, El Salvador's government had pushed through land reforms and nationalized the coffee trade, moves that threatened a ruling class whose financial and political dominance was built in large part on growing coffee. ARENA controlled and directed death squads during its early years.
>
> On March 24, 1980, Oscar Romero, the archbishop of San Salvador and an advocate of the poor, was celebrating Mass at a chapel in a small hospital when he was assassinated on D'Aubuisson's orders, according to a person involved in the murder who later came forward.
>
> The day before, Romero, an immensely popular figure, had called on the country's soldiers to refuse the government's orders to attack fellow Salvadorans.
>
> "Before another killing order is given," he advised in his sermon, "the law of God must prevail: Thou shalt not kill."

But for profit, why not kill? A future presidential bid might be on the line. So much hidden stuff, or not so hidden, is swept under the presidential sweepstakes rug. Even if we knew everything, it wouldn't change the overall vote. This means, too, that Romney's recent hobnobbing with the wealthy in Jerusalem is just another presidential sweepstakes rug. The Western Wall will be swept underneath it, too.

How far we have come when Republicans court the Jewish vote. Unheard of when I was a kid. Israel changed the American Jewish voting landscape. True, there are more Republican votes from Jews, but the main deal is still with the Democrats who are more pro-Israel than some of our Jewish brothers and sisters. If the Democrats hadn't played ball with their Jewish constituency, would the Republicans be getting a majority of Jewish votes or would Jews have had to bite the Israel bullet and see where it was all going?

On the political front, who cares if the world goes to hell in a hand basket? Just promote your career. Hint that the American embassy will be moved to Jerusalem, then denigrate the Palestinians and any movement toward justice. Take money from death squad politicians from another country to make your fortune. Bury any misgivings. Just do it.

Israel's connections with Roberto D'Aubuisson and all he represented. Dollars in the bank. Political capital. Assisting themselves and the US, which assisted them again. Arms sales circle completed. Dollars/Aid/Protection/Prestige. Help yourself and your main benefactor. Ethics and heart can't figure into that equation. It's too dangerous on the political front.

Of course, the practical can turn around in a New York moment, then where would Israel be? This isn't on the horizon, I know, but one can't be sure of the future yet to be born. My Palestinian student certainly doesn't have much hope. She thinks my idea of revolutionary forgiveness is stillborn. As do I. She's writing her paper on the different versions proposed for peace but says she knows that none of them will come into being. Asked by my Israeli student to suggest the solution she wants, my Palestinian student is defiant. Says she won't. Why give away her hand when nothing is in the offing?

Also talked with my Israeli student. American background as well. Farewell meeting. Good stuff. We went through how she wouldn't live in Israel for any length of time again – hasn't lived there except for short stays for the last ten years – and how her identity will be assaulted more and more in the coming years. I told her she has a choice to stay away from Israel and deflect the questions she has or delve right into them and hope for the best.

Israel is unstable, as Jews are, I don't think any more or less. It's part of our (prophetic) fate which a Jewish state can't change. The dream of normalization for Jews is just that – a dream. Pursued too intensely the dream becomes a nightmare. Call it the (Jewish) normalization nightmare.

There's a huge difference between a hard and soft exile. If you have experienced both like I have, you'll know the difference. So, too, with the dream and nightmare of the normalization of the Jewish condition. Whichever side of the normalization divide you're on determines the kind of fidelity necessary. Context isn't everything, to be sure, but it helps shape our lives in small and large ways. I told my Israeli student that we have to give everything we have to the present to see if we can land on the soft side of the Jewish normalization divide. She was listening intently. But what to do in real life?

Another Jewish divide. Like the Empire Divide, where we are and where we can land is important to figure out. Since stability for Jews is out of the picture, the illusion of stability is essential to demystify. With the illusion out of the way, we move into deeper realms of thought and some practical politics as well. Both are necessary now.

Last session today, then my afternoon class is walking to a nearby pub for some Austrian beer. All has gone well, considering the difficulties involved. The students are involved in other matters as well, including who will sleep with who this night and the next. Living intensely is loving intensely. Perhaps.

Life goes on in this neck of the Austrian Alps. Tomorrow in Innsbruck, I'll take a cable car up the mountain for a mountaintop view. I'm not much into cable cars – not by a long shot – but hey, when you're in Austria do as the tourists do.

Also a good meal or two. Went by the hotel I'll be staying out. It's old and kitschy, with a solid state crucified Jesus surrounded by mounted animal heads in the stairwell. Quite a scene.

How better to end my Austrian visit? Soon I'll be leaving on a (Nazi-German) jet plane. I don't know when I'll be back again.

But before I leave, I've been following the latest from the Wagner festival site in Bayreuth. You know the one Hitler hung out at and has been the center of Wagner's music ever since. The Russian bass-baritone Evgeny Nikitin had to withdraw from his upcoming appearance because of swastika tattoos that were etched into his chest some years ago when he was in a heavy metal band. Over the past days his story has changed. Instead of the swastika, the tattoo in question might be Scandinavian runes that were co-opted as SS symbols during World War II. The report is as inconclusive as Nikitin seems to be.

On the Nazi past, or, better, the pre-Nazi past of Wagner and his festival, the report in the *International Herald–Tribune* is clear: "Proto-Nazi ideals of racism, rabid nationalism and ethnic cleansing were at the core of Wagner's Bayreuth, a conception carried through with intense loyalty by his family after his death in 1883." The addition of an exhibit – "Silent Voices" – which seeks to question some of Wagner's ideals, while welcomed, does not diminish his initial impulse: "To view 'Silent Voices' and then look up at the proud, implacable Festival Theatre is to feel only sadness and revulsion, to question whether the wounds can – or should – ever heal."

This describes Austria and Germany for me, even as I know it is unfair. To look up at the proud nations that once – well my feeling are evident. Count it as generational baggage.

Leaving Austria soon with the (same?) question my Palestinian student implied when she refused to speculate on a future that isn't going to happen. Thus the case at hand: to look at the proud history of the Jewish people today is to "feel only sadness and revulsion, to question whether the wounds can – or should – ever heal."

No comparisons. Only sadness.

EXILE AND THE PROPHETIC
part three | *volume one*

Stairway
CAPE CANAVARAL

Johann Wolfgang von Goethe
FRANKFURT

AUGUST 25

WHEN THE JEWISH STUDENT IS READY

Returned home today. Long flight. Many thoughts.

On Romney's blood money, Romero's life. Our blood money, the Congo's life. Israel's blood money, Palestinian life. The Wheel of Blood Money. Everyone has to have their place on the Wheel, otherwise they are down and out. Finished. Not a rosy picture.

The last nights in my hotel in Innsbruck – the crucified Jesus and the crucified animal heads as his partners. They've been hanging there together for a long time.

Turns out the hotel is older than old, going back to the 1500s or so. The famous have stayed here and I was upgraded – are you ready – to the Goethe Room where – if this could really be so – Goethe stayed on occasion. Sans indoor toilet I assume.

Perhaps my stairway friends, as I came to know them, were already here or in the process of being collected. One of the preserved animal heads appears to be from a bison. But there are others, including a ram's head, all arranged alongside the huge wood-carved crucified Jesus. An unusual combination. I've never seen hunted animals and the hunted man arranged as a family portrait. Doubt you have either.

The hotel breakfasts were terrific. Real bread and an assortment of cheeses plus many other items you'd never eat at breakfast except at a tourist hotel. So good stuff, and meals on the town as well, mostly pizza and beer, served European style. Did I forget my ride up the mountain with cable car as transport? The ride wasn't bad at all. Beautiful landscape. Steep climb. Tall trees. Cool breeze. Thoughts of winter. The winter must be bitterly cold.

Europe is Europe, though changing. Tourism is tourism, hasn't changed. Air travel is air travel, changed for the worse as everyone who flies knows.

Word on the street is that Romney has chosen Paul Ryan as his VP choice. Romney is trying on the conservative economic hat after his Middle East foray. Debacle?

Disappointed with Obama? Try Romney for the next four/eight years.

From the European and global angle here in the program, any enthusiasm about Obama is over. Enthusiasm about America ended eons ago. Romney would just set us back further. Details unnecessary. The Republican package is a disaster.

Though my Israeli and Palestinian students are now in my rear view mirror, I can't help but think of their future. The Israeli will trot the globe, trying to cope with the Israel she can't return to. The Palestinian will return to Ramallah, trying to cope with Israelis who stay and those who leave. She won't show her solution hand because there isn't going to be one

she or her people can live with. Though it is also true that my Israeli student can't live with the non-solution Israel proposes. Their difference in not being able to live with this or that non-solution betrays a similarity. One is captive in the land, the other is free as a bird. They are joined at the Israel-Palestine hip.

Our last beer session with students before my hotel stay, again joining the non-resolution of the German/Austrian - Jewish divide. There aren't enough European Jews left to move toward revolutionary forgiveness. Yes, we were discussing this until the alcoholic end. There is a possibility in Israel-Palestine since, though the situation has gone too far, it hasn't gone far enough to make forging a new history impossible.

Really, though, I think the nomenclature of revolutionary forgiveness has gone far enough. Need to scrap it. So, too, with Jerusalem as the broken middle of Israel-Palestine where Jews and Palestinians can gather as two traumatized people and begin again. The path of justice seems impossible now. Probably should just bury the prospect of a future different than the present.

Yet a future will come into being. Over time, it can't look too much like the past. How long that "over time" will take is an open question. Even our small Israel-Palestine/Jewish dialogue in the program is part of a larger change that one day will turn the corner.

Turning the corners of history. Jews aren't present on the Austrian/German horizon. Still, there was a corner turning on the Jewish question, a corner turning made easier without the presence of Jews. So, the fact that no revolutionary forgiveness is possible doesn't preclude a new sensibility. While revolutionary forgiveness and turning the corner can be combined, they can also be separated. As in so many arenas, though context isn't everything it's a lot. I suppose the lesson is to take what you can. Take what is left. Do something with the leftovers.

Tired. Traveling the world is a violence to the body and the psyche. Necessary travel, yes, though ninety percent of the airlines are full of Disneyland tourism wherever their particular destination happens to be. People trying to escape their humdrum life. No matter that the planet might go under as you enjoy the tourist side show. Why let the thoughts of global warming ruin your whole day?

The heat struck me as I landed in Orlando. I grew up with the heat, so no problem for me. As I have remarked to others, in a decade or two my Cape accommodations might be waterfront property. An increase in net worth. However, the following decade might find it in the middle of the ocean. Downward mobility is part of our planetary lives.

Did I mention that I met my Fijian student in the city for coffee? She's on the decolonizing of her religion track for good. Told her that she needed to hang out in liberation circles in Latin America for a while. Yes, they continue to exist. Across our warming globe.

A Jewish theology of liberation. Few takers then. Few takers now. Even the twenty-fifth anniversary of its arrival hasn't spurred an (un)revival of interest.

When my Fijian student thanked me for my teaching, I shared the Buddhist saying –

"When the student is ready, the teacher appears." The teacher has already been on the scene, sometimes for thousands of years, but before the student takes the teaching to heart, she has to ready herself for the teachings's arrival.

Jews aren't ready for the teaching we need. When the (Jewish) student is ready, though, the teacher will appear in an intensity that shocks us. Too late, no doubt. But then when it happens, it is right on time.

The Isles of Palestine
OCCUPIED TERRITORIES

AUGUST 26

ARCHIPELAGO PALESTINE

For the first time in weeks, dawn without mountains. The sun here rises against a wide open sky. Clouds filter the sun light. Colors galore.

The daunting mountains. Forbidding beauty. The oceans with unlimited horizons. Beauty that opens the world.

Tropical Storm Isaac – soon to be Hurricane Isaac – is on the way. It's been raining here, overcast skies throughout the day. Winds are picking up. The ocean is roaring. The Republicans are gearing up for their convention in Tampa. I wish them the worst of luck.

One of my courtyard companions said hello to me this morning and asked me if I was living here now. He met Isaiah when he was here several months ago and has seen me around for a couple of months. He didn't know if I was a short-time renter. We talked about the coming storm. It seems they shut the causeways down when the winds reach fifty miles an hour. He told me that he just purchased some butane so not to worry. He had enough fuel to cook for "us" if the power goes out.

How's Isaac for a storm's name? Binding. Being bound. Trust. Fidelity. To be honest, though, when an acquaintance mistakenly refers to Isaiah as Isaac, it scares the hell out of me. I've never been drawn to the Isaac story, even when Aaron, studying the Bible this summer, told me that the silences in the text were fascinating and changed our traditional meaning of the story. Being quite traditional, I can't quite get the possibility of sacrificing a son to demonstrate a belief in anything, including God.

To 7-11 for some breakfast provisions, a banana and apple, some Greek yogurt and, lo and behold, fresh lime. 7-11 is a truly one percent healthy place that caters to the ninety-nine percent. Coffee on the run, candy, various gambling opportunities, cigarettes – the great bulk of their sales.

I have the *New York Times* delivered through the week. It resumed this morning with my carrier including back-issues I missed on my travels. An act of random kindness.

I took my morning walk with the tourists and the regulars. I see the regulars standing outside their apartments for a smoke, walking at dawn, sleeping on the beach. After a while you separate who's who. Even the policeman who pulled me over some years ago for riding my bike in the middle of the street at dawn – without identification, imagine that! – smiles at me knowingly when we pass in the street.

The depressing news continues to hit the news wires. The White ticket, Mormon Mitt and Gut-em Ryan, the kind of ticket that has the likes of Ken Starr and his White Christian

America band salivating. The reason: it devastates the poor and those anywhere close to poverty while keeping the big bucks flowing to the wealthy. Sure, the wealthy "give back" to the community through donations for university football stadiums. Corruption is the theme here, with the "I use you, you use me" dance prominent in these endorsement transactions. Think of it as an endless ATM world. For the wealthy.

The political campaign this time around is like the political campaigns of the past. An American merry-go-round where the poor and the working class are lauded only for their upward mobility desires, as they are condemned for their real life misery. The poor and the unemployed desire to be somewhere else. They are where they are because they aren't somewhere else.

On the Middle East, forget it; don't think about something happening politics-wise. Even thought-wise. Not a fake peace process trial balloon on the horizon.

Have you noticed the absence of any rhetoric of the peace process during these last years? In years past, at least Jewish progressives could ramp up their "peace is just around the corner" pamphlets from yesteryear, tweaking a point or two, then hitting the Facebook thumbs-up fantasy world. Where have all the Tikkun flowers gone?

So, yes, the Egyptian president has hit the delete button on some top military officials. That's news worth thinking about. Muslim Brotherhood types seem to think Egypt is for Egyptians. Good luck with that. I hesitate to pre-judge the move, though, since there's a lot of Egyptian blood under the bridge and, no doubt, more to come. Reporters are being arrested for opposing what's going on. Nothing new here, I'm afraid. I leave it to the Egypt watchers to weigh in on how serious this is and in what direction Egypt might be heading.

Speaking of censorship. Do you see that Rabbi Lynn Gottlieb is on the firing seat? Seems like the Republicans are singling here out for her support for Obama. And her justice struggle for Palestinians. And her travel to Iran. Enough said?

Rabbi Lynn is a Renewal rabbi – a mark against her! – but don't compare here to the Michael Lerner or Arthur Waskow crowd. No way. She's a pioneer and she actually reads books, something most rabbis haven't done in years. More on her later, but first let me offer her a safe-haven at the Cape. My place is small but I have a large living room couch. Since she's a pioneer, I might even offer my bed. I love sleeping on couches. Especially when I'm honoring a rabbi on the run.

Rabbi Lynn may even have to turn the page. Perhaps we need to form a community of page-turners. Page-Turners Anonymous (PTA). Hmm.

Turns are interesting. They can as easily go Left as they go can Right.

Obviously the Egypt situation is an Austrian mountain climbing situation rather than a Cape Canaveral beautiful dawn sky that stretches out to infinity. Will the Islamic faith flourishing restrict the air Egyptians breathe or open Egyptian life to a world beyond Islam – and America? Surely, the Israel air Egypt rhetoric has been breathing for years has been tainted with hypocrisy. The abandonment of Palestinians has been defining. New justice air to circulate?

Without getting overly down on Islam as a cultural and political force and without restricting religion to the confines of the mosque or church or synagogue, wearing religion on one's sleeve is a limitation. It already raises the question of how much whomever's religion will play its game in the political sphere. The prophetic is different than religion, of course, but here we are talking about prayers and laws and everything else that regulates what cannot be regulated. Pretty soon we're talking about women and soon after the male Promise Keepers of every denomination and faith community arrive. You see the trajectory.

Sure, I have to point out that those "free" of religion have their own hang-ups and legalisms, even if it's freedom of everything that restricts the exercise of individual autonomy, like traveling across the globe to see the Statue of Liberty and Disneyworld as one and the same thing. The "global tourism as civilization" game is everywhere as our new freedom. It seems to dominate even my travel home on the Nazi/German jet plane.

Speaking of fascinating (un)equations, have you seen the new map of Disappearing Palestine by the French cartographer Julien Boussac? Floating in greens and blues, Boussac imagines the West Bank as an archipelago. Julian Rake who reports on the map thinks that the Palestinian map resembles the Caribbean or Indonesia – without water. Or Israel is the water that separates the Palestinian enclaves.

Boussac's map is more or less the same as the maps that I have presented on my PowerPoint presentations since Oslo but, hey, here's another one, and this one plays reality against the imagination.

Another attempt to map the territory. Now I challenge someone– have I already issued this challenge in writing as I have done orally for years? – to map the territory of Palestinians in Israel proper, Gaza, then the refugee camps in Lebanon and Syria for example and watch Palestinians float in leaky lifeboats surrounded by the Israeli, Egyptian, Lebanese and Syrian sea. And I haven't even touched on Palestinian life in Jordan.

Palestinians as an archipelago nation? Archipelagos, a group or chain of islands surrounded by the sea. The five largest archipelago nations – Indonesia, Japan, the Philippines, New Zealand and the United Kingdom. Unlisted – Palestine.

Reminding me of the fourth largest Jewish population in the world – residing within the borders of the Palestinian Authority.

Cape Canaveral, as you approach, surrounded by ocean, bays and rivers. So beautiful. My very own imagined archipelago.

We all need our territory mapped. It's a way for us to view the world.

Researching archipelagos, I note they're often created as islands. In the geological literature they are referred to as oceanic islands, continental fragments and continental islands. Oceanic islands are mainly of volcanic origin. They have separated from a continental mass due to tectonic displacement.

Sounds like a definition of Palestinian life. The continental mass has become Israel. The tectonic displacement, the Nakba.

Archipelagos, of volcanic origins, for the moment dormant. Mass expulsion oceanic islands at Israel's doorstep.

Oh my, spelling correction. I first typed Teutonic instead of tectonic. In my jet lag mind, the Austrian Alps are still outside my window.

Rabbi Lynn Gottlieb
FAITH HOUSE MANHATTAN

AUGUST 27

ONLY EMPTY SUITS
AND OLIVE TREES

In anticipation of the Tampa stage-set. I'm thinking about the Isaac weather – bucket loads of rain and high winds I hope for them. Since they're pouring on the poor and everyone in between the poor and the very wealthy, they deserve the worst of Florida's weather.

The weather is worsening here, too. Yesterday I went for a walk on the stormy beach in my bathing suit. Returned soaking wet. Well worth it. Sky dark, the sound of the water crashing on shore, visibility only a few feet. If it stays within a safe range, storms are wonderful.

Not so in Haiti with a number dead. What a global scandal that things were like they were and remain so. Even Sean Penn can't seem to get the job done. He couldn't handle Kabbalah Madonna either.

On the moon beat, Neil Armstrong is dead. The first moonwalker in 1969, after the Great Society had faded in the jungles of Vietnam. On earth we remain where we were. Or some steps behind.

Another shout out for Rabbi Lynn, the latest assault victim of the right-wing. Yesterday a friend of a friend suggested that I might be a good lecturer on cruise ships. She knows a cruise ship lecturer and wants to suggest my name. I think it's a hoot and a real possibility for Jews of Conscience on the run. So as I contemplate my cruise future I also thought of Rabbi Lynn. Shall I recommend her?

It's a sign of humility to sing for your supper. Can you imagine me singing Martin Buber for my supper? Indeed, Buberian encounters can happen at sea. Still, I have to be careful of meeting someone on Buber's narrow (b)ridge. You never know what secret agents might be lurking. Ellis overboard!

On the political, really 1950s beat, reporters have been trying to pick Paul Ryan apart. Or trying to find some scandal to pin his name on. Not much on the sex. They take for granted his marrying into wealth. When they checked out his wife's corporate lobbying it turned up some very Republican credentials i.e., like most of them, for years she was a well-paid corporate lobbyist in Washington. Her clients included the cigar industry, a logging company, drug makers, the health insurance industry and a nuclear power plant. Oh well, sounds like Newt Gingrich and Vice President Cheney. Sounds like all of them. The list is endless.

Typical (un)political reporting of our day – the story didn't go anywhere. Since I have just come from more than a decade among folks like Ryan, I'm weighing in on what these

reporters might find – if they knew how to look.

You see, for the most part, with Paul Ryan types it isn't where you look. Sure people like Ryan engage in everything everyone else engages in, though when they participate in behaviors reporters want to find, they're usually well hidden. Like being a closeted Gay or having an office wife. On the university level, such behavior involves faculty, chairs of departments, directors of programs and administrators. It even extends to the legal arm of universities.

Listen carefully to Maureen Dowd – she's got Paul Ryan down and the others I've been dealing with: "I'd been wondering how long it would take Republicans to realize that Paul Ryan is their guy. He's the cutest package that cruelty ever came in. He has a winning air of sad cheerfulness. He's affable, clean-cut, with the Irish altar-boy widow's peak and droopy, winsome blue eyes and unashamed sentimentality. Who better to rain misery upon the heads of millions of Americans?"

Believe me, Dowd is right. She's all over the conservative landscape but know, too, they protect their own. To protect themselves. However, more important is the "empty suit" phenomena, people devoid of personality or anything that would hint at a crisis that involves living. When you enter the empty suit landscape probing belief structures won't lead past one sentence qualifiers. As in, I am a Christian. Or, I believe that Jesus Christ is Lord and Savior.

As a reporter, you have to remind yourself that the one sentence affirmations cover a host of sins. Don't think that strongest held beliefs means belief in anything. Most of the time, people in leadership structures don't believe in anything but their own paycheck. Don't be fooled by conservatives. Their (un)belief is palpable.

I'm beginning to write about this in another format. For now, I warn reporters that it isn't so easy for those who think the great questions of the day are about to be debated to realize that in fact a charade is about to begin. Though Hillary Clinton's belief in a vast right-wing conspiracy was way too strong, I have learned that the people who tried to do her husband in were empire enablers who simply wanted their time at the trough. Think of conservatives as waiting their turn. It isn't about beliefs. It's about power and money.

That and whiteness. How dare a Black man like Obama think he has the right to eat at the table of power!

My message to reporters – think closet, emptiness and money. Think whiteness. When you connect the dots you might be underwhelmed. The challenge for reporters is to write a story that is faithful to the truth and a story that someone somewhere is interested in reading. Typically this is done by saying – "Okay, believe it or not, this guy/gal believes that, on the domestic front, destroying Social Security, Medicare and Medicaid etc., etc., and, on the foreign policy front, nuking Iran and keeping America armed to the teeth until eternity – that the greatest nation on earth will remain the greatest nation on earth." When reporters know that they are stretching the truth because there is nothing of substance to deal with, they might throw in their "belief" that Israel is the center of everything that is right with

America. If America abandons Israel, the story continues, well, that would be the end of America's right to govern the world. Where would our city on the hill be then?

Empty suits also pervade the American Jewish establishment(s). Let others in America and around the world fend for themselves.

But, then, the saber rattling turns serious. I see that Israel is demanding that the world community declare that Iran hasn't towed the line. As preparation for an attack on the American political system, election time, trying to unseat the European socialist, Saul Alinsky radical, secret Muslim, Barack Obama? The great foe of Israel: Obama, who increased every level of support for Israel imaginable? The friend of Elie Wiesel?

Remember Obama's great opening to the Muslim world. Remember where he flew right after his speech? Buchenwald, a seemingly unrelated destination, where Wiesel joined him. This would have been fine, I suppose, if before or after Obama had visited a Palestinian refugee camp. For my tastes, Obama could have even taken Wiesel along on the Palestinian leg of his journey. That would have been groundbreaking, don't you think?

Better to head toward yet another diversion, like the Pope's butler, who sees himself as an agent of God trying to expose the corrupters of God's real agent on earth, the Pope. Sounds fishy, the whole thing, and no doubt Israel is somewhere in the mix in the ever expanding VatiLeaks investigation.

Seriously, though, traveling Jewish doesn't get any easier when you have to present your American passport at the credential's counter of the global classroom. Jewish/American – hybridity is assumed with the emphasis on American. If emphasis is assumed to be Jewish, the negative ratings zoom upward. A strange combination in today's world. Those of you who don't travel Jewish don't want to know. Is that why Jews have mostly disappeared from territories outside America and Europe except for the Palestinian archipelago we control?

While we're on the subject of American Jews, did you see Philip Weiss's video tour with Jeff Halper, the Jewish/American/Israeli, who pointed out the magnificent olive trees stolen from Palestinian lands replanted as decorative objects for Jewish settlement beautification? With Ace Hardware and the Library of Peace in the background?

Speaking of the Wheel of Colonial Life, thinking of Halper and my last discussion with my Fijian student in Innsbruck. It went something like this: Can she be liberated with the (Christian) colonial religion she inherited? Since she has been conquered by the Bible. Our (Jewish) question is thus related. Can an American/Jewish/Israeli like Halper become the conduit for understanding the Israeli empire he enabled and now opposes? In the end, is there a difference between the conquered and the conqueror when both awaken to the nightmare of history?

Because, you see, when both Halper and my Fijian student seek to return to the before of all of this, they have no ground beneath their feet. There is only after.

Uprooted Fijian woman, meet my uprooted American/Jewish/Israeli friend, Jeff Halper. Somewhere in between is an uprooted Palestinian olive tree waiting to return home.

Empty suits hang together. On the racks of injustice. They use the same butlers, more or less. Does it matter where olive trees are planted?

I have a picture of beautiful Hannah, Henry's daughter, planting an olive tree in the West Bank. The (re)planted (now settlement) olive tree has only four hundred plus years on Hannah's tree.

We are left here for now. With volcanic fragments, Archipelago Palestine, Ace Hardware and the Library of Peace.

The Holy Land has always been strange. (un)Holy.

Rachel Corrie
CHILDHOOD

AUGUST 28

RACHEL CORRIE
RISING

Stormy weather continues. More rain and wind today. This morning the beach was deserted. Even the regulars stayed home. A sight to behold as I looked out over the ocean, rain blowing in my eyes, a huge cruise ship, lights on, steaming into Port Canaveral. An omen about my future cruise lecture life?

The Rachel Corrie case is coming to a head. Adam Horowitz, a delightfully bothersome Jew of Conscience, is keeping his eye on the Israeli justice system. I never met Rachel but I have spoken at her alma mater, Evergreen College, on a number of occasions. What an education the Evergreen faculty provides and their arguments about having (or not having) Jewish Studies are legendary. Since – can you believe how far we have come – introducing a real live Jewish scholar in Jewish Studies would probably function as a brake on their radical outlook on the Two-Thirds world. And American empire. Let alone Israel's empire.

I've met parts of the Corrie family. How delightful and committed they are. On the Jewish side, I think of Rachel as I do Edward Said. Part of the Jewish future, if there is one. Or part of a future without declared Jewishness, if it has to be. In my mystical eye I see Oscar Romero, Edward Said and Rachel Corrie rising together

Thoughts about "strategic depth," what Jews of Conscience need to survive the corruption and the slime that surrounds us. Years ago my teacher, Richard Rubenstein, spoke about my need for "drop-dead" money. Security when the knives came out. Obviously I couldn't go the money route, but what he was really talking about is the ability to survive the onslaughts that come your way if you practice conscience in the Golden Age of Constantinian Judaism.

Strategic depth – a place in the material and spiritual realms that can sustain you when you're on the ropes. I'm not a dualist – a strategic depth has to be material and spiritual.

The empty suits we have become. It doesn't matter that Alan Dershowitz has more personality – and a deeper voice – than the squeaky Ken Starr. Or that one is a Harvard Law prof and the other, having lost his standing in the national legal community, is building a football stadium on the backs of the offspring of slaves.

Yes, empty suits look alike on the injustice rack. You find them in a long row, one after another, their price reduced when the buyers are few. They're hoping for another payday.

Empty suits talk civilization when the check is in the mail.

Carrying the white and Jewish burden is (now) hand in hand. Into the teeming (un) White world. Such a difficult and demanding job isn't for everyone. Knowing that they're backed by every conceivable weapons system known to man, they stand tall. How courageous conservatives are!

"Heil," the derivation of which an Austrian student of mine started to research. In her village the greeting is still used, hence the curiosity. At her first glance it seems that heil is more or less a shalom word, meaning hail fellow, all's well, but no doubt it needs further research. Somewhat like Goethe, whose personal relations with Jews seems not bad at all for the time, though he opposed certain public liberalization regarding Jews.

Mixed messages from history. The norm.

Returning to Jeff Halper's comments on the olive trees that line the settlement boulevards via my Fijian student whose people were conquered by the Bible, or more specifically by the Gospels. Even if the Christian violence that overcame her people was hidden or "clean" as Richard Rubenstein asserts the Nazis preferred, clean violence being the type of violence that is regulated and logical, once the Christian missionary-industrial complex entered the scene it was more or less over. So what does she have in common with Jeff Halper whose people were never conquered by the Gospels?

Crimes of passion give way to crimes of logic. Albert Camus described this as the peculiar transposition of our time. Are both my Fijian student and Halper victims of those crimes of logic, where Christianity reigns without firing a shot and massive olive trees are uprooted so efficiently that their replanting takes place as if the tree had always been where it is(n't) supposed to be?

The question here is to whether my Fijian student and Halper are now on both sides of the Empire Divide or the same side turned upside down and around. Her being conquered by the Gospels and he being an agent of conquering the Palestinians, both carry a colonial and imperial identity, the outward shell of which were imposed on both of them. Or in Halper's case, initially he didn't understand what he was volunteering for when he left America to live in Israel. Now he recognizes the situation and is opposing his colonized position. Does that excuse and align him with victims of colonialization?

Argued another way, is Halper, in his dissident yet still empowered position, in solidarity with my Fijian student? Or, because of his position and regardless of his personal choice, is Halper unable to return to a time when Jews were in an embodied solidarity with the colonized?

I ask, then, is there a way back for Jews? Halper, who remains in Israel as a Jew of Conscience, is a Still/Former. Is that enough? Or is there a decolonized place where Jews cannot go regardless of their personal intentions?

Clearly, you can't ask of someone what he or she can't do. You can't become someone you aren't. The defining moment of solidarity is only partly up to us. This means that we do with that solidarity moment what is possible for us to do.

Back on the Romero Road for a comparison. Romero did not and could not become a peasant. In this way he could not become one with his own people. However, I have

no doubt that he did rise in the history of the Salvadoran people – as an Archbishop. He couldn't rise any other way. I doubt, too, whether the people would have wanted him to rise in any other way.

We rise where we can. Even when we rise in another people's history, especially when we aren't even supposed to be there, we rise as who we are. There are Jews – Halper may be one of them – who will rise in the history of the Palestinian people. Will Halper's fate, like Ezekiel's, taste sweet just like honey?

Rabbi Lynn and Jeff Halper – rising with Edward Said and Rachel Corrie? New Diaspora risings?

Rising where you aren't at home. Rising in the history of another people. That's another element of exile and the prophetic. Another (un)known territory that Jews and Palestinians are beginning to explore together. For when Palestinians oppose certain forms of Palestinian power and are exiled, where do they rise?

It isn't only the fact that Israel created a Palestinian Diaspora. Within the Palestinian Diaspora is another displacement, one that comes from within.

I still have memories of the Oslo Accords and the return of many Palestinians to work for the new Palestine in the offing. The frustration with Israel's interpretation of Oslo is well documented but, as well, many Palestinians returned from their return. They couldn't abide the maneuverings, compromises and corruption within the Palestinian Authority. Though unstated, once outside of Palestine, many could not return to the cultural and religious restrictions of their native homeland. Though laid at the feet of the PA, I always thought it was more complicated. Exile always is more complicated, isn't it?

Once outside, forever outside, even when your people need your energy and talent. So when I told my Israeli student that her intellect and passion was needed to think through the situation we are in, I might have been advising her to dedicate herself to a cause she couldn't win and probably couldn't abide. After all, her leaving Israel wasn't only about politics. Nor is her inability to return only political. Once outside Israel, she experienced the peculiar and complicated freedom of exile. Adjusted for very different circumstances, it may not be so different for Palestinians who have the freedom to leave and remain outside Palestine.

Once out, never to return, more or less. Statistically. Psychologically. Thus, traveling Jewish/traveling Palestine. At some point, we have to be honest enough to say what's in our hearts and minds. But how can a truly honest exchange occur – even within ourselves – when the oppression continues without missing a beat? The fact is that most Jews and Palestinians who live among others want to – live among others. They don't want to be compressed back into a Jewish – or Palestinian – culture/life – only. Jews and Palestinians want to have their freedom and eat it too.

Cosmopolitan Jew. Cosmopolitan Palestinian. The Jewish/Palestinian Diaspora(s). But first, let's admit it, before the cosmopolitan streak, Jews and Palestinians had to cut their collective teeth on a history of violence and atrocity that came from without and from within.

If we ditch the rhetorical pride of place and tradition, within the disparity of experience, the common place we meet is outside, among others.

So, then, at a moment when everything is on hold, with the toll that continues to mount, what lessons do privileged Jews and privileged Palestinians have to offer themselves, each other and the world?

Since we may be rising together in this the evolving history of the Jewish/Palestinian Diaspora, we might as well spend a little time being honest with ourselves and each other.

Before the violence, at least on a massive scale, begins again. Or, as importantly, within the violence that never ends.

On the Jewish side, think Shabbat, as the eschatological sign that within an unredeemed world, one day, here on earth, justice and peace will reign. We can do it without the candle lighting or the prayers and on any day of the week. We don't have to mention the Jewish holy day or other holy days of any religion or nation.

Call it Lessons Learned Day – where Jews and Palestinians ponder our collective fate. Of exile. And the New Diaspora.

The message of Lessons Learned Day is for ourselves and each other. Perhaps, then, a joint communique to the world?

Such a communique might begin this way: "This message from the Jewish/Palestinian Diaspora emanates from (un)Jerusalem, the (un)united (un)capital of (un)Israel, (un)Palestine. The Jewish/Palestinian Diaspora in the making would like to communicate the following to all parties, including ourselves, on what we are learning in our individual and collective lives..."

Or we could call it Lessons (un)Learned Day. More accurate?

Rachel Corrie rising. Her day in the court of (empire) Jewish justice has arrived.

Rachel Corrie Street
RAMALLAH

AUGUST 29

RACHEL CORRIE
RIGHTEOUS GENTILE

Now Hurricane Isaac, unbelievably so, is heading straight for Katrina(ed) New Orleans. Not like Haiti but still not rebuilt. That's amazing, too, isn't it?

Walkers are back on the beach here at the Cape. Fishing resumed. And the older gentleman who seems unable to see too far in front of him and who golfs on the beach – with real golf balls – well, he was back and gave me a wave of his club after striking a ball that whizzed by me at far too close an angle.

And, to be reported on later, I've been asked to lecture at a Body Worlds symposium, you know the exhibits where real bodies are featured on display and have caused a boatload of controversy. Like where do the bodies come from and under what circumstances are they obtained? The patented process of preserving the bodies is called "plastination." It was developed by Gunther von Hagens, yet another German, birth year 1945. Continuing on the Nazi front, his father was a cook for the Nazi SS.

Touring corpses. The idea is that the more we know about the internal workings of our bodies, the more we'll pay attention to our health and well-being. Shall I start my lecture with a rendition of the corpses at Auschwitz? Or I could begin with Rachel Corrie's corpse, yesterday rendered as a nobody who didn't make the right decisions. Perhaps I'll start with both.

Yes, the Rachel Corrie verdict is in. The state of Israel: not guilty. As *Haaretz* reports, the judge rejected the civil suit against the government with these words "There is no justification to demand the state pay any damages." Noting that the soldiers had done their utmost to keep people away from the site, the judge continued: "She (Corrie) did not distance herself from the area, as any thinking person would have done. . . ."

"As any thinking person would have done" – to allow state power to have its day unimpeded by action guided by conscience? What kind of judge, a Jewish one at that, in post-Holocaust Israel has no time for the "We didn't see/We were just following orders" routine of the not so recent past? What "thinking person" would have helped Jews? Those Righteous Gentiles, who did not distance themselves from the danger, we have honored them for committing civil disobedience on behalf of Jews.

Rachel Corrie. Righteous Gentile. In the Nakba Memorial Museum. When it is built. Also in the Jewish historical museums of the future, a separate part of the museum that honors those non-Jews who cried out in the Golden Age of Constantinian Judaism that no human being, let alone a Jew, should displace another human being, let alone a people.

Yes, to the Corrie family, your loss is immeasurable. But, if I might say, Rachel is remembered in the history of Jews and Palestinians of Conscience, now and always. A victim of state power, in this case Jewish, and a stain on Jewish history, including this verdict, Rachel Corrie is a light unto the nations. A light unto the Jewish people.

As the saying goes, we deserve the leaders we have. And the judges. What should we expect from an Israeli legal system that endorses apartheid in the present but also accepts historic and ongoing ethnic cleansing of Palestinians as a given? The trite statements from an Israeli judge are reflective of Jewish history as it is presented to us in its dumbed-down, trivialized way.

This verdict only deepens my sense that we must think a future that isn't happening and already has begun.

On the one hand, it might seem slightly off-kilter to speak about lessons learned on the Israel-Palestine issue when the lesson isn't even thinkable because the suffering continues. On the other hand, that is what exile in diasporas are about. Exiles reflect on what happened and didn't happen when choices were made. The verdict in the Rachel Corrie case only illustrates the dead-end we've reached. Our need to think ahead is pressing.

So some more reflections below – in honor of Rachel. What say us about her life and this verdict? Rachel is part of a history in the making. Along with others who have committed themselves to justice.

Most people in the various exile diasporas of our world aren't powerful. Like others, residents of diasporas live vicariously through the decisions made above their pay grade. Diaspora folks live the consequences. There are those who make decisions because they have power or made decisions when power was being used unjustly against them. Too, there are those in exile diaspora communities who haven't learned any lesson save one – take care of yourself, get what you can.

If we think about the exile diaspora folks who exercise conscience then or now, does it matter when they've come to the conscience/justice table? Since there aren't enough people who survive exile to practice conscience another day, diaspora junkies can't be picky. And besides, when did the ones judging learn their lessons? We don't want a "When did you learn your lesson'" metric applied.

Diaspora metrics are endless. Besides, we'd probably all fall short on the conscience scale. If not one particular scale, there is always one we'd fall short on. Measuring a person's interior life is different than measuring their actions. If you've been awakened to the complexity of life you might have noticed that actions are difficult to measure, too.

When you judge someone else know in a similar situation you might have done what was done to you. Once you let the ego down, it's easier to let the strange and complicit one in your tent. When conscience is involved, there's a need for numbers and some kind of leeway.

Hannah Arendt wrote beautifully about forgiveness. In the end, though, she couldn't forgive Adolf Eichmann. Arendt concluded that there are some actions that cannot be forgiven. I agree.

Shall we now include in these unforgivable actions what happened to Rachel Corrie?

In the circle of the bereaved there's another level of mutuality which balances the unforgivable. Losing a child changes everything. Sharing that loss across enemy lines highlights the absurdity of conflict. Winning loses meaning. Losing enters another realm. The (un)thinkable can also bring people together.

Sure there is abuse of power, collusion, empty suits, paid informants/witnesses and holier than thou types. No doubt the Rachel Corrie case was full of that. There are those who answer the master's bell to (re)assure themselves of their self-righteousness. All of this is real whether on the corporate, university, military or state levels. There's no use minimizing these evils. I'm suggesting that at the end of the day we give over to the master and their enablers only what cannot be taken away from us – our integrity.

Simply stated. Difficult to live. So it is with those of us in protected diasporas. Easy to discern lessons because we are safe and sound? You object? Tell me another way.

Diaspora is the place where exiles gather. It is where culture, religion and life in general get a second chance at getting things right. Possibly this is because the power to define is given up. Possibly this is because the power to be defined is absent. Or perhaps the power to define and be defined shifts and is newly experienced.

The diaspora is a situational change that allows or forces another look at life – from a different point of view. This doesn't mean that life is hunky dory or that the existential questions of identity are answered. No way. In exile diasporas, life and identity become existential necessities. Everything of the old remains and is heightened since the world is turned upside down and around.

I'm belaboring the point because exile diasporas are the strategic depth of nationalities, states, religions and ideologies gone awry. First being in exile, the practice of which ensures that almost nothing will ever be the same, Jewish identity forms in the diaspora. Jews have been in a diaspora situation for so long that documentation and interpretation are plentiful. Palestinian identity forming in the diaspora is so new that documentation and commentary is minimal. On that subject, think Edward Said, the Palestinian who had to learn Palestinian history in America. This as he spoke for a homeland that he lived in only a brief and marginal way. Would Said have been possible inside Palestine?

Think Edward Said without the Palestinian Diaspora. Now think the Palestinian Diaspora without Edward Said.

Think Palestine without Edward Said. Now think the Jewish Diaspora without Edward Said.

Many narratives were and are possible within Palestine. Many narratives were and are possible within Israel. They simply don't add up to what we need without the Jewish and Palestinian Diasporas. So much the better if the diaspora is thought Jewish and Palestinian together. There I've said it: the Jewish/Palestinian Diaspora.

Lessons learned in the Jewish/Palestinian Diaspora: Jews and Palestinians know now that nationalism is a dead end; the friends of your nationalism are as destructive as they come and sooner or later, and often at the beginning, your nationalist friends are more interested in themselves than they are in you. This means Map Makeover whenever your powerful friends, who also breed powerful enemies, decide they need something to do.

The Jewish/Palestinian Diaspora knows the details. The Jewish/Palestinian Diaspora connects the dots.

So Israel has used the colonial template for its own devices but also check out the circle of the bereaved and ask them how things look from their vantage point. Palestinians have been abused by the colonial template outside and inside the Arab world. Talk to Palestinians about how the rhetoric of support from their friends hasn't helped them out of their ongoing Nakba jam. You can also research how they've been actively betrayed on all sides. This is part of the discussion that the *After Zionism: One State for Israel and Palestine* book is generating. Betrayal of everything. On all sides.

Strange twists in the Jewish/Palestinian Diapsora: both Jews and Palestinians are safer the more distant they are from home ground.

I am open to correction but it seems to be the case that Jews and Palestinians are better off in current and former empires that support Israel almost without qualification. Of course, these same empires are a pox on Jews of Conscience and decry Palestinians almost without qualification, hence a pox on the entire Palestinian nation. Weird world.

Better to whisper these lessons in this new and fascinating Jewish/Palestinian Diaspora. To be overheard is to risk a demotion from the Diaspora powers-that-be. Which there are, you know. Like the powers-that-be everywhere, they're watching every move you make.

They're also watching the Rachel Corrie verdict I'm sure. But be wary of superficial understandings. What happened to Rachel Corrie was an injustice like any other. And, from my perspective, something more. That "more" has to do with Jewish and Palestinian history in the land and the history of Jews and Palestinians far from the land.

The question before us is the lessons we have learned. What is the Jewish/Palestinian Diaspora to make of Rachel Corrie's life and death? Of the verdict which claims that Israel is innocent?

Here's one take that plays history against itself while projecting a just future: Rachel Corrie as a Righteous Gentile.

Righteous Gentiles, then saving Jews from the Nazis, now saving Jews from ourselves.

In a teacher's guide to the Holocaust a simple definition of Righteous Gentiles: "Non-Jewish people who, during the Holocaust, risked their lives to save Jewish people from Nazi persecution. Today, a field of trees planted in their honor at the Yad Vashem Holocaust Memorial in Jerusalem, Israel, commemorates their courage and compassion."

One day in a teacher's guide to Jewish and Palestinian life after the Holocaust and Israel

an expanded definition of Righteous Gentiles will appear. It will read like this: "Non-Jewish people who, during the Golden Age of Constantinian Judaism when Israel's empire expanded at the expense of Palestinians and Jewish dissent was crushed, risked their lives to save Jewish people from their own abuse of power. Today, a field of trees planted in their honor at the Yad Vashem Holocaust and Nakba Memorial in Jerusalem, Israel-Palestine, commemorates their warning, courage, sacrifice and compassion."

Write it down. Pass it along to your children. One day.

Hacia Una Teología Judía De La Liberación
COSTA RICA / PUERTO RICO

AUGUST 30

SHOAH BUSINESS

Isaac is now a hurricane battering the New Orleans area. With the storm passing into the Gulf and beyond, the weather here is hot and humid. On the religious scene, some rabbi of distinctive lineage is providing the invocation for the Republican convention while a conservative Cardinal is doing the honors for the closing bell. Birds of a feather.

Interfaith dialogue love fest. Or what I call the Interfaith Ecumenical Deal. Empire Jews and Christians gather to celebrate their conformism to power. No Muslims in sight but they're standing on the sidelines itching to be called in to do their bit. It's the ticket to mainstream White America.

Rachel Corrie. The internet chatter about her verdict is huge. News passes quickly on our easily forgetting news cycle but Rachel's witness remains.

Contrast that with the invocation rabbi. I shouldn't be shocked. Years ago when my *Toward a Jewish Theology of Liberation* was translated in Spanish, I traveled to Costa Rica for the book launch. The group that published my book arranged a visit to the local synagogue. When I met the rabbi, who was of Latin American descent, he proudly informed me that he was a supporter of Pinochet, the torturing dictator of Chile. With that he handed me a prayer book and a kippah as Sabbath services were about to begin. I put them both down and left.

On Skype with Aaron and Isaiah, they've arrived at their respective universities for the new academic year. Isaiah wants to get a job bartending to help with costs. Aaron is contemplating his future after his graduate degree. In the mood of mentor, I sent both words that came to me via a friend some years ago: "Try not to think about work and the future. Instead, think of the monastery of contemplation, thought and action. You're not going anywhere in particular, only deeper, which is where you need to go."

My friend's words bring to mind Thomas Merton, the monk, and the contrast with so many "important" figures today. Like Fareed Zakaria, who can be found in every media outlet imaginable. He was found plagiarizing an article published in the *The New Yorker*. Like Jonah Lehrer who resigned from the same magazine because, among other things, he wrote a book using manufactured quotes ascribed to Bob Dylan. Thoughts, too, of the rabbis who pray for White Mitt and the public figures who are calling out Rabbi Lynn. The judge at Rachel Corrie's trial. Those who manufacture scandals in order to reap millions in donations. The list is endless.

Stealing from others and making stuff up – well the story is the same. I can't imagine discovering that I thought someone else's words were my own. It's amazing that Zakaria and

Lehrer are gurus for thoughtful people when, in fact, they're primarily on the make for status and money.

Then there's Claude Lanzmann whose memoir was recently reviewed in the Sunday *New York Times*. Lanzmann, of the documentary film, *Shoah,* fame, always struck me as an unsavory fellow. His memoir confirms this. As it does my sense that contemporary Jewish life is vacuous. Even in his own description, Lanzmann comes off as a bully.

As I read the review, I thought of the recent incident in Jerusalem's Zion Square where a Palestinian was beaten unconscious. In Lanzmann and in Jewish life, I see a direct connection. I will write more about this in the future but just as a preview, my run-in some years ago with Rabbi David Forman, the founder of Rabbis for Human rights, or as I like to think of them, Rabbis for (Jewish) Human Rights, reminded me of Lanzmann.

Like Lanzmann, Forman was a bully. Sure, Lanzmann didn't wear a kippah like Forman. Nonetheless, they were peas in a pod. This is true of much of Jewish life today. So why show surprise when systematic state violence against a people – with a Holocaust backdrop – erupts on the individual level in Zion Square? Or when Israel is found innocent of Rachel Corrie's death?

Following his life's arc Lanzmann appears hollow and without an ethical anchor. In many ways, *Shoah* exhibits the same character. Everyone nods their assent to *Shoah* as rote obeisance, as if we are standing up in synagogue when the Pinochet rabbi announces the next pages of text. In real life everyone stays as far away as they can.

Shoah made its debut just a few years after the Israeli bombing of Beirut. It was a Holocaust comeback, just as Holocaust remembrance was taking on water. And with a rebranding terminology, shoah, Hebrew for catastrophe, struck a nerve. Parts of the Jewish community were beginning to distance themselves from the Holocaust because it was being used as a blunt instrument of discipline against others and even against Jews who were stepping out of line. On the other side, the Jewish establishment perceived the Holocaust had gone universal because it was being used to name other catastrophes.

On the Jewish establishment side, the Holocaust becoming universal was a threat to the use of the Holocaust as a lever for Jewish power. For establishment types the Holocaust was being dumbed down and shared with other communities. The Holocaust was losing its distinctive identity. Better find a "Jewish only" term for the mass death of European Jews.

Rebranding means a credibility problem is at hand. Rebranding means something that once meant one thing now means another. Rebranding is, on one hand, a return to the origins and, on the other, it wants to shift the ground upon which the origins can be accessed. In the end, rebranding the Holocaust succeeded in more or less the same way that the rebranding of Israel did some years later. It delayed the inevitable in the immediate time frame while tarnishing both in the long run.

Typical of the Holocaust/Shoah as it extends itself in history, Lanzmann shows ruthlessness in getting his story across. In the search for truth, ruthlessness is sometimes

allowed, primarily if it's done in the service of the marginalized and oppressed. One can agree or disagree with this or that tactic and still admire perseverance. Yet by the time Lanzmann finishes his film, the Holocaust was on the march, was organized institutionally and was so powerful that punishments for criticizing Israeli policies were linked to Holocaust denial and anti-Semitism. The Holocaust wasn't being forgotten by history.

Lanzmann's film checked in at more than nine hours in length. By the end of the film you don't have the energy to say Palestinian, let alone the courage. By remembering the Holocaust in this way, the hope was that you would forget all about Palestinians. More or less, Lanzmann accomplishes this goal.

Lanzmann's documentary shuts down discussion related to Israel and the Palestinians. It also shuts down discussion about life beyond the Holocaust and how the Holocaust, if it is to retain any meaning at all, must be a bridge toward all those who are suffering, including and especially the Palestinian people.

"There's no business like Shoah business," a rabbi once shared that with me in reference to Elie Wiesel – I wrote of this earlier. But Lanzmann's Shoah business is more serious and perhaps more destructive. There is no pretense to hope or light or interpretation in *Shoah*. We are just there. *Shoah* functions as a dead weight on Jewish dissent. It closes down the Jewish prophetic.

Shoah is an asceticism – but (un)like the training of a fighter in Emmanuel Levinas' evocative understanding of the prophetic. True, it is starker than stark, using only present remains of the Holocaust, including interviews with Nazi protagonists that don't realize what's going on. Reality doesn't always emit light, so the prophetic gathering of light can become idealized, like a scripted Hollywood movie. But, then. place *Shoah* and *Romero* in motion. You'll see the difference. In each ask to what destination you are traveling.

The Holocaust/Romero in life, as in film, our first question shouldn't be how they function. However, since they seek to represent a wider historical lens, they make little sense without that question. Both feature an austere asceticism. What kind of asceticism do they depict? It is only a short step from depicting to proposing, or they are already connected, if not one and the same.

Shoah isn't only about the Holocaust.

Shoah business – even as an anti-meaning film that drags the viewer through the muck of the death camps without placing us there historically/visually. We are somewhere, though. We are stuck in hour upon hour of no movement/no hope/no redemption. No rising.

In the "monastery of contemplation, thought and action," *Shoah* doesn't rate the asceticism we need. For the prophetic. It isn't the training of a fighter. For the future. This means the Holocaust, as our major export and as the defining moment of Lanzmann's ambition – even with the rebranding name change, *Shoah* isn't going anywhere fast. It isn't going anywhere slow, either.

If *Shoah* was made in the present, with no archival footage, as indeed is the case, then Israeli soldiers also have to be depicted as they march into Lebanon with Israeli fighter planes lighting up the Lebanese sky. Along with the still living Nazis and survivors, interview Israel's invading force. Film Nazi railroad lines. Film Israel's invasion troop lines.

ShoahLebanon – how's that for a title? Full picture, mix it up, deconstruct the meaning of both. Then the asceticism needed for the present would be on the big screen for all to contemplate, think and act.

That would be the courage Lanzmann is lauded for and lacks.

Think of Lanzmann's courage. Then think of Rachel Corrie's courage.

Full picture. Mix it up.

The Field of Battle
PALESTINE

AUGUST 31

RACHEL CORRIE
ON THE FIELD OF BATTLE

I awoke this morning at four in the morning, my apartment shaking, a loud noise outside my bedroom window. I was startled, then I remembered. A rocket launch, delayed because of Isaac, was lifting off. I scrambled out of bed and hurried outside. I saw the rocket lifting into space.

I couldn't fall back asleep. I lay awake trying to wrap my mind around some big-time cognitive dissonance. It continued through the morning hours.

I was thinking about Rachel Corrie. Then I thought about Republican members of Congress on a recent junket to Israel. After dinner, they decided to go for a swim in the Sea of Galilee. One of the Congressmen went skinny dipping. It was huge news. The *New York Times* reported: "For eight expense-paid days, House Republicans visited Israel's holiest sites, talked foreign policy with its highest officials, and dined at its most famous restaurants, including Decks, known for its grilled beef, stunning views of the Sea of Galilee, and now, for an impromptu swim party."

So what if an entire people next door are being walled in by the Congressmen's hosts?

The reason for these junkets – to keep the lid on the truth and American foreign policy on Israel's side. So we learn that the American Israel Education Foundation, an offshoot of AIPAC, has organized more than seven hundred all expenses paid trips for members of Congress since 2000. Included, of course, are the top-tier hotels and private tours to Yad Vashem and Bethlehem.

I wonder where these hundreds of Congressional junketeers were when the Rachel Corrie verdict was read. Some may have been junketeering when she was killed. Did they know who she was, what she stands for, the meaning of her life and death?

After a fantastic night rest at a beautiful hotel, the dual whammy of the Holocaust and the birthplace of Jesus must be something special. I'm sure the private Congressional tour eliminates the bothersome view of Palestinian Christians, now surrounded by walls in their own city. Why spoil the religious sensibility of our Christian members of Congress with the Christians of the land?

The reporting features the political nature of these junkets. But they don't mention Palestinians – Palestinians don't appear in the *Times* article. Disappearing Palestine. Disappeared Palestinians.

Good to know, though, that these trips are bipartisan. Representative Hoyer of Maryland, the second-ranking House Democrat, endorses the tours as a "rigorous, serious,

and educational opportunity to understand the complex challenges Israel faces and the resiliency of the Israeli people in building a vibrant democracy through which to meet these challenges."

Must be difficult for Hoyer and his fellow Democrats to pronounce the words "apartheid" and "Palestinian." Haven't heard it in the Republican convention either.

The Rachel Corrie verdict strikes me the same way. The powers-that-be want to keep a lid on her fate. It's a bipartisan affair. Why spoil the American love affair with Israel?

The verdict was predictable. Israel as innocent. But even if a guilty verdict was returned, would Israel's policies have changed? Would the junkets have been discontinued or radically changed?

It makes you want to throw in the Holy Land towel. It makes talk of the Jewish/Palestinian Diaspora seem a theoretical construct. Without political teeth.

Should we throw in the Holy Land towel? My good friend, Keren, that indefatigable Jewish convert, hasn't. Still, she spends much of her days now baking challah bread and tending a peace garden with a Palestinian friend in Washington, D. C.

Like many of us, Keren is coming to an end of sorts, though I'm not sure she knows it. She's hit a stone wall on the justice theme. Recently she has become quite sensitive to incendiary language about Jews in the Middle East war of ideas. Like many Jews of Conscience she's in an impossible situation. Her courageous ISM's work for justice – like Rachel's – isn't bearing fruit in any discernible way.

So Keren is knee-deep in the practice of exile. She embraces the New Diaspora fully. There isn't a bone in her body that thinks she's going back home. Only the future is still-born.

In the Four Quartets, T. S. Eliot pictures Krishna, a divine incarnation, instructing Arjuna, on the field of battle. Surveying the scene, looking toward the past for wisdom, knowing also the fate which awaits him and his companions, Arjuna hesitates. Krishna implores him. "Not farewell/but fare forward, voyagers." Doubt is resolved. Arjuna commences battle.

The prophetic doesn't accept fate or instruction – as definitive. We always have choice – to turn within history. In the Jewish Bible rather than the Hindu Bhagavad Gita, fate is chosen rather than endured. Yes, Arjuna reflects for a moment. There seems to be a possible break in the action. Perhaps he can break the action and change the script in another direction. Krishna has other ideas.

Arjuna – the fine archer and peerless warrior – on the field of battle. Keren – Jews of Conscience – on the field of battle. Rachel Corrie – on the field of battle. Not farewell but fare forward – voyagers?

Transpositions in time. Rabbi Irving Greenberg writing in the 1970s: "After the Holocaust, no statement, theological or otherwise, should be made that would not be credible in the presence of the burning children." To which my son, Aaron, at the tender

age of 14, and as a response to an Israeli spokesman he heard speak at my university as Star of David helicopter gunships struck Palestinian towns and villages in 2000, wrote: "You are now undermining the 'Name of God' as I see it."

Here in stark contrast, the inability to speak of God. With children burning. Jewish. Palestinian. Young Aaron asking the question the venerable Rabbi Greenberg is unable to ask: Aren't the burning Palestinian children also our own?

Rachel Corrie giving her life. For the burning children. Of Palestine.

Since there are burning children, burning at our hands, so the impossible question – if it makes sense in the presence of burning children of the Holocaust – is impossible to speak if it doesn't make sense to the burning children of our time, whom we are responsible for.

As voyagers, prophetic conscience is our guide. Our asceticism is like the training of a fighter – with conscience. We move in different directions, against the grain of history and toward the suffering, even and especially when it is caused by us.

We aren't bound to a history that unfolds before us. We aren't directed to overcome doubt. By a God. And if we are so directed, we can speak back and argue. We can and must disobey.

As actors within history, where we stand, where we move and don't move is defining of our prophetic freedom.

Prophetic freedom. This is our Jewish fate – on the field of battle.

Aaron admonishing Rabbi Greenberg – on the field of battle.

Keren – on the field of battle – burning children everywhere.

Rachel Corrie's prophetic freedom – on the field of battle – practiced.

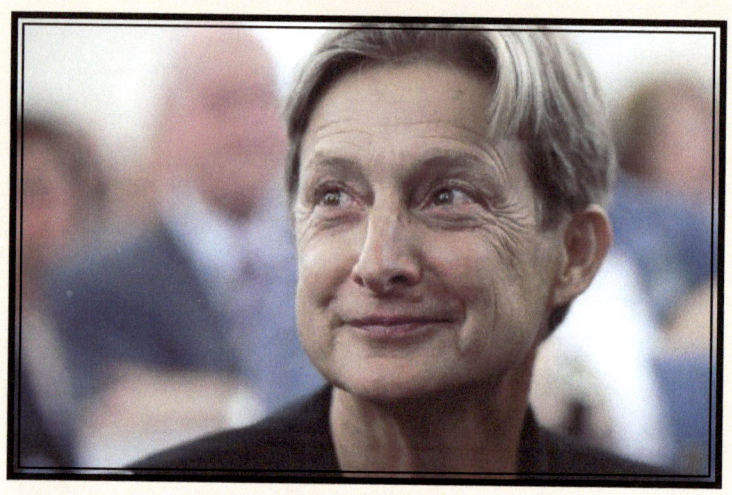

Judith Butler
PARTING WAYS

SEPTEMBER 1

WAR CRIMES

Should we hold a coming out party for Judith Butler? Her new book is raising quite a stir. Yes, she's late to the table but there are always extra chairs to be found. It isn't every day that someone of her renown officially comes out.

From the advance publicity on her book she seems to emphasize "Jewish." No doubt this will bring out the universalist types who can't handle Jewish particularity. But, who knows, Butler's star quality might overwhelm them.

As the Rachel Corrie verdict continues to resonate, I share other quotes from Aaron's 2000 letter to the Israeli Consul of Houston. This as Star of David helicopter gunships patrolled the Palestinian skies.

I share his words because they're profound and because they come from a young person. Like Rachel Corrie was. Rachel was killed less than three years after Aaron's letter. Those of us of a certain age have failed. Including, now, Judith Butler. Here's Aaron:

> I understand that Israel is a democracy. If you say that, that you are forcing Palestinians to move out because you are more militarily advanced than they are, you create a totalitarian government, much like that which was created in Germany in the 1930s.
>
> You, in essence, are saying that whoever has the most powerful thugs, Gestapo, Army, or secret police, should rule regardless of their political views. This is exactly what led to the suffering of so many fellow Jews and others. This, also, is what's happening to the Palestinians even as you read this, only on a smaller scale.
>
> I don't know how you really support your views, except for the fact that Israel is more powerful than the Palestinians, and therefore should rule over them, which is of course just down right stupid for anyone to think this, much less an entire nation.

Then the clincher: "Thank you for your time, and I would greatly appreciate a letter back, as I am trying to find out the truth."

So kind and considerate Aaron is, after burying this Israeli spokesperson – on the field of battle. I realize that as part of the Israeli consulate headquartered in Houston, the speaker's address had the power of the state at his back. In real life, Aaron was defenseless. Yet, reading Aaron's words, one feels a seismic shift taking place.

Sure, you can chalk it up to parental pride that I quote from my son, but if you stop and think, where in God's name could such a letter come from if not the prophetic persisting through time? I return to my Palestinian friend's announcement that the Jewish prophetic voice will never die. In his words, you can feel a seismic shift has already taken place – on the field of battle.

Israeli power will never be safe from the Jewish prophetic. Never. The prophetic will haunt Israeli power and Jewish power in America until the end of time. And when certain Jewish prophetic voices are sidelined by the empty suits of our world, through the typical and transparent ploys of power, that voice and other voices like them will pop up out of nowhere. More or less like the Biblical prophets do.

Like Rachel Corrie. She was murdered. Her memory and witness is alive. When you read her letters home, don't you feel the same seismic shift taking place?

So the expansive prophetic. Rooted in Jewish. Now coming back to haunt Jewish power.

If you're not Biblically savvy, not to worry. Reading the Biblical text isn't mandatory for embodying the prophetic voice through time. In fact, the Bible-toters on the Right and the Biblical deconstructors on the Left carry on their own civil war about religion without touching the voice that continually appears unannounced. So engrossed in their warfare they miss the point. Why dally there when you can have the deepest exile imaginable by exercising conscience against the powers-that-be?

More on Aaron's letter. If you read the full text, you'll notice there is only one paragraph where God is mentioned. His God paragraph is a clincher to be sure but it is previewed and followed by a moral politics that is strictly on the up and up. Couched in Jewish history, of course, Aaron swings the historical axe. He cuts the brush that the Israeli Consul waded into, leaving them naked to the world.

Unlike Lanzmann's *Shoah*, Aaron isn't stuck in the Holocaust. He invokes the pre-Holocaust 1930s and intimates that the Israeli Consul is already there, as are Jews in general. It's not about whether we are going to take the next step. It's about our imitation of discriminatory and exclusionary policies adopted by Hitler's government as they seized and consolidated power. Which raises the issue about whether fascism has to wear a brown shirt to be fascism.

"Whoever has the most powerful thugs." Is that enough for our state-backed mouthpieces? "You create a totalitarian government, much like that which was created in Germany in the 1930s." Response?

The coup de grace: "I don't know how you really support your views, except for the fact that Israel is more powerful than the Palestinians, and therefore should rule over them, which is of course just down right stupid for anyone to think this, much less an entire nation."

Standing there, the Israeli Consul is stripped naked and with it empire power is, too. He is faced with the prophetic Jewish conscience, also stripped naked. No question who wins – on the field of battle – right now. There also isn't any question of who wins – on the field of

battle – in history. From the moment of confrontation it's only a matter of when the empire's power to create burning children is lost. Then what?

So the Rachel Corrie verdict. Well, Israel isn't the only court in the world. In the broader world a different verdict has already been announced. History, too, is weighing in. How do you think Israel will do in history's court?

Listen to Jeff Halper checking in on the Corrie verdict with notes from international law. Note his (un)religious analysis:

> Sending IDF American-made Caterpillar bulldozers to demolish Palestinian homes in Gaza or anywhere in the Occupied Territories is a war crime. To what degree Israel ignores, violates and distorts international law was particularly evident in the testimony of Pinhas "Pinky" Zuaretz, the brigade commander who supervised the illegal "clearing" of Palestinian homes from that area of Gaza. "There are no civilians in military conflicts," he testified, directly contradicting one of the most fundamental principles of international law, the duty to protect non-combatants.

War crimes. The Israeli occupation is. Which brings us back to the recent Holocaust past.

You see, stripped naked, empire power has a shelf-life. Which isn't listed. The prophetic doesn't have a shelf-life. No listing when it kicks in either. It isn't that empire power runs its course and then the prophetic wins. History isn't like that. Empire power and the prophetic are wrestling all the time. Even when empire power is winning hands-down. Even when empire power has the prophetic knocked to the mat. Even when the referee is counting the prophetic out. Especially then.

You see, this is the time when the asceticism of the prophet kicks in, when all the resources of the prophet are brought to bear, when the history of the prophetic is galvanized. When the collective junk of the millennia and the individual junk of a lifetime are called upon.

On the field of battle. The victor always knows that the prophetic is lurking. Out there.

War crimes are judged in history's court.

One of Rachel Corrie's emails home. I can hear Aaron's voice here, too:

> Anyway, I'm rambling. Just want to write to my Mom and tell her that I'm witnessing this chronic, insidious genocide and I'm really scared, and questioning my fundamental belief in the goodness of human nature. This has to stop. I think it is a good idea for us all to drop everything and devote our lives to making this stop. I don't think it's an extremist thing to do anymore. I still really want to dance around to Pat Benatar and have boyfriends and make comics for my coworkers. But I also want this to stop. Disbelief and horror

is what I feel. Disappointment. I am disappointed that this is the base reality of our world and that we, in fact, participate in it. This is not at all what I asked for when I came into this world. This is not at all what the people here asked for when they came into this world. This is not the world you and Dad wanted me to come into when you decided to have me. This is not what I meant when I looked at Capital Lake and said: "This is the wide world and I'm coming to it." I did not mean that I was coming into a world where I could live a comfortable life and possibly, with no effort at all, exist in complete unawareness of my participation in genocide.

On the war crimes scene, I doubt even Judith Butler can say it better than Aaron and Rachel.

Encyclopedia Judaica
CAPE CANAVERAL

SEPTEMBER 2

WHAT ABOUT AN ENCYCLOPEDIA PROPHETICA?

A huge sea turtle on the beach this morning. It was heading back to the ocean when it couldn't go on. The vultures are out, picking the body clean. About thirty yards away, two young lovers who slept under the stars are just waking up. Life goes on.

This morning I am thinking of the prophetic and the stream of history it occupies. How the prophetic becomes a tradition. How it deconstructs itself. How the prophetic tradition pays homage to the past. How it evolves. How, even with this ancient tradition, the prophetic is always startlingly new.

The prophets are recognizable through time. The prophets can recognize themselves. In the prophetic historical mirror.

In its fundamentals, the mission of the prophets hasn't changed over time. In its fundamentals, the cost to the prophets hasn't changed over time.

The prophetic community. Its internal building blocks. Passing the torch from one generation to another. But also reaching back and within historical time zones.

Think of Henry's letter that I wrote about a few weeks ago. It was the 1980s. Israel's invasion of Lebanon. Henry resigned from the editorial board of a Jewish journal and said good-bye to Jewish life. Henry had enough. Then Aaron's letter, 2000. A re-engagement.

Henry would have loved Aaron. Aaron would have loved Henry. In my mind's eye, I see Henry on the resignation mat, looking up at Aaron, Aaron extending his hand, Henry clasping it, rising. Henry's daughter, the beautiful Hannah, looking on from a distance.

The prophetic ballet – on the field of battle.

The prophetic torch is always being passed, reaching back and regaining strength. It's always up and running somewhere – on the global field of battle. Now we remember Rachel Corrie's letters. Those who witness for justice today extend a hand to her. They lift her up. She is also lifting others up – on the field of battle.

Henry, Aaron, Rachel. They are defined by their time. Their witness also exists beyond their specific time. The prophetic has its own time.

I picture Keren's life as a letter. On what it means to choose "Jewish." Never looking back. My favorite convert. Signing up early on with the International Solidarity Movement in the West Bank, she sheltered Palestinian bodies from the blows of Jewish soldiers and settlers. Always off and running for justice.

If she ever published her letters from the West Bank and Egypt when she was trying to get into Gaza, well, there's a whole prophetic world there. Think of Keren as Rachel Corrie, just older.

Moving backwards in real time, but staying within the prophetic time zone, I think of Etty Hillesum's last letters which she dropped from the train on the way to Auschwitz. Choosing to go with her people. Never looking back. Memories of her during these last days.

Etty's story isn't as known as Anne Frank's. Etty discovered her Jewishness as the Netherlands were infiltrated by Nazis. Then when she could have escaped, Etty stayed with her people. She volunteered for Westerbork, the Nazi transfer camp to points east. There Etty wrote about creating a new world after the cataclysm facing Jews and all of Europe. A world where all humanity would live in peace and harmony.

She thought of the war as a purification of the evil found in the world. Experiencing the evils of the war, the world would wake up and embrace a new way of life. She was convinced that her sacrifice was worth this new world. In July 1943, Etty wrote:

> The misery here is quite terrible; and yet, late at night when day has slunk away into the depths behind me, I often walk with a spring in my step along the barbed wire. And then time and again, it soars straight from my heart—I can't help it, it's just the way it is, like some elementary force—the feeling that life is glorious and magnificent, and that one day we shall be building a whole new world. We may suffer, but we must not succumb.

Etty pictured herself – on the battlefield. She wanted to absorb the violence of the world and refashion it into a new world. Her dreams were full of catastrophe. They were also full of hope.

In the last few days there have been commentaries comparing Rachel Corrie with Anne Frank. Just yesterday, there was a perceptive essay – another prophetic letter – by yet another Jew of Conscience, Jennifer Loewenstein, whose father-in-law grew up with one of Anne Frank's "secret annex" companions. But, really, the better comparison is Etty. Rachel and Etty were more or less the same age when they began to see the world through different eyes. This occurred in Etty's case, as it did it Rachel's, when they placed themselves in harm's way. Once they saw the world differently there was no turning back.

Etty's life was interrupted – by justice. And compassion. As was Rachel's. We picture Rachel arms raised, trying to halt the bulldozer. But that was the outer manifestation of an inner commitment. Reading Rachel's letters you see a justice filled with compassion for the suffering. Rachel was well aware of the war crimes being committed. What motivated her stand for justice was compassion for the suffering.

Jennifer Loewenstein, herself, stands with the prophetic tradition. As she raises up Anne Frank and Rachel Corrie, she is also staking a prophetic claim. Loewenstein lived in Israel for some time during her childhood; her father, a musician, played in the Israel

Philharmonic Orchestra. She returned to Israel as a college student. Over the years she has lived in Palestinian refugee camps in Lebanon and traveled extensively in the West Bank and Gaza. In the early 2000s, Loewenstein worked at the Mezan Center for Human Rights in Gaza City. She writes often and radically in support of Palestinian rights.

Prophetic lives. Jewish prophetic letters in a time of deep darkness. They're worthy of publication. Together.

Possible titles – *Jewish Prophetic Letters: From the Field of Battle. Prophetic Letters: At the End of Jewish History.*

Prophetic letters from every time and place. From every people.

To Whom It May Concern. Is this the generic opening the prophets use since they're addressing power and the state? They're also addressing God, the Jewish people and all those working toward justice around the world. The prophets cast a wide net. The cast of characters they catch all have their individual names and times. The catch is also generic.

Look for the catch on the morning beach. You'll find an assortment of characters in the same net. When you find Hitler, Stalin and Franco in your net, it can startle you. But you can also find satellite figures, Benito Mussolini, George Bush and their act-a-likes, David Ben-Gurion and Henry Kissinger's crowd. Even the ones who have been recycled as university presidents like Robert Gates and Ken Starr.

You'd be amazed at what washes up on the beach. But we needn't dally over what gets caught up in the prophetic net.

A global encyclopedia of prophetic letters throughout history. It could replace the print edition of the *Encyclopedia Britannica* which just went belly-up.

Encyclopedia of Prophetic Letters. If we go historical and global, I wonder how many volumes we would need.

Encyclopedia Prophetica.

Subtitle: *Prophetic Letters Across the Millennia.*

Rachel's prophetic letters – on the field of battle. They fit in well with Henry's, Aaron's, Keren's, Jennifer's.

And let's not forget our Decolonizer of Peace. She's still waiting for the United Nations to stop posturing and cross their soldier's Congo prostitution line. The offending soldiers seem to be whisked away in the dead of night when the commander's bell is rung.

The prophet knows the powerful's score. Never believe that transparency or investigations will uncover the cover of injustice. For more than a New York moment. It's just a cover for another cover.

The indigenous Jewish prophetic continues to check in with its diverse guises. To remind whoever the powers-that-be are that the indigenous Jewish prophetic is still around and has gone global. In the Golden Age of Empire Judaism the prophetic is still writing

letters – to unjust power.

Give the prophetic its due. If it is anything, the prophetic vocation is stubborn. It doesn't know when its time has passed. When it should shut up and sit in the corner. It doesn't even know how to restrict itself to Jews.

The (un)Jewish prophetic letters – on the field of battle. They remind Jews of the vocation we don't want and can't shake.

Etymology – ica – Latin – when used as a suffix meaning a collection of things that relate to a specific place, person or theme. As in erotica, Hebraica, Judaica.

Prophetica.

A nice ring to it, don't you think?

Eugen Herrigel
GERMANY

SEPTEMBER 3

ZEN AND THE ART
OF SPECIAL BOOK COLLECTIONS

Last night a heavy rain with thunder and lightning. Up this morning and out for a walk while still dark, stars clearly visible in the sky. Then beachside, walking, passing the early-to-rise fishermen, past a couple who slept on the beach, then sitting cross-legged waiting as the sun begins to filter through the clouds.

The sea-turtle remains on the beach now marked up with red paint to be studied by marine biologists. The scientific battle for survival continues. We now know more about disappearing species than ever before in history. Especially when they weren't disappearing through human degradation of the environment. Like the transparency that is another cover for corruption, our studied planet is yet another ironic part of our time.

Skyped with Aaron and Isaiah last night before the rains, catching up on things and chatting about the year ahead. Against my will, Isaiah confessed that he is now studying German. A rebellious child!

Isaiah also just finished reading *Zen in the Art of Archery,* an assigned text for the Asian religion class he is embarking on. Initially I thought the book was an offshoot of *Zen and the Art of Motorcycle Maintenance.* But rooting around on the internet, I see the reverse is the case.

Another interesting and disturbing tidbit. *Zen in the Art of Archery* was written by Eugen Herrigel, a German, who, after teaching philosophy in Japan during the 1920s, wrote a short essay on the subject. He, then, returned to Germany, expanded his essay and published it as a book in 1948. Though credited by some as bringing Zen to Europe, the other shoe, his Nazi past, has apparently been hushed up. I came across this response in the journal *Encounter* (February 1961) by the noted German-Israeli Jewish scholar, Gershom Scholem:

> Zen-Nazism?
>
> With reference to the article by Arthur Koestler,"A Stink of Zen," in your October issue, I think I ought to make a remark illustrating his point concerning the amoralism of Zen teaching. Koestler goes in for a lengthy criticism of Eugen Herrigel's Zen in the Art of Archery and some other texts by Zen adherents. About one he says that what he quoted could "come from a philosophically-minded Nazi journalist." It has obviously escaped Koestler's attention that Eugen Herrigel, who wrote this widely-discussed treatise, had in fact become a member of the Nazi Party after his return from Japan and having obtained whatever Zen illumination he might have got there. This fact

has been carefully hushed up by the circle of his admirers after the war and it is thus small wonder that Koestler did not hear about it.

Herrigel joined the Nazi Party after the outbreak of the war and some of his former friends in Frankfurt, who broke with him over this issue, told me about his career as a convinced Nazi, when I enquired about him in 1946. He was known to have stuck it out to the bitter end. This was not mentioned in some biographical notes on Herrigel published by his widow, who built up his image as one concerned with the higher spiritual sphere only. Herrigel's case is an excellent illustration of what happened to many high-minded German intellectuals.

On the other hand, when in 1954 I asked Dr. Suzuki point-blank whether someone who had passed through a true Zen experience could have become a Nazi, he flatly denied this possibility. At the same time, however, he also denied having known any Westerner who—in his opinion—had achieved true Zen illumination or satori. This left me not a little baffled–which of course may be just the right state of mind for a student of Zen, or for that matter, for any student of the history of mysticism in general.

Gershom Scholem

The Nazi can of worms again, this time relating to Zen and the university-industrial complex. Where does the naiveté end? Not that Scholem isn't a handful. A German Jew, Scholem immigrated to Palestine at the same time that Herrigel was in Japan. Scholem was an artful scholar and dodger on the subject of Jewish mysticism, a subject he pioneered in the academy. He also spent a lifetime lecturing others on the value of Zionism. Like many others, Scholem changed his name when he arrived in Palestine, in this case only his first name. Gerhard became Gershom.

Shortly after exposing Herrigel's Nazism, Scholem questioned Hannah Arendt's Jewishness. This criticism – essentially charging Arendt with self hate – was in reference to her writing on the Eichmann trial. Scholem's criticism reads like a laundry list. Scholem accused Arendt of exposing the dirty laundry of Jewish leadership during the Holocaust, not being Zionist enough and thinking that the mass murderers of Jews were careerists. Scholem's deepest cut was that for Arendt, Nazis like Eichmann weren't unadulterated Jew-haters.

The self-hate/Jew-hater dynamic that Scholem introduced continues to play big-time in the Jewish war of ideas. I noticed a recent celebration of Scholem's teaching and life at Hebrew University. Apropos of the *Great Book Robbery* documentary I first saw in the program in Austria – remember Hebrew University collecting the books in Palestinian homes after the Palestinians had been cleared out – check this out from Yehudah Mirsky on the celebration of Scholem's book collecting after the Holocaust:

Several weeks ago, Hebrew University, in whose development he played a formative role, marked his 30th yahrzeit with several days of discussions of the man and his legacy. The topics were as wide-ranging as he was, including magic in antiquity, early medieval mysticism, the Lurianic Kabbalah, Sabbatianism, Hasidism, and Zionist intellectual history, and the list could have been longer. Some of the most fascinating presentations concerned not Scholem's Kabbalistic research as such but other facets of the man.

One of those facets, discussed by the great paleographer and historian of the Jewish book Malachi Beit-Arieh, was Scholem's book collecting, the stuff of legend. Arriving in Jerusalem in 1923 with 2,000 volumes, at his death, he left 20,000 to Hebrew University and Israel's National Library. One of the National Library's first librarians, he traveled to Europe after World War II to retrieve the Jewish books that survived the Nazis and was among the first to grasp the need to create a microfilm library of the manuscripts holding the hidden treasures of Jewish history.

Then there was Scholem's Zionism. The writer and kibbutz historian Asaf Inbari observed that Scholem's enterprise negated the "negation of the Diaspora," classic Zionism's view that the New Jew could take what he needed from the Bible, leapfrog over 2,000 subsequent years of Jewish history, and land securely in the present. Zionism would have to reckon with Judaism, Scholem thought, including its darker, even demonic dimensions, while the religious would have to deal with the myth, sensuality, and freedom deep within the tradition. Precisely because Scholem was so schooled in the history of messianism, he feared its effects on politics—and knew that a blithe dismissal of the non-rational forces in human history was a dangerous delusion.

Hmm. Hebrew University. The hidden treasures of Jewish and Palestinian history. Both "rescued" by Jews for posterity. One rescued from the ethnically cleansed of Europe, the other from the ethnically cleansed of Palestine, at more or less at the same time. Did Scholem know of the Palestinian book "rescue?" If so, what did he have to say about it? What did he do about it?

Where was Scholem during the 1948 war? What were his views about what he witnessed happening to Palestinians? Polemics aside, what were his views about Israeli expansion in the 1970s and beyond? He died in 1982; what would his views of the Lebanon war had been? What a hoot, rooting around for Scholem and the Palestinian question, I googled "Scholem and Palestinians." Up came the National Library of Israel site which features two special collections. Here they are as described in Wikipedia:

> Special collections
>
> Personal archives

Among the library's special collections are the personal papers of hundreds of outstanding Jewish figures, the National Sound Archives, the Laor Map Collection and numerous other collections of Hebraica and Judaica. The library also possesses some of Isaac Newton's manuscripts dealing with theological subjects. The library houses the personal archives of Martin Buber and Gershom Scholem.

Palestinian Books

Following the occupation of West Jerusalem by Haganah forces in May 1948, the libraries of Palestinian notables who fled the country were transferred to the National Library. These collections included those of Henry Cattan, Khalil Beidas, Khalil al-Sakakini and Aref Hikmet Nashashibi. About 30,000 books were removed from homes in West Jerusalem, with another 40,000 taken from other cities in Mandatory Palestine. About 6,000 of these books are in the library today indexed with the label AP – "Abandoned Property". A campaign has been launched by Benny Brunner to return the books to their owners.

Love the footnotes, don't you? But I wonder if the librarians there have checked the site recently. Obviously some conscientious hackers have made sure that the National Library of Israel is accorded its due. Scholem must be rolling over in his grave, his collection, and then the Palestinian collection, one after the other.

The Scholem rescue mission in Europe, how should those books be classified? Abandoned Property (AP)? Or Rescued Property of the Cleansed and Murdered (RPCM)? I suppose the designation on Palestinian books would be more accurately rendered, Stolen Property of the Cleansed and Denigrated (SPCD). Or better, Stolen Books of the Cleansed and Denigrated Palestinians (SBCDP). Though that's too many letters for book spines. See if this works: Stolen Palestinian Books (SPB). If the letters are already taken we can change their capitalization – (sPb). Or (sP) For stolen Palestine.

Still working on it. The mind races. Perhaps a special designation "P" with an olive tree next to it. That would simplify the design and free up plain "P" for other books. The olive tree is also a nice touch for a special collection. When cruising the stacks, Jewish students will wonder what's up with the olive tree. (But then, as we've seen, the olive tree, now also stolen and placed in Israeli settlement boulevards, may be mistaken as Israeli. Like most of Israeli – really Palestinian – food. So many problems when the Wheel of Ethnic Cleansing spins!)

I certainly had no idea that checking in on the kids would lead to Zen and Nazism, then further down the road to the question of what a great Jewish scholar (and other Jewish scholars) were doing/thinking as Israel and its national library augmented its (surprise, surprise) two special collections. You do have to ask the Watergate question in its Jewish covering to Scholem - on the ethnic cleansing of Palestinians, on the Palestinian book front and beyond. What did Scholem know and when did he know it?

Applied now: What did Jewish scholars know about Palestinians and when did they know it?

I think of the great reversal of the German sons and daughters relationship in the aftermath of World War II. They never knew what their fathers did. No one was talking. No one wanted to know. Thus the void – Europe without an identity – what I experienced in the last weeks in Austria. Or rather, Europe with an identity infected by atrocity. Uprooted. Uprooting others.

Jews, too? The Jewish identity void, now covered by a Holocaust and Israel conveniently outside history. Some of that history is to be found in the special collections of the National Library of Israel.

Cruise the stacks. Go to (sP). Then compose your prophetic letter. Make it confessional.

What you knew and when you knew it.

Isaiah the Prophet
AT SCHOOL

SEPTEMBER 4

NOW ISAIAH KNOWS

Now Isaiah knows. What shall he do about the wonderful book, assigned as required reading, authored by a convinced Nazi? Telling what he knows lands Isaiah right in the lap of his quite extraordinary teacher. If he speaks what he knows, will the Nazi connection be seen as relevant or special pleading? After all, the Nazi, Martin Heidegger, another highly educated university professor, is still taught in the rarified philosophical atmosphere of our major universities.

Isaiah's first response ran like this: "Well, Dad-o, it sure is troubling. I must point out though that 'true Zen illumination, or satori' has to do with one's enlightenment in a singular moment, regarding a singular focus of mediation – so this illumination seems to not be permanent." But, of course, the issue isn't with Herrigel. The issue is the persistence of literature authored by Nazis, as if books have no history or as if this history is irrelevant.

But, then, if we take the Ethnic Cleansing and Worse Road of political correctness all the way to the end, shall we ban Jewish-Israeli authors who cleansed Palestinians or stood idly by while it happened? Should the Jewish American authors who have remained silent or worse, actively enabled Israeli hegemony like Elie Wiesel and and more or less any contemporary Jewish writer on the Holocaust, philosophy, Jewish history, also be banned?

Since most publishers and Jewish authors are mum on the Palestinians, the ban might include those incredibly expensive Holocaust text books that authors and publishers thrive on. It might also mean that every course on the Holocaust be mandated to include a section on Palestine during the Nazi era and that every Holocaust course discuss the aftermath of the Holocaust to include the aftermath of the state of Israel and its effects on Palestinian life.

Sounds like a Herculean effort that leads to another road. We might be returning to Highway 61 from another direction.

I can't imagine teaching the Founding Fathers without including their slave-holding or the ethnic cleansing of Native Americans. Sure the basics are still taught. Now, however, the basics are augmented, with extras included. Like the slavery of Africans and ethnic cleansing of Native Americans. I doubt, though, that African Americans and Native Americans think they're extras in the American drama. Like Palestinians, they probably think they're central actors without which the drama doesn't make sense. Imagine that.

I can't imagine Palestinians being included as extras in the study of the Holocaust and its aftermath. Even if they think they're central in how the Holocaust functions, a major reason the Holocaust is central in the American educational curriculum is to make sure Palestinians are entrenched in the American imagination as terrorists. Obviously, it can't be

the Holocaust itself that makes it central to contemporary American education. There are other events of great magnitude that don't have their own course set-aside.

Yes I am aware of the recent writings on the Arabs, including the Palestinians, regarding their views on Nazi Germany and Jews during that time. Most literature I've seen is aimed to bolster political support for a "beleaguered" Israel. Its aim is to show that Arabs are anti-Semitic rather than having a real political beef with a colonial (Jewish) movement that was about to take over Palestine.

Starting in the late 1800s, the early Zionist writers in Europe thought Jewish life in Europe would be limited in the future or worse. They feared there would be no room for Jews in the evolving European landscape. They were prescient. The Palestinians and Arabs outside of Palestine also predicted calamity regarding the burgeoning numbers of Jewish settlers reaching their shores. They, too, were prescient. Soon Jewish books were being rescued in the aftermath of the Holocaust. Soon Palestinian books were being "collected" in the aftermath of the Nakba.

It's all too familiar. And depressing. Among my favorite books I read in my Introduction to Religion course many years ago was Mircea Eliade's *The Sacred and the Profane*. At that point, Eliade's past was safely hidden from view. Prior to his coming to the United States after the war, Eliade was an enthusiastic member and intellectual savant of the Iron Guard, a fascist and anti-Semitic organization in his native Romania. During World War II, Eliade also associated with Nazi collaborationists in Vichy France and Franco's Spain. Like the Nazi scientists who built the American space program, Eliade embraced America as the land of second chances.

When I read his book, Eliade was at the pinnacle of his career, hanging out at the vaunted University of Chicago. So universities go. He never lost his standing in the American Academy of Religion. A giant! Now that I know, how do I deal with my early fascination with the Eliade's writings? Would I assign them to my students?

I just looked up another of the German romantics that was huge in my university life and many other young Jews of that time period – Herman Hesse. In college, I had a number of his books, more than twenty, I think. Hesse's wanderings went well with the music of Bob Dylan and Neil Young. A time of searching, aloneness, spirituality, love and alienation, all wrapped up into one Rolling Thunder Review (which I saw, by the way, in Tallahassee, at the old basketball gym in 1975.)

Hesse passes the Nazi test. By the time the Nazis rose to power, Hesse was living in Switzerland, that bastion of (un)neutrality. Hesse aided Berthold Brecht and Thomas Mann, both opponents of Nazism, as they came across the border into exile. Hesse's third wife was Jewish; he publicly condemned anti-Semitism early on. In the 1930s, German publications stopped publishing his work. Eventually the Nazis banned his writing.

You see, German romanticism moved in different directions, as all things do – toward empire or community. During the 1930s, romanticism traveled toward or away from the Nazis. But then, the attraction to the land of Israel was also part of this German and, in

general, European romanticism.

Martin Buber was highly influenced by this trend. On the one hand, it moved him to reject fascism and embrace a Jewish communal sense in Palestine. On the other hand, Buber's romanticism had little room for Palestinians as rooted in the land. True, Buber opposed the Jewish state and argued against the injustices done to Palestinians. At the same time, he claimed Jewish priority in the land. The reason was a romanticized one. Jews were joined to the land though Israel's origins in a way that Palestinians could not be. The Jewish "return" to "our" land was essential to the recovery of Jewishness being lost in the Diaspora.

The Catholic Worker movement in the United States also embodied aspects of European romanticism toward the land. However, this was tempered by service to the poor and adopting a life of poverty. Choosing community, the Catholic Worker became a radical, anarchistic and pacifist community. God works in mysterious ways.

Here is the dilemma for my Isaiah, my little one who isn't little at all. Now that he knows that the Zen mind can go empire and since he knows that Jewish can and has gone empire, what is he going to do with the neon "No Exit" sign flashing in front of him?

Shock & Awe
ISRAEL

SEPTEMBER 5

ZEN AND THE STAR OF DAVID
HELICOPTER GUNSHIP MAINTENANCE

I'm still ruminating about Gershom Sholem's expose of Herrigel's Nazi proclivities: "Herrigel's case is an excellent illustration of what happened to many high-minded German intellectuals."

Now transposed to include Elie Wiesel: "Wiesel's case is an excellent illustration of what happened to many high-minded Jewish intellectuals." Substitute almost every known Jewish intellectual on the scene today. To be "known" it seems you have to succumb to an ideology that characterizes you as "high-minded," i.e., positive enablement or silence on what happened and is happening to the Palestinians.

Epitaph time, again transposing Scholem's critique of Herrigel: "[Wiesel] was known to have stuck it out to the bitter end. This was not mentioned in some biographical notes on [Wiesel] published by his widow, who built up his image as one concerned with the higher spiritual sphere only."

For Jews, the higher spiritual sphere – the memory of the Holocaust. Sticking it out to the bitter end meaning – silence on Palestinians.

Epitaph time, now applying Scholem's critique of Herrigel to himself: "Scholem also stuck it out to the bitter end. This is not mentioned in some biographical notes on him published by his admirers, who built up his image as one concerned with the higher spiritual sphere only."

Isaiah knows not to stick it out to the bitter end. But what is he to do, write his own prophetic letter?

Zen in the Art of Archery. The Nazi/German connection.

Zen and the Art of Star of David Helicopter Gunship Maintenance. The Jewish/Israel connection.

For the Miscellaneous file: A few days ago I heard a report on NPR that there would be no High Holiday services in Cairo's synagogue this year. Haven't seen further news on the subject. But I wonder, how can the few Egyptian Jews left start the new year without fetishizing the most hypocritical days of the Jewish calendar? Since we don't confess our real sins regarding Israel, why bother?

On the "lucky-find" trail, I was about to order a book I wanted to read and, lo and behold, I found it at the public library when I returned from Austria. Author: Kay Larson. Title: *Where the Heart Beats: John Cage, Zen Buddhism, and the Inner Life of Artists.*

I'm not the only Jew who's thought Zen is a way through the maze of Jewish life. Have you noticed that some of the best practitioner commentators on Zen in America are Jewish? In the post-Holocaust years, Zen replaced conversion to Christianity as the way out. The most chosen way out is simply disappearing from Jewish authority into secular Europe and America. The Jewish establishment has been complaining about this for years.

Yes, the prison that is Jewish. Which Jews want to escape. Also, the prophetic that is Jewish. Which Jews can't escape. You can't have the prophetic without the prison. Obviously worthwhile. Or the prison without the prophetic. A useless trap. It's only normal to want to be free of the prison and the prophetic. At least, for a Zen interlude.

Is the New Diaspora a place where that freedom can be found? If the prison is shared or distributed so the weight of prison isn't too heavy on any one community and the prophetic is shared or distributed so the weight of the prophetic isn't too heavy on any one community, then we might have less prison and more of the prophetic. The added bonus would be a saner atmosphere for individuals and their diverse communities.

So back to my (un)diversion, Cage and Buddhism. The first chapters are vignettes on the major early figures of Zen in America – Gary Snyder, Allen Ginsberg, Jack Kerouac and Allan Watts. The leading light was the already elderly Japanese Buddhist missionary, D. T. Suzuki.

Reading the early chapters, I am struck by the randomness of the growth and influence of Buddhism in America. This one stumbles upon a certain text or book, meets another one who stumbled upon a certain text or book and then together they stumble into experiences that define a generation. What didn't make sense, does. Renewed and invigorated consciousness comes alive in a new and creative way.

When we look back at what is now defined as important, we don't remember how seemingly random things are until they're not. Like the Beats. Like the New York School of painting. Like John Cage and the revolution in music and dance he helped inspire.

There are lessons here for every movement under the sun, including the issues surrounding Israel-Palestine. Here are two lessons I glean from this:

1: What is taken for granted after rarely begins as a focused intention. What begins with focused intention doesn't always come to fruition. Things happen. Things don't happen. What happens in one place and doesn't become known may crystallize somewhere else. Why one understanding takes off and another doesn't is hard to know.

2: We rarely know if what we're doing will move beyond ourselves. If it does, we rarely know if it will be credited to us or even if it will be used for good. What starts somewhere else may seem destined to fail. It may also succeed, for better or worse.

Conclusion: Start where we are. Try to think and act in the best way we can. If possible think and act with others. If the time isn't right, think and act on your own. Pay attention. Continue on. Let the historical chips fall where they may. Since the historical chips will fall anyway, no matter what we do and no matter our intentions.

History is an entangled affair. Our only protection is conscience. Obviously conscience isn't equivalent to a stealth bomber or even an armored vehicle. If we take the French philosopher, Michel Foucault's definition of power – that "truth isn't outside power, or lacking in power" and that "truth isn't the reward of free spirits, the child of protracted solitude, nor the privilege of those who have succeeded in liberating themselves" – at least we have a foundational level from which to begin on the protection front. Foucault continues: "Truth is a thing of this world: it is produced only by virtue of multiple forms of constraint. And it includes regular effects of power." This may be the next level of evaluation. What can protect us and what can't.

But, then, since we know that no power can protect us always and everywhere, vulnerability is the name of the power game no matter what side you're on. Our Zen archer, Herrigel, and our Nazi philosopher, Heidegger, thought they had signed on to the latest and best thousand year Reich. They were protected and elevated – for a decade or so of the (un) thousand year cycle.

Herrigel/Heidegger. The historical chips fell their way for a while. Then they came crashing down on them. Both are still read. For the most part, without the questions they deserve.

The same for our faint of heart Jewish big-wigs who signed on to Israeli and American empire thousand year reign? Will they be read with the questions they deserve?

Free Palestine
MELBOURNE

SEPTEMBER 6

PREPARING OUR DEFENSE
FOR THE COMING DAYS OF AWE

Middle of the night – pool party outside. Condo life. It happens.

Were they celebrating the Democratic National Convention? Doubt it. More than a few White Romney signs in the neighborhood. Black isn't everyone's favorite color here.

Adam Horowitz is reporting on a blow-up on the Israel-first campaign trail, though the Democratic Party plank on Israel reads as if it was ghost written by AIPAC. If they didn't write it, they apparently approved the language. I suppose AIPAC doesn't count as the lobbyists President Obama promised to restrict. Perhaps AIPAC is better understood as part of the government. They should have their own seat in the House of Representatives. And a Senate seat, too.

Then the NPR report on hunger in America. The report cited the growing number of food stamp recipients and used the category "food insecure." Amazing bureaucratic terminology for the chronically overfed to employ.

Don't know whether it was the pool party that woke me up or I'm still tossing and turning with my Zen discovery of a true Nazi. I can't find other details of Herrigel's Nazi past; it's well covered up. Remembering Adrienne Rich – whatever is undepicted, censored – will be recycled.

Check out Amazon's Nazi-washing of *Zen in the Art of Archery*:

> It is almost impossible to understand Zen by studying it as you would other intellectual pursuits. The best way to understand Zen is, simply, to Zen. This is what author Eugen Herrigel allows us to do by sharing his own fascinating journey toward a comprehension of the illuminating philosophy.
>
> In Japan, an art such as archery is not practiced solely for utilitarian purposes such as learning to hit targets. Archery is also meant to train the mind and bring it into contact with the ultimate reality. If one really wishes to be master of an art, technical knowledge of it is not enough. One has to transcend technique so that the art becomes an "artless art" growing out of the Unconsciousness. In this way, as the author simply, clearly demonstrates, archery becomes a path to greater understanding and enlightenment.
>
> This program is an outstanding way to experience Zen – and an intriguing, influential work of literature.

Transcending technique. Artless art. An intriguing, influential work of literature.

We've known for a long time that sophistication and barbarity often go hand in hand. The literary critic (and anti-Zionist), George Steiner, explored this many years ago. The appreciation of Beethoven and the death camps can co-exist. Relaxing with the classics in the evening is one way of preparing for the next day's death work.

Atrocity by the learned. At the Wannsee Conference, where the final solution of Europe's Jews was decided, most of the "deciders" were lawyers. They weren't the peasants of Poland or the Ukraine, most of whom were willing to do their bit.

The wretched of the earth continue to multiply. The threats to the wretched and those notches above continue as well. Even the educated get caught up in cycles of violence and atrocity. When power is on the move, everyone in the line of fire is forewarned.

Think of the casualties over the years in the Middle East. Those with connections anywhere have fled the scene. Think of those left behind, many maimed in body and soul, not to mention the dead. Think of the bereaved in Palestine, in Israel, Lebanon, Syria, Jordan, Egypt, Iraq and Iran. Think of the wars that have lasted on and off for decades. The threat of more to come.

Did you see that Desmund Tutu turned down a boatload of cash to address a conference and instead suggested that George Bush and Tony Blair be tried in The Hague for war crimes in Iraq? Referring to the invasion of Iraq, Tutu writes: "Those responsible for this suffering and loss of life should be treading the same path as some of their African and Asian peers who have been made to answer for their actions in The Hague."

The Middle East is suffering post-traumatic stress syndrome – as a region. Or rather traumatic stress syndrome, since there isn't any end to the violence in sight.

Middle East leaders play the PTSD card with flags and religion. Perhaps what is needed is a massive medical and psychological hospitalization of the wounded and the bereaved. Hospitalize the leaders, too. Call it a medical truce if you will, one that allows healing and a new beginning.

What is needed in the Middle East is another round of standing tall and dishing it out. That's what the leaders' say, Jewish leaders in Israel and in America among them. Transposing Tutu: "Those Jewish leaders in Israel and America responsible for Palestinian suffering and loss of life should be treading the same path as some of their African and Asian peers who have been made to answer for their actions in The Hague."

Platitudes from exile? Platitudes from the prophetic? Yet, what can one do but struggle against these policies and understandings, survive the fire-fights and think in a new key? Though history seems to have an iron-clad rolling logic, it is also open, not predetermined, with forks in the road. We need to spend time preparing for a future that can't be seen and may yet be in the air ready to land.

I am reading my John Cage biography in this light, as a fork in the road detour that might shed light on a future. In relation to the Middle East and the prophetic.

Working through aspects of Zen and the prophetic – through Cage – as we approach the High Holidays. Not searching for a coherent narrative. Just beginning. Sectional.

More on Zen

Cage begins by taking Henry David Thoreau into the musical future through Zen and, interestingly enough, the I Ch'ing. For many years, Cage hides his homosexuality, especially after he sees a good friend jailed for the sin of loving another man. Then, in the twilight of his life he admits his various loves. The change – Stonewall. Stonewall, a Gay hangout that one night erupts. Call Stonewall a local skirmish in a global field of battle.

But Zen? We've already looked at how Zen can be seen in a Nazi light. Now, *Zen at War*, the book, by Brian Victoria. Have known about it for some time. Amazon describes it this way:

> A compelling history of the contradictory, often militaristic, role of Zen Buddhism, this book meticulously documents the close and previously unknown support of a supposedly peaceful religion for Japanese militarism throughout World War II. Drawing on the writings and speeches of leading Zen masters and scholars, Brian Victoria shows that Zen served as a powerful foundation for the fanatical and suicidal spirit displayed by the imperial Japanese military. At the same time, the author recounts the dramatic and tragic stories of the handful of Buddhist organizations and individuals that dared to oppose Japan's march to war. He follows this history up through recent apologies by several Zen sects for their support of the war and the way support for militarism was transformed into 'corporate Zen' in postwar Japan. The second edition includes a substantive new chapter on the roots of Zen militarism and an epilogue that explores the potentially volatile mix of religion and war. With the increasing interest in Buddhism in the West, this book is as timely as it is certain to be controversial.

Turning East as I did with an entire generation of Jews looking for a way out and a way in, it's all mixed up and contradictory, as the description points out, which then demands apologies. Notice how Zen militarism has been transformed in postwar Japan into "corporate Zen." This means, apologies all around, now pass the hat for a religion that will support a rapacious appetite for the spoils of war - without declarations and outward manifestations of war. Familiar, isn't it?

Corporate Zen. Corporate Judaism. Our transformation has been on the corporate and military fronts. Judaism – Jewish – has bit the conformism bullet to our financial and status benefit. Jewish power now has its own heartbeat.

JuBu's handle this corporate sensibility well. Jews without the silence do even better.

Getting Ready for the Coming High Holidays (Without Mentioning Them)

Synagogue is the place where corporate and militarism co-mingles without mentioning

its existence. Consider synagogue as a time-out from the *New York Times* while the *Times* has your back. You know it in advance, as a rote prayer comfort zone that exudes power without having to show it off. Call it an ethical snobbery that can't be challenged because it's already in the bank earning interest. Jewish power is tied up in securities backed by the United States government. Like Israel.

Corporate Jewish. Frayed around the edges because of Israel's sinking reputation? Doesn't seem that way. Inside. Or from the outside either.

Zen at war, now through other means. Jewish at war, with the world. With itself?

Gershom Sholem wrote that he didn't have a biography, only a bibliography. Of course, this isn't true for him or Herrigel or states, religions, nationalities or ideologies. He hoped he would only have to disclose what he wanted the world to know about him, his scholarship on Jewish mysticism. His Zionism and the state of Israel was mostly for Jews. His bibliography tells part of the story. His biography exposes the accusing images of a displaced man who enabled the displacement of others.

Coming in a few weeks, another bibliographic cover, in the guise of religion. So others – and ourselves – won't delve into the accusing images of a displaced people who precipitated the displacement of others.

Bibliography – know us by the books we've written. What we have contributed to the world. By our actions in the past which we romanticize as if we're doing them now. Know us by our suffering. Which was. Respect our days of reflection where we pledge to be silent on what needs to be spoken.

Back to the Nazi Trail and Fellow Traveling

On the Herrigel, Nazi trail from Shoji Yamada's, *Shots in the Dark: Japan, Zen and the West*. Listen to his reviewer, Victor Sojen Hori, sum up Yamat's treatment of Herrigel's Nazism. Sounds a lot like Heidegger's:

> In the picture which Yamada paints, prior to his departure for Japan, Herrigel had had significant opportunity to learn about Zen from informed people. However, it is Yamada's account of Herrigel's life after his return from Japan which will shock people. Interested parties to date have deliberately attempted to suppress details of this period. Yamada confirms that Herrigel was a card-carrying member of the Nazi party (his party membership number was 5499332). He officially joined the Nazi party on 1 May 1937 and thereafter he rose quickly through the ranks at the University of Erlangen. He was head of the Philosophy Department from 1936 to 1938, vice rector from 1938 to 1944, became an official member of the Bayern Science Academy in 1941, and was rector of the University of Erlangen from 1944 to 1945. Yamada says that Herrigel could not have enjoyed such a successful career without being a member of the Nazi party. After the war, Herrigel wrote a defense of his actions for the deNazification court, but the court concluded that while

Herrigel had not been a committed Nazi, he was guilty of being a Mitläufer, a passive fellow traveler.

Quite a court ruling, wouldn't you say? Since we have so many Jewish fellow travelers, the Jewish community should listen up to the court's judgment. Local rabbis should secure a translation of Herrigel's defense. For whatever it means in real history, learn well the distinction between active and passive fellow travelers. That might come in handy for the Jewish community when it is called to task for its own behavior. It's already happening at the international court in The Hague where Israeli policies have reached the docket. Best to be prepared.

The "Fellow Travelers" defense. There are more than a few Herrigel's and Heidegger's on our campuses. Many of them are Jews. Speaking up can land you on the street. Why risk what you teach?

Herrigel's official party number – 5499332. Did his Zen Nazi mind memorize the career card he punched? Think now. The career card punchers of our day.

Successful careers. Fellow traveling. Preparing our defense.

Thoughts for the coming Days of Awe.

Julian Rides the Rails
GERMANY

SEPTEMBER 7

EINSTEIN
ON (MY) BEACH

The news over the last weeks. Reminders of the world now. South African miners shot dead by the police of the (un)Apartheid South African government. Not to worry, apologies all around. Tribal folks in the north of India leaving by the droves. Bulk text messages warning them of eviction and worse. China in Africa, saturating the news cycle with their intrepid state reporting. Looks like Africa is in for another round of imperial "assistance."

And poor Julian Assange, granted asylum by Ecuador, holed up in London, with the Brits threatening to get around diplomatic immunity. The Ecuadorian embassy announces defiantly that they're not a British colony. I wonder who will win this round.

The news cycle is still on the Russian rock group, Pussy Riot. Several members of the group will be serving prison sentences. Others are on the lam. All for defying – on a Russian Orthodox Church stage – the President/Dictator of Russia.

The Middle East seems condemned to a continuous cycle of violence and atrocity. The government of Syria is just another bad apple ready to fall. Where, oh where, will the Syrian President/Dictator flee to?

On the Democratic convention platform wire – "Jerusalem is and will remain the capital of Israel." So AIPAC did write the platform after all.

Nonetheless, if you've traveled to Jerusalem lately you know the score. It's a highly contested city. Always has been. The victors one day are the defeated the next day.

Provocative Zen. Reading John Cage's biography, Zen style, I am coming to the conclusion that John Cage was a Zen provocateur.

Take in this scene. In 1974, on the day that Richard Nixon resigned the presidency, Cage gave a debut performance of part four of his musical composition, *Empty Words*. The venue was Naropa, the Zen learning center in Colorado. Though the crowd was boisterous, assuming there might be a celebratory sing-a-long because of Cage's reputation and Nixon's resignation, Cage assumed the opposite. Engaged in a Buddhist environment, Cage thought a disciplined work about silence would get a sympathetic hearing. He was wrong.

Let me set the scene. Cage sat a table on a makeshift dais, his back to the audience. The projection screen was in front of him. Cage then presented segments of Thoreau's journals through a mixture of vowels and consonants, punctuated by extended times of silence. It wasn't easy to make sense of what Cage was reading and the silences were long. After a few moments, it was clear that the crowd wasn't getting into Cage's performance. Or they were, but in a wholly unanticipated way.

As Cage's biographer, Kay Larson describes it, some in the audience began to let loose with "deafening shrieks, bird whistles, catcalls, and screams. Some twanged guitar strings or played their flutes, or threw things onto the dais." A few stormed the stage, danced and sang. Cage remained in place, displaying an intense concentration on his performance, as if nothing was happening around him.

When his musical piece was over, Cage turned and faced the audience. To the question of whether he expected a hostile reaction and perhaps courted it, Cage responded: "I know it. I know what limb I'm out on. I've known it all my life, you don't have to tell me that." It seems like he was throwing it back to the audience: "Do you know what limb you're out on?" Later, Cage wrote about the incident. Cage recalled that the Bodhidarma, when he came from India to bring Buddhism to China, sat facing a wall for ten years: "So thinking along those lines, I sat in Boulder with my back to the audience. Well, after twenty minutes, an uproar began in the audience, and it was so intense, and violent, that the thought entered my mind that the whole activity was not only useless, but that it was destructive. I was destroying something for them, and they were destroying something for me."

Ever get that feeling when you're traveling Jewish in the Golden Age of Constantinian Judaism? The audience of whatever stripe expects to hear what they want to hear and if you, figuratively, turn your back to the audience, you get what John Cage received in the heart of Buddhist America. If you don't say what is expected, which means no thought allowed, or push whoever's envelop a little too much, you'll find yourself out the door on your ear.

Our rabbis, did you ever think of delivering your Rosh Hashanah and Yom Kippur sermons turned away from the congregation? Did you ever think of sitting cross-legged on the bima facing the Ark of the Covenant for ten years? (Since you might even be bringing the prophetic to the congregation like the Bodhidarma brought Buddhism to China, this might make them curious. It might also convince them that you're serious about the prophetic.)

Sure, your contract won't be renewed and you might be hauled off by the police and taken to jail in handcuffs. Before that you might be jeered with deafening shrieks, bird whistles, catcalls, and screams. Some might throw their bulletins at you or storm the stage. With Cage, you might think it was all useless and destructive. You might destroy something for the congregation. The congregation might destroy something for you. Like what it means to be a rabbi and a Jew?

Call it Jewish Theatre of the Empowered. Advertised for the upcoming High Holiday season:

> Flash Mob
>
> Dance Around the Ark
>
> Those interested meet at the synagogue on 4th Street, 8:15 for High Holiday services. Do not wear your synagogue best. Proceed to the Ark of the Covenant, gather around it and, using mime, begin building an Apartheid Wall. As some continue to build the Wall, others should start flying around the Ark making the sounds of helicopter gunships on the prowl. In a friendly

way, send a delegation to encourage the (startled) rabbi to join the dance around the ark. To make it clear you might want to sing those words to the old rock'n roll favorite, "Rock Around the Clock". Have the rabbi mime a bull horn and call the congregation to denounce all injustice, including injustice done to Palestinians. After five minutes exit the synagogue peacefully. Gather in the parking lot where a festive organic meal will be served.

Even on Yom Kippur? Leave it to the (un)schooled Jewish activists to forget the fast. Or, like the Feast of Fools in Medieval times, should everything political and religious be turned upside down? Showing the utmost disrespect for the respectable because the respectable has become criminal? Not to worry, you establishment types. After the High Holidays Flash Mob all will return as it was. After all, there's a reason for (un)prophetic order. How else can the community survive its own indigenous? The pull of the indigenous. As the Days of Awe come ever closer.

Speaking of which, if Dancing Around the Ark is too much, another option might be the revived performance of "Einstein on the Beach," the opera. It's returning to the Brooklyn Academy of Music just a couple of days before Rosh Hashanah. There doesn't seem to be much about Einstein in the opera. More or less the opera plays on Einstein's iconic status. The audience fills in the universe Einstein ponders. But since we know Einstein was an internationalist, more or less a pacifist and if a Zionist, a homeland type, then we can fill in his Jewishness in the synagogue setting.

Filling in Einstein's (Jewish) universe. Some possibilities.

Einstein in Synagogue – on Rosh Hashanah.

Photo Op. Caption: "Einstein dancing around the Ark of the Covenant."

Einstein in Synagogue – on Yom Kippur.

Photo Op. Caption: "Einstein standing in front of the Ark of the Covenant.

Einstein at the pulpit. Getting ready to deliver his sermon. Priceless.

Einstein walking on my beach. Einstein's universe. Passing the mezuzah on the beach.

Albert Einstein
UNITED STATES OF AMERICA

SEPTEMBER 8

PLUS SUFFERING

I'm drinking water with limes that I bought at my local co-op. They're unsprayed and local, like you find on a tree in your backyard. I'm savoring this small wonder on a rainy afternoon.

Earlier in the day, I decided to leave my writing aside but in the John Cage biography I'm running across the inner life of my artist self. I'm back thinking how Cage applies.

That's after my walk on the beach with Einstein yesterday. You may not know it but I was once compared with Einstein. No, not in science. With regard to Israel. Here's how it happened.

A few years ago I wrote a book, *Judaism Does Not Equal Israel*. At about the same time, Jerome Robbins wrote a book analyzing Einstein's views on Zionism and the state of Israel. The books were reviewed together by Glenn Altschuler. The review appeared in *Ha'aretz* and the *Forward*. In Altschuler's mind Einstein had ideas that were important to communicate today. He thought I did, too.

Here's Altschuler's summary of Einstein:

> Einstein's writings underscore that he was not a systematic political thinker. His idealism, moreover, often crossed the border into naiveté. His views on a Jewish state, however, were rather consistent. Alarmed by the rising tide of antisemitism in Eastern Europe at the end of World War I, Einstein declared himself a human being, a Jew, an opponent of nationalism and a Zionist.
>
> Militantly secular, he maintained that the bond uniting his people was "the democratic ideal of social justice, coupled with the ideal of mutual tolerance among all men." Einstein's Zionism used the "fact" of Jewish nationality to promote self-knowledge, self-esteem and solidarity. But it was "immune from the folly of power" and "the obsession with race" that dominated Europe in the first half of the 20th century.
>
> Einstein supported a "homeland" for Jews in Palestine, but he opposed a Jewish state "with borders, an army, and a measure of temporal power." Since two-thirds of the population of Palestine consisted of Arabs, he preferred bi-national status with "continuously functioning, mixed, administrative, economic, and social organizations." Only cooperation with Arabs, led by "educated, spiritually alert" Jewish workers, he wrote, "can create a dignified and safe life ... What saddens me is less the fact that the Jews are not smart

enough to understand this, but rather, that they are not just smart enough to want it."

Altschuler's take on me begins like this:

> "Judaism Does Not Equal Israel" is a sharper — and shriller — version of Einstein's critique of the Jewish state. A "post-Holocaust" theology, according to Marc Ellis, professor of Jewish studies and director of the Center for Jewish Studies at Baylor University, has conflated Jewish identity with allegiance to Israel, justified the "ethnic cleansing of more than seven hundred thousand Palestinians," and muzzled "even mainstream, moderate critics" as "self-hating Jews."

His conclusion:

> Mourning can be a sign of hope, in which God returns or doesn't, Ellis emphasizes, rather abstractly. And "too late can be right on time — when the time is right." For now, though, he's a self-proclaimed prophet in exile. His book is often over the top, but Ellis's concerns about the ethical obligations of the State of Israel are, at times, worth listening to, even by those with a powerful urge to doubt, dismiss or destroy him.

Well, considering everything, I didn't do badly. First, it's clear that Altschuler agrees with Einstein and me. Though he notes that Einstein can be naïve and I am sometimes over the top, those are covers for Jews who want to survive the Golden Age of Constantinian Judaism. Altschuler wants our ideas out there and, for the most part, describes them fairly. He also wants distance from both of us. Altschuler doesn't want to be destroyed by those with a "powerful urge to doubt, dismiss or destroy" me.

The attempt to destroy me has already taken place – and failed. I am back in the ring, honing my asceticism, and coming back stronger than ever. After my walk on the beach with Einstein yesterday I feel relaxed. What prophetic company I – and we – have in exile!

A suggestion for Jews of Conscience: Take a day off and stroll with Einstein on the beach of your choice. If you're landlocked, take a stroll in your mind. *Zen Mind, Einstein's Mind*. Try it.

I'm relaxing on my (un)writing day, reading Cage's lectures on something, then on nothing. They're titled that way, "Lecture on Something; "Lecture on Nothing." In her biography, Kay Larson traces the evolution of these lectures. As it should be, she's gets somewhere and nowhere, at the same time.

Cage explores the process of "going nowhere." He speaks: "I am here, and there is nothing to say. If among you are those who wish to get somewhere, let them leave at any moment." On Israel-Palestine, such a lecture might begin: "I am here, and there is something

to say. If among you are those who wish to get nowhere, let them leave at any moment."

The dramatic exits I've experienced during my lectures! The disgruntled ones who stay seated huffing and puffing. The angry ones who begin talking loudly to no one in particular. Those who stomp out shouting expletives. The Israelis who have left. Israel military types who threaten to kill me.

Jews of Conscience know the exits, staged and otherwise. Getting somewhere?

I am thinking of my Palestinian student in Austria who said getting somewhere was a fantasy. My Israeli student needed that somewhere, though she knew it was an illusion.

Larson italicizes the process – *going nowhere*. Possible lecture title: "The Process of Going Nowhere in Israel-Palestine."

I hear the howls already. How dare I suggest that going nowhere is acceptable in the present situation? I'm not suggesting that as a politics. I'm trying to wrap my mind around a future different than the present.

In our instant electronic world, it is more and more difficult to take a longer view. It seems that in the Blogosphere, the responses are relentlessly negative to nuanced thought, especially from a Jew, I might add. This leads me back to my European tour a few years ago, the one where I encountered the anti-Semitic BDS leadership in Ireland and Scotland. Just before those encounters, I experienced another shock.

It was right after the Gaza invasion, in the spring of 2009. My first lecture was in Geneva, then on to various venues in France. From Paris, I flew to Ireland and Scotland. I was traveling Jewish through a very strange terrain. With Gaza on their mind, the audiences were large. A good number of European Jews attended. Everyone was convinced that Gaza was the turning point of the Israeli/Palestinian crisis. The world wouldn't tolerate Israel's behavior any longer. I told them they were wrong. They were.

I found the Jewish side of things as startling as the BDS side. After my lecture in Geneva, I had a long discussion with my Israeli-born host who was now living in Geneva. I asked him if I had it right: the Jews I encountered weren't simply against Israeli policies or only arguing for the end of a Jewish state, that, in fact, they were ashamed of being Jewish. He replied, "They are."

This was before I encountered the other side of the coin in Ireland and Scotland. On the plane home, I felt like exiting the entire scene. Talk about the process of going nowhere.

This is where Cage is caught up short. At least, I don't know what to do with the truths this Zen provocateur speaks. When he thinks through the "process of going nowhere," I think – plus suffering. When he says, "I am here, and there is nothing to say. If among you are those who wish to get somewhere, let them leave at any moment," I think – plus suffering. Plus suffering. This means we have to get somewhere. Nowhere won't do. But, most of the time, nowhere is where we are anyway. Let's mine that direction and see where nowhere takes us.

It's 1959 and Cage is still moving. Nowhere. Also getting somewhere. What is to be said? "People and sounds interpenetrate." They do – plus justice.

Zen – plus justice. Can Zen be in history – without justice?

Perhaps this is the challenge of all religions, as religions. Religions project themselves into the heavenly spheres. In the heavenly spheres, there's no substitute for conformism to power here on the earth.

So what is a Zen provocateur, a religious provocateur, a secular provocateur – minus justice? So far in the Cage biography, the justice-oriented commitment is mute. But searching I find another side of Cage who is deeply involved with the question of history. This involves his theory of interpenetration "in order to thicken the plot."

Justice thickens the plot by calling us to another level of engagement. The music of the spheres is not enough. But since, even with the best of intentions and all the hard work and commitment imaginable, we fall short, the thickened plot is not enough, either.

Justice – plus limitations? Justice – plus silence? Justice – plus compassion?

Israel-Palestine. The need for justice – plus?

Only justice – mindlessness. The revolution devouring its own.

The revolution that isn't a revolution.

Rabbi David Forman
RABBIS FOR HUMAN RIGHTS

SEPTEMBER 9

RABBIS
FOR JEWISH RIGHTS

Skyped with Isaiah last night. He's glad to be out of his summer doldrums and on his own. We chatted about our Nazi Zen archer and his chat with his teacher. It turns out that his teacher knows the score. A teachable moment all around.

What more is there to be said about the Zen arrow, become a Nazi salute, now read in Empire America? That's everyone's question. For Isaiah, the question resonates on another level. Since he's looking for his life's path and is drawn to Asian religions partly as his Jewish exit strategy, the Zen Nazi connection isn't a "who cares" moment. But, then, since the Jewish community is mobilized against others, the Jewish Israel connection can't be a "who cares" moment either. Isaiah knows he can't read Jewish writers innocently either.

Our Zen Nazi archer went through the denazification process and received his certificate. He was retired, so his fellow traveler status was judged to be of some significance. Nonetheless, in real Nazi time, our Zen Nazi archer's career was enhanced by his Nazi membership card.

I think now of our Jewish Studies types gathering in convention after convention and even my Society of Jewish Ethics colleagues. They're all kippahed up and ready to ride. Will they one day have to go through a dezionfication process? Perhaps most of them have already, at least internally. Their internal dezionification process has more to do with washing their hands of the accusing images pointed at them by others than any solidarity they might have with Palestinians. This, too, should be seen as a career move. They've seen the future handwriting on the wall. Israel isn't very popular anymore.

On the academic front, and by extension deep into other parts of Jewish professional life, I've encountered very few Jews who figure Palestinians into their ethical calculations. Just the opposite, almost to a person, Palestinians are looked down upon. Typically, they are relegated to an inferior status as part of the "Arab problem."

Most Jewish intellectuals are more or less where Romney is on Palestinians – ignorant and racially charged. Isaiah has a mountain to climb in his lifetime. He'll need to become his own archer.

Rabbis for Human Rights isn't going to be of much assistance. I've known this ever since I ran into the founder of the group, Rabbi David Forman. Some years ago he camped out in Central Texas for the High Holidays to make some big bucks. Now deceased, Forman contacted me in advance of his arrival, asking to speak at my Center for Jewish Studies. I agreed. Then the locals informed him that I invited Palestinians to speak at the Center, the

sin of all sins. So Forman sent me a nasty email withdrawing the invitation he had solicited.

Of course, Rabbis for Human Rights have done some good work. Some of the rabbis went in with the best of intentions and left. Others have stayed but their views have moved beyond the organizational framework. Nonetheless, what needs to be said should be stated, because our Rabbis for Human Rights are in the news again.

The "lynch" incident in Jerusalem's Zion Square is still making the rounds. There a group of Jews gathered around a few Palestinians, shouting, "Death to Arabs." Several Palestinians were beaten. One was rendered unconscious and brought to the hospital. It wasn't the first time. It won't be the last.

Shocking? Not really. To really know where we are as Jews, check out the Rabbis for Human Rights, North America, website for their response:

> In the wake of a violent attack by Israeli teenagers on Palestinian youths, Rabbis for Human Rights-North America calls on rabbis, cantors, Jewish educators, and community leaders to teach our children that hate is not a Jewish value.
>
> Today, a mob of dozens of Israeli teens attacked three Palestinian youths in Jerusalem's Zion Square. One of the victims was beaten so severely that he required resuscitation and remains in critical condition. Witnesses described the scene as a "lynching" and said that the perpetrators shouted "death to Arabs" and other racist epithets.
>
> As rabbis and cantors, we are shocked and embarrassed by the behavior of these teens. Regardless of our political opinions or our desired resolution of the Israeli-Palestinian conflict, we have a responsibility to teach our children that Judaism condemns the shedding of blood, as all people are equal creations in the divine image.
>
> We applaud the swift action of the Acting Jerusalem Police Chief, General Menachem Yitzhaki, in already setting up a special investigative team for the case. We urge the police and prosecutors to thoroughly investigate and prosecute the perpetrators of this horrific hate crime. And we praise the Magen David Adom rescue team who administered first aid, and the doctors and staff at Hadassah Hospital who continue to care for the victims. These medical personnel embody the Torah's command, "You shall not stand against the blood of your neighbor."
>
> On this Shabbat, as we enter the reflective period of the month of Elul, we ask rabbis, cantors, and educators to spend a few minutes speaking with our children and our communities about today's incident in Jerusalem. These conversations should emphasize that political differences are no excuse for bigotry. We pray that our children will help us to realize a world free of hatred or violence.

"Hate is not a Jewish value." Nonetheless, it has become a value in the Jewish community,

just as long as you don't express it openly.

"The Rabbis and Cantors are shocked by the behavior of these teens." Instead, they should be shocked by the behavior of Jewish adults, themselves included, as perpetrators and enablers of this kind of behavior. Who sets the structure that encourages and sanctions this behavior on a systemic level? Not the teenagers. They're just acting out the system. On the Torah's command, well, rabbis and cantors, the learned of our community, the "authentic" Jews of the world, be wary of the slippery slope you enter. Because if Palestinians are our neighbors, then they have to be accorded equal political rights. Human rights without political rights is the non-starter of all non-starters. It leaves individuals and communities helpless. It's not about being rescued after you're beaten because the political and ethical system sponsored by Israel and Judaism relegates Palestinians to the nether world of human rights. It's about justice, which is nowhere to be found in a self-righteous condemnation of others.

Entering the Rosh Hashanah/Yom Kippur season, the rabbis and cantors appeal to Jewish educators to spend a few minutes with the children they teach. Emphasis: "Political differences are no excuse for bigotry." A more apolitical discrimination enabling message I can't imagine. I think it would be more honest to say that the rabbis and cantors of our community and Rabbis for Human Rights support the ethnic cleansing and segregation of Palestinians to small enclaves in the West Bank and Gaza as our right and as our destiny. But, as with our household help, we are reminded to be respectful of the humanity of the Other.

The message from the Rabbis for Human Rights reminds me of Yitzhak Rabin's description of Baruch Goldstein, the murderer/martyr of recent Jewish history, as an "errant weed" who grew up in the swamps of Jewish life, by which he meant New York, I believe. The real lesson of Goldstein was that he wasn't errant at all. Nor was he a weed, at least a weed that flowers. Goldstein was a totally predictable outgrowth of Israeli state policies and Jewishness as it is taught and embodied in the Gold Age of Constantinian Judaism, of which Rabbis for Human Rights, like *Tikkun*, is its Left-wing.

What a Golden Age. Where we spend a few minutes with our children. To wash away our sins.

Wouldn't it be more accurate to call them Rabbis for Jewish Human and Political Rights? When things get too outrageous or, better, when things are too obvious, then we must talk to our children about hate.

Rabbis for Jewish Human and Political Rights. Speak the truth to our children.

A Prophetic Gong
JOHN CAGE

SEPTEMBER 10

SOUNDING
THE PROPHETIC GONG

For the approaching High Holidays, I return to the prophetic via our Zen provocateur. Here's John Cage, June 1955. Eisenhower time. Going nowhere:

> A sound does not view itself as thought, as ought, as needing another sound for its elucidation, as etc.; it has no time for any consideration – it is occupied with the performance of its characteristics: before it has died away it must have made perfectly exact its frequency, its loudness, its length, its overtone structure, the precise morphology of these and of itself.
>
> Urgent, unique, uninformed about history and theory, beyond the imagination, central to its sphere without surface, its becoming is unimpeded, energetically broadcast. There is no escape from its action. It does not exist as one of a series of discrete steps, but as transmission in all directions from the field's center. It is inextricably synchronous with all other sounds, non-sounds, which later, received by other sets than the ear, operate in the same manner.
>
> A sound accomplishes nothing; without it life would not last out the instant.

And then:

> An experimental action, generated by a mind as empty as it was before it became one, thus in accord with the possibility of no matter what, is, on the other hand, practical. It does not move in terms of approximations and errors, as 'informed' action by its nature must, for no mental images of what would happen were set up beforehand; it sees things directly as they are: impermanently involved in an infinite play of interpenetrations.

When I read these statements, I wonder. Has our musical friend, via Zen, stumbled upon the prophetic?

Listen to Cage transposed:

> The prophetic does not view itself as thought, as ought, as needing another politics for its elucidation, as etc.; it has no time for any consideration – it is occupied with the performance of its characteristics: before it has died away it must have made perfectly exact its frequency, its loudness, its length, its overtone structure, the precise morphology of these and of itself.

Morphology is the study of the structure of anything made up of interconnected or independent parts. We usually think of the prophetic as a one-off and here it seems to be – but not only. On the field of battle the prophetic is its own sound, thus itself, but it is also bound up with the other sounds of humanity, including the sounds of suffering. The prophetic is pre and post-political without being apolitical. It performs itself as itself, for itself and for others:

> Urgent, unique, unconcerned with the limitations of history and theory, beyond the normative imagination, central to its sphere without surface, the prophetic becoming is unimpeded, energetically broadcast. There is no escape from prophetic action. The prophetic does not exist as one of a series of discrete steps, but as transmission in all directions from the field's center. The prophetic is inextricably synchronous with all other, sounds, non-sounds, which later, received by other sets than the ear and mind, operate in the same manner.

Cage strikes home, again transposed: "The prophetic accomplishes nothing; without it life would not last out the instant."

Which brings me once again to my Prophetic Doxology: "Without the prophetic there is no meaning in life." And its corollary claims: "There may be no meaning in life. The prophet embodies the possibility of meaning in life."

Central to its sphere, the prophetic has its own sound and frequency. It is without surface. For the prophetic there is no veneer to disguise itself. This is the prophet's asceticism. The prophetic becoming is unimpeded, energetically broadcast. This is why the clarity of the prophetic is so disturbing. It isn't its uniqueness or its intellectual rigor, that field is reserved for the transmitters of knowledge and information. The prophetic is disturbing because its very sound doesn't mind its own business or look for cliques to confirm its authenticity. This is also the reason the prophetic isn't going anywhere. The anywhere the prophetic isn't going is unique. It isn't somewhere. It isn't nowhere.

Synchronicity – the coincidence of events that seem related but are not obviously caused one by the other. Prophetic synchronicity – speaking and living justice even though there isn't a successful payoff in a specific time and place. This means that the prophetic is most often a witness to others who tap into the prophetic somewhere else which is considered nowhere.

Imagine prophetic synchronicity as the sound of one hand clapping heard – without a second hand, or the falling tree in the forest – heard even though it seems there's no one there.

Now Cage's second statement rendered in the prophetic:

> The prophetic is an experimental action, generated by a mind as empty as it was before it became one, thus in accord with the possibility of no matter

what, is, on the other hand, practical. The prophetic does not move in terms of approximations and errors, as 'informed' action by its nature must, for no mental images of what would happen were set up beforehand; the prophetic sees things directly as they are: impermanently involved in an infinite play of interpenetrations.

The prophetic isn't based on calculation. The prophetic must empty its mind of results. By emptying the mind of results, the prophetic becomes one with other prophetic movements. Because the prophetic has emptied its mind of the mental images which are defining, the prophetic defines practicality rather than listening to the critics of utopianism.

Being released from the illusion of permanence, which, of course, doesn't exist except in argumentation, the prophetic sees directly to the heart of the matter. Unconsumed with causality, the prophetic is released from conformism to even the expectations of fellow travelers. The prophetic is the sound of sounds, among others. The prophetic witness goes where it goes. Then moves on from there.

The prophetic voice is not alone, even in its singularity. It may be crying out in the wilderness as Isaiah 40:3 – depending on the translation – seems to indicate. Though it seems with transposed Cage, it might be better to see the prophetic as having a distinctive sound that would be unfamiliar in its familiarity from tradition. True, the prophetic isn't accepted locally according to Jesus in Matthew 13:57, but then, acceptance or non-acceptance isn't the prophet's aim.

The infinite play of interpenetrations is the ultimate result of prophetic singularity – which means tragically that the prophet doesn't solve the problems at hand or restore what has been taken away. The end of the Job story, where restoration is emphasized, is fiction. In real life, restoration doesn't happen. If it does, restoration comes through another cycle of theft and destruction.

As it is with Jewish empowerment after the Holocaust. Job-like, what was lost to the Jewish community was "restored" and multiplied manifold. That restoration was accomplished through a deal with the devil. Where once Jews sat on the dung heap, others sit today. To call the Jewish restoration just is to go (un)Rabbi Forman on the Palestinians. Israel as restoration, as justice for the Holocaust, means becoming unglued when it's even hinted that the price for Jewish restoration was too steep.

Rabbis for Jewish Rights. I don't hear them in the John Cage transpositions. In Rabbis for Jewish Rights I hear a conformism to power. With their rabbinic imprimatur, Jews have an official license to speak (un)truth to power.

Rabbi Forman – may I have permission to speak? You say that your permission is needed because the voice of my dissent isn't yours. It goes too far. Do you mean to the heart of the matter?

Cage slightly adjusted: "The prophetic does not view itself as thought, as ought, as needing permission for its elucidation."

A Cross on the Beach
CAPE CANAVERAL

SEPTEMBER 11

A CROSS
ON THE BEACH

Beach shrine. A Cross on the beach. This morning I stumbled upon it behind a sand dune during my morning walk. It seems to have been recently placed there, perhaps for a remembrance ceremony. The Cross is fashioned out of the kind of darkened plasticized bamboo you find at Michael's and is decorated with plastic pink butterflies. A ribbon with an inscription runs across it. The inscription reads: Sara 3/17/99 Love Mom Miss You.

Walking up from the beach shrine are the Four Winds apartments, a dressed up name for what appears to be a men's dormitory. the Four Winds consists of three rows of small efficiency apartments that haven't been upgraded since they were built in the 1950s. The tenants are middle-aged men who seem down on their luck. Often there's a guy outside tinkering on a car or a small boat. No doubt, much drinking at night but not raucous.

My neighborhood puts our inflated election year politics to shame. We need a politics that places (real) ordinary life first.

Isaiah continues on the Zen Nazi trail. It's great to stumble on a religion or ideology that is innocent, at least in your own mind. What a release from the hum-drum complicity of every system that has ever been devised by humanity even if it is attributed to God or destiny. But, then, realizing its taint, we are thrown back and out of our reverie. To where?

Did I tell you the story of the time, some years ago, that Aaron was demonstrating against a house demolition in the West Bank? When confronted by Israeli soldiers, one of the friendly soldiers told Aaron he agreed with the protests. He thought Aaron's protest was important. I asked Aaron what he thought of the soldier's remark. His response startled me: "Daddy, I lost my faith in humanity."

We had quite a back and forth on his conclusion. I told Aaron that you could take the soldier's comment in another direction and derive a different meaning. Given a different structure the soldier would willingly do justice. He would build houses rather than destroy them. Aaron's take: "if you're willing to carry out orders that you don't believe in, conscience isn't free. If you're waiting for someone else or some other system to do the right thing or refuse to do the wrong thing, then you're – we're – lost."

Our intrepid Decolonizer of Peace is facing the same problem on the UN front. Having written of child prostitution and UN Peace Keepers who father children in far-off places and then disappear, she received the UN's cold shoulder. She was contacted by some high ranking UN officials who investigate such cases once they are brought to their attention, but now, well, it's pretty obvious that the UN is glad to bury its own sins. Even some UN women are compartmentalizing the prostitution/children issues. They're operating as if investigations,

policies and training are properly separated by bureaucratic oceans.

The patriarchal model of separation continues to flourish. It is quite capable of being upheld by women. How ingenious these systems are. Should our Decolonizer of Peace also lose her faith in humanity?

We could go "institutions" or "systems." We certainly don't want to go "original sin." That would be way too traditional and Christian to boot. As an alternative, we look eastward, toward Zen but, as we have seen, the Zen/Japan/war thing didn't work out too well.

The Middle East is hardly a model of religious insight. Judaism and Islam are so militarized there that some Jewish Renewal folks prove their credentials by trumpeting their son's induction into the Israeli military, like Michael Lerner's son did some years ago. Aaron's response might move beyond his lost faith in humanity. As in: "Are you kidding me?"

No, I'm not kidding you, Aaron. Nor am I kidding you about the *New York Times*, Jerusalem, reporter of many years whose son also joined the IDF.

Corruption is all around us. Others encourage us to stake out their conscience while they obey orders. Is it possible to pay for or rent another's conscience to keep our sanity afloat?

Sometimes we separate responsibility or bring it together in a conspiratorial way. Like the banker on the beach I mentioned a while ago. For him everything that ever happened is connected with corruption. Everything in the world is a plot. He was just one step away from the Protocols of the Elders of Zion when I left him with a wave and a smile.

We can't lose faith in humanity. This is the message of our prophetic provocateurs, Jewish, Zen and otherwise. Just the sound of the prophetic voice recalls the possibility of another way. When embodied, the prophetic voice interpenetrates everything, simply as itself. It exists and performs its singular note of hope for humanity in distress. Which is all of us.

That singular note is justice. Yet that same note creates a place where the grieving mother and Aaron, our intrepid Decolonizer of Peace and our conspiratorial banker meet in their broken humanity.

On September 11th, just days before the Jewish New Year, distressed humanity and the prophetic voice embodied. Is there anything more we can do or hope for?

Muna Hamzeh
TEXAS

SEPTEMBER 12

MISSING MUNA

Well I've found Rabbi Forman's High Holidays diatribe against me. I retrieved it by way of a newspaper article which was published in the local press. You see I had the audacity to invite – along with the local rabbi – a German and a Palestinian to speak in my Holocaust class in 2001. During the High Holidays in 2004, Forman heard about this from the local Jewish informants. He went ballistic.

The German speaker was Susanne Scholz, a "Diasporic German feminist," as she calls herself, and a friend of many years. Her story about what her relatives went through as the war drew to a close is horrifying. Understandably, Scholz and her generation want to distance themselves from the Holocaust. They want to get on with life. Yet there is little room in the vaunted halls of German academia for women in general and feminists in particular, thus their conflicted voice is heard mostly in the United States. Scholz is one of those Biblical scholars who deconstructs the Hebrew Bible into fragments yet, in my view, is quite the traditionalist in matters Christian. She's also a gamer on the Middle East. As you might imagine, Susanne and I have an interesting relationship.

The Palestinian speaker was Muna Hamzeh. She came to me via a friend's recommendation. Muna is another story altogether.

Dispensing with Scholz, Forman focused on Muna: "I was in shock that she would be your guest to commemorate the murder of 6 million Jews. I found it not just inappropriate but obscene." Forman took "great" offense that I would invite "someone who would dare put forth the comparative drivel between Nazi Germany and the Jewish state in order to make some lame social comment about Israeli guilt and responsibility. Such a comparison defies logic, fact and truth."

Well the truth of the matter is that Muna didn't make any such comparison, but, hey, why let the facts of the matter get in the way? What she did do, as the article states, was, with Scholz, talk about the after-effects of the Holocaust on their families and communities. This is accurately stated in the article: "Hamzeh's experience as a refugee in her homeland is an after-effect of the Holocaust, she told students then. She even compared her people's treatment at the hands of the Israelis with other oppressed minorities throughout history," Ellis recalled.

Muna's book had just been published when she spoke in my class. Forman is right; it is an "obscene" read. To begin with, check out the title: *Refugees in Our Own Land: Chronicles from a Palestinian Refugee Camp in Bethlehem*. Form the title you can see where that "obscene" indictment is leading. She dares to speak her own history in relation to Jewish history. Who does she think she is?

On the topic of who she thinks she is, here is the "obscene" description of her book:

> This book is an eye-witness account of what it is like to live in Palestine as a refugee in your own homeland. Born in Jerusalem, Muna Hamzeh is a journalist who has been writing about Palestinian affairs since 1985. She first worked as a journalist in Washington DC, but moved back to Palestine in 1989 to cover the first Palestine Intifada – the war of stones. She then settled in Dheisheh, near Bethlehem, – one of 59 Palestinian refugee camps that are considered the oldest refugee camps in the world. Immediately accessible and fully up-to-date, the first part of the book consists of a diary which Hamzeh wrote between October 4th and December 4th 2000, telling the story of the second Intifada.
>
> Facing the tanks and armed guards of one of the best equipped armies in the world, the Palestinians have nothing. They fight back with stones. The anguish and terror that Muna and her friends face on a daily basis is tangible. Who will be the next to die? Whose house will be the next to burn down?
>
> This deeply moving personal account brings to life the harsh realities of the Palestinian struggle. The second part of the book provides the background to these current events. It describes what life has been like for Dheisheh's refugees since 1990, and explains why the second Intifada was a natural development of the Oslo peace accord. "Refugees in Our Own Land: Chronicles from a Palestinian Refugee Camp in Bethlehem" is a rare insider's look into the heart and minds of Palestinian refugees. It is a tribute to the bravery of the Palestinian people, and a wake-up call to the world that has ignored so much of their struggle and their suffering.

Muna doesn't stop there. As she spoke at my Center, she was about to embark on yet another "obscene" book about an event that occurred after she spoke her "drivel". This also contained some "lame social comment about Israeli guilt and responsibility" for her people's plight. The title: *Operation Defensive Shield: Witnesses to Israeli War Crimes:*

> On March 29, 2002 the Israeli army launched Operation Defensive Shield, the largest military offensive against Palestinian civilians since the 1948 Arab-Israeli War. During the operation, the military used the most advanced weaponry at its disposal: Merkava tanks, Apache attack helicopters and F-15 fighter jets. When the operation ended on April 21, Israel had destroyed the Palestinian economic and social infrastructure, leveled large swathes of residential area, killed 220 people, and injured hundreds more and arrested thousands.
>
> This book documents these events through a collection of electronic witness narratives written by Palestinians who were under attack and by Israeli and international peace activists who witnessed the results of these attacks.

Deeply moving and courageous, these narratives offer a uniquely powerful and intimate account of the daily reality for Palestinians who endured Ariel Sharon's military strategy, and the death and destruction that strategy has caused throughout the Occupied Territories.

Most important, the witnesses' voices bring to life the aggressive nature of this strategy — they belie the noble motives ascribed to Sharon and those in his government and military that designed and carried it out. The editors argue that Operation Defensive Shield is a prelude to Israel's ethnic cleansing of the Palestinians. They provide historical context, a chronology, and an analysis of the conflict that situates the horror of these days in their proper perspective. Operation Defensive Shield: Witnesses to Israeli War Crimes is an essential record for those who want to understand what happened in the West Bank in the spring of 2002, and what it portends for the future of the region.

Note this passage: "The editors argue that Operation Defensive Shield is a prelude to Israel's ethnic cleansing of the Palestinians. They provide historical context, a chronology, and an analysis of the conflict that situates the horror of these days in their proper perspective." Israel's ethnic cleansing – can't be, can it? After the "lynch" incident in Zion Square, the Rabbis for Jewish Rights asked Jewish educators to spend a few minutes with the Jewish children in their care. Will they now issue a statement that Jewish educators should discuss this historical charge of ethnic cleansing in the founding of the Jewish state?

The bigger question. The question that unlocks other questions. This is exactly what Jewish leadership, including the Rabbis for Jewish Rights, wants to keep a lid on. Forman's mission: allow criticism up to a point; declare the deeper question off-limits. Rabbinic limits of thinkable thought.

I miss Muna. Haven't seen or heard from her in ages. She appeared one day, black hair out there in a Palestinian Afro, and started the class with a simple evocation. As a child she read Anne Frank. She wondered out loud what Anne Frank would say if she looked around and saw Muna and her people on the run.

She told her true life story. Like Anne Frank.

In the last internet mention of Muna I can find, she is at a peace rally in Portland, March 18, 2007. She wrote of her time there the following year:

> Now it is fast and easy. You hear the news on cyberspace. You let your friends know on cyberspace. They can't see your shaky fingers. They can't hear your choked voice.
>
> You tell them about Zeinab's mother. She was kidnapped and tortured in Baghdad on April 12, 2007. She was shot six times in front of her family. But not all her family because Zeinab wasn't there. She didn't have to see the mutilation, the warm blood and the mangled corpse of the woman who carried her for nine months.

Zeinab is safe in America. She looks out the window to a well-manicured lawn. She can tell what time of the morning it is when she sees the mailman. He always shows up on time. Her neighbor walks his dog and bends over to scoop the poop in a plastic bag. He would be fined if he did not. Will they wear gloves when they scoop the pieces of her mother's flesh? Will they place them in plastic bags? Will they fine the men who made her scream in torment before they shot her dead? I search online for news about her. She is nowhere to be found. She's lost in the latest Baghdad bombing and the number of US soldiers killed. She is now a statistic added to the count. Have we reached 600,000? Is it more than 400,000? Or is the number less? Do we feel safer now? Are the Iraqis liberated? If they don't democratize, will they meet their death? Is Zeinab glad to be here, or is she wishing she were dead?

The sun has risen. It is the dawn of a new day. The trees are in bloom and the roses are beginning to bud. The tulips fill the landscape with their white, yellow and pink. Welcome to America. We have beauty here and a multitude of color. Over there in Iraq, Palestine and Afghanistan, they see only one color. It is always red.

Muna's "lame" social comment about American guilt and complicity. Muna was still on the hunt.

Missing Muna. It isn't like Muna to disappear without a fight. Maybe Muna went corporate. Or maybe Muna took up arms and went to the hills of Palestine or Iraq or a dozen other places. Perhaps, instead of Anne Frank, she began thinking of the Warsaw Ghetto fighters.

Muna's "obscene drivel." Missing it. Missing her.

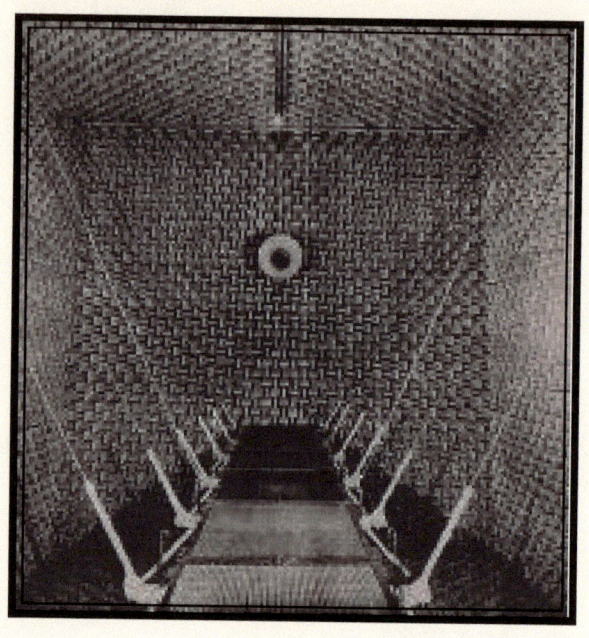

Beranek's Box
HARVARD

SEPTEMBER 13

OUR JEWISH
ANECHOIC CHAMBER

Visited the Cross on the beach this afternoon – with an (almost) mystical vision. The beach was quiet, only the sounds of the waves reaching shore. Standing in front of the Cross, I noticed a woman picking flowers nearby. Everything slowed down. Sorrow and beauty, death and life intermingling.

Silence – with sound. I felt my night reading of the Cage biography coming alive.

It was 1952. Cage was searching for silence in life and music. Harvard had a state-of-the-art anechoic chamber which was the most "silent" place on the planet. Kay Larson, Cage's biographer, describes Harvard's anechoic chamber as a "sound proof box lined with sound-absorbing baffles, guaranteeing the most perfect silence on earth." The chamber absorbed 99.8 or more percent of the energy of a sound wave. Cage arranged a visit.

At Harvard, Cage entered the chamber expecting what was advertised – perfect silence. Instead he hears a "dull roar" and a "high wine." Alarmed, Cage demanded an explanation from the engineer. The engineer explained that the whine is the firing of Cage's neurons. The roar is Cage's blood flowing through his veins.

Cage is taken aback. His Zen studies convinced him that silence existed. When silence was put to the test, it failed. Silence had so intrigued Cage that he anticipated the next question: What does silence sound like? Now Cage understood that silence doesn't exist. His question was stillborn.

Cage was "stupefied." This was his turning point. Cage had to rethink his Zen journey.

The turning point: "There is no split between spirit and matter. And to realize this, we have only suddenly to awake to the fact."

Larson writes: "In the quietest place on earth, he hears himself. Seeking silence – looking for the vacuum where 'he' is not – Cage hears the ceaseless buzz of being." Cage reflects: "Silence is not acoustic. It is a change of mind, a turning around."

Cage's turning leads to his most famous and controversial composition - 4'33". The composition lasts four minutes and thirty-three seconds, hence the title. Yet music there isn't, at least as it is known as a performance art. Instead, *4'33"* consists of the following: For four minutes and thirty-three seconds a pianist sits at the piano, opens and closes the keyboard lid twice, studies the score without playing a note; when the time is passed, the pianist stands and exits the stage.

What does Cage's musical silence signify? Like the anechoic chamber, the lack of music

isn't silence. Being in the performance space without a performance allows the audience to experience the noises of their bodies and the world. Cage's musical "silence" collapses the division of art and the world, spirit and matter. For the rest of his life, Cage tries to "write in such a way that it won't interrupt this other piece which is already going on."

Quite controversial it was, the music that wasn't music as it is understood to be. There are always those who don't want to hear the music of life. "Listen" to the letter to the editor that was published anonymously after the performance:

> This form of phony musical Dadaism built up by sensational publicity, frightens audiences away from the real music of our times. The arrogance of its nihilistic sophistries might be amusing to most people. But there is a war of nerves against common sense today, particularly in all fields of art. And if we don't check these insipid fungus growths that eat into the common sense of our people, their destructive influence will grow and gradually undermine the health and vitality of our civilization.

Sound familiar? Such "sounds" can be transposed into other areas of life. Think of Muna speaking in my Holocaust class. Think of those who don't want to hear her "insipid fungus growths that eat into the common sense of our people." We certainly don't want her "destructive influence" to be felt, lest it "grow and gradually undermine the health and vitality of our [Jewish] civilization."

The countdown continues, apropos of Cape Canaveral. In a few days now, Rosh Hashanah arrives.

Our Jewish anechoic chamber. Where we could hear our ethical blood pulsing and our historical neurons firing if we weren't so afraid. We could listen to the silence that isn't silence and thus face our turning point.

We know the rote greetings and prayers, the sweetness of the New Year and all of that. Let's suspend them, along with membership dues, High Holidays' paid seating and the Yom Kippur false fast.

Instead, let's make the synagogue an anechoic chamber for the High Holidays. The congregation can arrive with its expectations of the religious performance and then, in its place, listen to the sounds that are the real stuff of our lives.

Who knows, the silence that isn't may be justice and compassion.

Condi Leads the Way
GEORGIA

SEPTEMBER 14

MAHATMA CONDI

Sometimes diversion is the best antidote to hypocrisy, so I've decided to change the High Holidays focus today. In the anechoic chamber the expectation of silence is doused. It's on to the next question. Same applies to the High Holidays. If Rosh Hashanah and Yom Kippur aren't times for communal reflection, what are they?

A few years ago I composed a poem for the High Holidays. I imagined the local synagogue re-decorated in a Weather Channel motif. The Ark of the Covenant was decorated with weather instruments. The rabbi was the weather person. His main function was to check the congregation's barometric readings. Inside the Ark was the week's weather forecast. The door of the Ark was opened when the congregation's devotion reached a certain "apathy" reading. The tipping point was measured by the "Devotional Metric."

You'll be glad to know the poem has gone missing.

So on our High Holidays misdirection why not check the latest sports news with a racial and political twist?

No doubt you've heard that Condoleezza Rice has become the first women admitted as a member at Augusta national Golf Club, home of the Masters' golf championship. Until recently African Americans, male as well, were barred from membership in the club.

Condi's breakthrough brought memories of my writing of some years ago. For three years I wrote daily commentaries on everything going on in the world. When I finished writing the words totaled almost two million. It remains a multi-volume unpublished Candide-like romp around the world.

My commentaries began the day after Hurricane Katrina hit New Orleans. It continued through the Israeli invasion of Lebanon. This is where I picked up my Condi narrative.

Isaiah and I stopped at a rest stop for gas and food driving through Florida. Inside a television set was tuned to CNN. There was Condi, Bush's Gal Friday, making a dramatic announcement regarding a UN site in Lebanon that had been bombed by Israel. Many civilians were killed. Condi was doing her usual: "Horror of it all," "This shouldn't happen," "We will commence an investigation," "A just peace is essential" routine. It was the typical stuff from an imperial power broker with a black face.

As I was watching Condi, Isaiah came up behind me. I asked him if he knew who she was, feeling this was a teachable moment. His response was immediate: "Yes, I know Dad-o, its Mahatma Condi."

For the last months, Isaiah and I had been practicing baseball so he could equal his

brother's baseball prowess. During practice, we would chat about the commentaries I was writing. During one of our practice sessions, I shared my dream vision of burying Arafat and Sharon together. Isaiah loved my riffs on names and situations. With Mahatma Condi, he initiated his own.

I was off and running. I envisioned Mahatma Condi in Lebanon, dodging missiles fired by Israeli jets and scurrying for cover as the debris and bodies piled up around her. Then, I pictured her in civilian convoys with the fleeing Lebanese. On some nights, I had her sleeping outside in makeshift tents. Other times, she was taken in by Lebanese families. They found it strange to find a powerful African American woman, with perfect conked hair, wondering around the Lebanese hills.

During the time in Lebanon, Condi started a diary. She also broadcasted pleas to the international community. Her own imperial assumptions about Israel and the Arab world were being challenged. Her questioning turned to US foreign policy and then, like Martin Luther King, Jr., to America's role in the world. She used phrases like "purveyors of violence," "America's global reach," "Israeli expansionism." Because she was on the run, Condi entered the slippery slope that her previous Washington life insulated her from.

Condi went rogue. She began to grow an Afro. Mahatma Gandhi became her idol.

Isaiah saw the contradiction in her, hence his ironic naming, Mahatma Condi. He intuited the "converted" Condi. If she ever unclenched her fist, she might become who she was called to be.

The riff is endless. Think of the recent Skinny-dipgate, the Republican Israel junket where a group frolicked in the Galilean waters, one of them without his shorts. Now imagine Mahatma Condi stripping down and saying the hell with it. Cannonball!

Now Jock Condi joins Augusta and her dream macho golf match. Mahatma Condi is far away in the pages of imagined history.

For one brief shining moment the imperial Black face experienced the imperial power's rage. She became disoriented, as any powerful person would.

I assume she's accepted an invitation to a High Holiday service somewhere in the rarefied world of Constantinan Judaism. Which Condi will show up?

Thoughts of Constantinian Jews on the run in the hills of Lebanon. Living with Palestinians behind the Apartheid Wall. Trapped in Gaza with Star of David helicopter gunships firing rockets at will.

Imagine Constantinian Jews stripping down and saying the hell with it.

Those Who Have Gone Before
MATTANCHERRY, COCHIN

SEPTEMBER 15

LIVING
IN THE OPRAHSPHERE

As part of my High Holiday diversion, Mahatma Condi brings me back to the real Mahatma and my recent travel to India. When you think of prayer and devotion, India has to be high in the religious sphere.

There Gandhi is known and ignored. Such is the fate of the known. They are discarded even as they remain in the people's memory bank. Like the Jewish prophets, Gandhi hovers over everything that is done and undone in the nation he helped birth.

I've traveled Jewish to India several times. The first time was in 1986, when I went in search of a colleague named Siddhartha. You can surmise the rest of the story. When Siddhartha didn't appear, I bunked up with a Jesuit community who thought I was a Catholic priest because I taught at Maryknoll. Day by day I laid my life out to them. The second day I told them I wasn't a Maryknoller, the third that I wasn't a priest and so on. On the fifth day of my Jesuit sojourn, I told them I was a Jew.

Quite a travel log that first trip to India. Upon leaving I thanked the head of the Jesuit community for their hospitality and invited him to visit me in the United States. He was noncommittal. I asked him if he had ever been to America. He told me hadn't. Then he politely rebuffed my invitation: "I want to see if I can get to heaven without visiting the United States."

Humor with a bite, don't you think? My Jesuit friend placed redemption outside America's imperial power. He might have also been trumping America as a nouveau power. India was an ancient civilization.

Can Jews get to heaven without living in or even visiting Israel? Only a very small number of American Jews have ever lived in Israel. A small percentage of American Jews have visited Israel. Why, then, does our theology and communal consciousness tell us that Israel is redemptive?

In Israel, there is little vision beyond mere survival. There isn't much redemption consciousness there. The trials of ordinary life predominate in Israel as they do elsewhere. Redemption is for the mystics and the fundamentalists.

Among the Orthodox, sure, redemption counts. Yet what does redemption mean if you only live in the land under the protection of a militarized state? Call it *Sparta's Redemption*, the film. View it after *Shoah*. Make it short, though. More than eight hours of Holocaust reverie is already a supreme challenge for our attention-deficit redemption - breathing brethren.

There are so many accusing images regarding Israel today that Jewish audiences won't even want the *Shoah* sequel played. Perhaps just a scenic view of Jerusalem at the end of *Shoah* would suffice, a la Steven Spielberg's *Schindler's List*. *Schindler's List* offered audiences redemption without the inconvenience of travel. From Lanzmann's bully perch, Spielberg is on the Hollywood cheap, sugar coating the Holocaust and Israel for American audiences. Auschwitz as a hellish E T.

Roaming the internet highway, I see Spielberg's net worth is estimated at three billion dollars. Amazing amount of money for a sugar coater, don't you think? Sheldon Adelson bucks.

Spielberg grew up an Orthodox Jew and felt uneasy about it. He also had youthful anti-Semitism thrown at him. He did make it through, though, and has given back from whence he came, though always being careful of being bound to any Jewish religious authority. Billions of dollars buys you that freedom.

I've never been a fan of the Indiana Jones and the Raiders of the Lost Ark film franchise. I confess I haven't seen any of them all the way through, but I understand there there's a Nazi theme throughout and a race to find the Ark of the Covenant. When they find the Ark – don't tell me, I can feel the suspense – are there Star of David helicopter gunships inside?

On my next trip to India in 2001, I taught in a Christian seminary in Bangalore for three months. It was a Left-leaning seminary but, as it turned out, the seminary was riddled with infighting and was completely dependent on Europe for funding. Thus it perpetuated the colonial model they ostensibly struggled against. None of the students I taught had ever met a Jew, let alone be taught by one. It was quite fun at times. I also learned that I had a romanticized sense of liberation theology.

Last year I was invited to New Delhi. I visited a former student of mine, a true Christian missionary, who had a good relationship with all sorts of non-Christian folks in Kashmir. When that idiot fundamentalist in Florida burned the Koran, my student's life was in the balance. One evening as the news spread of the Koran burning, he noticed folks camping out in his front yard. Their presence was a sign that no retaliation should be taken against him and his family.

It must have been quite a scene, and so moving. Local folks protected someone from a different faith. Kashmir's very own Neighborhood Watch.

That story is one highlight of my travel. Another was a Muslim group from Afghanistan that had come to learn more about the Islamic history of India. My Christian missionary student was their teacher. My student isn't a proselytizing type. Instead he has become an expert in Islamic history. The Afghan students were from different universities who were part of a project that emphasized the freedom to think and debate the issues of the day. As you might expect, they had never been out of the country. They certainly hadn't met a Jew who, by their accounts, had to be an Israeli. Aren't all Jews Israelis?

In between my lectures, I toured with the Afghans. My student was our guide. As you might expect, the dialogue was fascinating, with questions like: "Professor, do you believe

that God is perfect?" To which I said, "No." Inevitably it came around to the Koran, and the question of its perfection. I gave the same response. Did I believe Muhammed was the last prophet? "No," again.

I was careful to preface each of my responses with the fact that they were mine alone. My answers didn't carry any transcendental truth they should consider as authoritative. After each question and response, we continued touring and speaking together.

I loved our visits to the Hindu and Sikh temples. I can't help but admire traditions that have movable Gods and a Book that is treated like a royal guest during the day and night. It also brought back memories of my former university where a head of department always insisted that America was the most religious nation on earth. In India, the whole American exceptionalism thing is even more absurd than it is inside America. Amazing stuff I lived with. We live with. India has a way of wiping clean the ridiculousness of our "knowing."

The highlight of my visit came unexpectedly. There were two Afghan women on the tour. Both were immaculate in their dress and manners. Each morning I shook the hands of the Afghan men. The women put their hand to their heart in greeting. The previous evening I talked to the group about my views on Israel. With the language, religion and cultural barriers, I wasn't sure what the students understood about the perspectives I shared.

The next morning I greeted the Afghans as they arrived for the day. Instead of putting her hand to her heart, one of the women put out her hand as if to shake mine. I was shocked and hesitated for a moment. I wanted to make sure I wasn't mistaking her gesture for another. As I hesitated, she clasped my hand. She held it for long while in full view of everyone. Then she smiled and placed her hand on her heart.

Traveling Jewish. The Indian Jesuit wanted to prove that God loved everyone, even those who didn't make it to America. Redemption doesn't run through Washington. The Afghan woman abandoned convention at her own peril.

Indeed Muhammed is not the final prophet. America – and Israel – is not redemptive. Steven Spielberg is a billionaire three times over, living somewhere in the Oprahsphere.

Oprasphere. Beyond Jewish power. Do you need to be a billionaire?

What Would Anne Frank Do?
AMSTERDAM

SEPTEMBER 16

JAMES BALDWIN'S
COALITION IS OURS

A sudden rainstorm and high winds struck this afternoon. Beautiful. Also a bit dicey. Walking on the beach, I could only see a few feet in front of me.

I'm in the final stretch of John Cage's bio. At this point, the early 1950s, he's just taught some years in the New School for Social Research. The New School's graduate school began in that fateful year, 1933. The early faculty were mostly refugees from fascist Italy and Nazi Germany. This included Eric Fromm, Han Jonas and, of course, Hannah Arendt. Its original name – University in Exile.

As universities regroup for the coming year, it's interesting to compare what was and what is. We can also compare on the Jewish side. Imagine being a student of Hannah Arendt who had just escaped from Nazi Germany. By all accounts, breakout sessions with her were intense. Arendt's *The Origins of Totalitarianism* was a real book, not the annotated textbooks marketed today. A few years ago a publisher requested I supply food for thought questions at the end of each chapter. This would make my text "reader friendly." What would Hannah Arendt have said?

You might not be familiar with the wrist bands in evangelical culture that carry the phrase, "What Would Jesus Do?" Obviously no one knows what Jesus would do. We don't even know what he did. Nonetheless, it's an interesting question that we can put to different religious and historical figures. Like Muna placed before us: "What would Anne Frank think about what's happened to Palestinians at the hands of the Jewish state?"

Well, Anne Frank might think more or less, though less philosophically, what Hannah Arendt thought. We could quiz her about the future, too. What Would Hannah Arendt Think About the Jewish Future?"

In a University in Exile we could all think together. We could also call it the University of the New Diaspora. This would bring the exiles of the world into a community where the future is discussed. Think about a curriculum in such a university and how it would differ from the Political Science 101 courses taught in universities today.

Whether we emphasize exile or the New Diaspora or combine the two – The University of Exile in the New Diaspora? – we need teachers who are on the run. And students who are willing to place themselves in the same exile boat. That is, teachers who are persecuted for righteousness' sake rather than the syllabi generating glorified High School teachers that fill the universities. As students, didn't our eyes light up and hair stand on edge when the teacher was obviously on the run from the powers-that-be?

Some talk about the Jewish intelligence factor when intellectuals are discussed. But what set Jews apart, at least up till now, is that Jews have existed on the margins of the powerful and the normative. Jews were on the run.

Though Jews are all over our modern universities, have you noticed how little real thought they produce today? Instead of being on the run, Jews have settled in. Few Jewish university professors today, would choose the University in Exile. The status and money flow are too low. Why teach those who will be on the run when you want nothing more than to hob-nob with whatever powerful clique can advance you to the next chair in Jewish Studies?

On the Jewish (re)education scene – since the Rabbis for Jewish Rights are so interested in our children after the Zion Square episode – we should send our young ones to a University in Exile. To see how the Other Half lives. Like Mahatma Condi on the run in Lebanon. It was quite an education for her, wasn't it?

Think of our heroic Henry Schwarzschild, resignation letter and all, sitting at the feet of the Civil Rights giants. That was a University in Exile right here in America. Henry was on the run from the Nazis, then gave his all for African Americans on the run in America. Henry, the exile, saw it all here in America. Sure Henry was in many ways a teacher, but he also had to be a willing student.

In a University in Exile it isn't always easy to figure out who's the teacher and who's the student. That's the way it is in the classroom of life. That's the way it should be in our universities.

I was in the same situation in my years at Maryknoll. Students came from all over the world. Once they understood their vocation was with the poor and oppressed rather than the empire, even some of the missionaries were on the run. Though they were sent out from the American empire with an empire religion, they studied the faces of those they baptized. They finally understood that the evangelization they pursued had been reversed. It was they, the missionaries, who had to be evangelized. Rather than teachers, they were the students of those on the run. The peasants and priests of the poor and oppressed were the teachers.

So it is with our Jewish sons and daughters. It's not for the parents of Zion Square(d) – the ethnic cleansers and those who enable it – to teach our children. They need to go to another school, a school with teachers and students who are on the run.

When the student is ready, yes, the teacher appears. I have a picture of beautiful Hannah, Henry's daughter, planting an olive tree in the West Bank. She is a teacher – for Jews. But she is also a student – of Palestinian teachers.

I wonder if Henry knew James Baldwin, one of my favorite writers since my youth. Baldwin lived his last years in France. Listen to Baldwin and see if it strikes you as relevant for Jewish students to hear once again, transposing his words into a challenge for Jewish ethics:

> I imagine one of the reasons people cling to their hates so stubbornly is because they sense, once hate is gone, they will be forced to deal with pain.

If we – and now I mean the relatively conscious whites and the relatively conscious blacks, who must, like lovers, insist or create, the consciousness of others – do not falter in our duty, we may be able, handful that we are, to end the racial nightmare, and achieve our country, and change the history of the world. If we do not now dare everything, the fulfillment of that prophecy, created from the Bible in song by a slave, is upon us: God gave Noah the rainbow sign, No more water, the fire next time!

I took my evening walk on the beach thinking of Baldwin and the University in Exile and the New Diaspora. In my imagination, the relatively conscious whites and Blacks Baldwin wrote about became Jews and Palestinians of Conscience. Ending the racial nightmare became the Holocaust and the Nakba. To achieve our country became a challenge to achieve an Israel-Palestine based on justice and equality. This would change the world.

Walking on a beach after a storm is wonderful. And yes, this evening a rainbow arched over the water. Clouds framed the translucent blue water.

Baldwin's question remains: the rainbow sign or the fire next time?

A Brand New Year
CAPE CANAVERAL

SEPTEMBER 17

IF ROSH HASHANAH
RETURNS

On the beach this New Year morning, the sky is like an artist's palette. The colors are pastel, various shades of pink and blue. A New Year omen I hope.

The world isn't as beautiful as the morning sky. Libya and Egypt lead the foreboding news cycle. Syria's war stalemate remains. Heading for America, Netanyahu draws his red lines in Israel's Iranian sand. Instead of meeting Netanyahu, Obama is received by David Letterman.

On the rote and trite Rosh Hashanah front, Obama and Romney issue Jewish New Year messages. I can't tell one from the other.

Politics makes for strange and meaningless High Holiday messages. Nothing to mull over. No pointers for self-correction. Trivialized challenges for the coming year. More of the same.

More or less, like the Rosh Hashanah sermons preached today. You can't tell one from the other.

Religion makes for strange and meaningless holyday messages. Like Pope Benedict on his Lebanon pilgrimage. Won't you please wish us well?

On the local front, the Cross on the beach lists in the sand. The weather is taking its toll. I've thought about taking it to my apartment for safekeeping. Then I realized it's become a mandala of sorts for me. Changing its physical location might change its spiritual meaning.

Mandalas are a series of concentric diagrams with ritual and sacred significance in Buddhism. When mandalas are constructed out of sand, they are destroyed by those who constructed them. The destruction of the creation represents the impermanence of life and the sacred.

Should we look at Rosh Hashanah as a Jewish mandala? The Jewish calendar, with its rites and rituals, and Jewish history, which we mark today of more than five thousand years, is heavy stuff. As a mandala constructed out of sand, "Jewish" is here and then not here. Jewish is omnipresent. Jewish disappears.

Auschwitz as a Jewish mandala. I remember when I traveled to Auschwitz, a rabbi suggested letting the death camp decay. Let nature take its course. Today, climate control experts preserve Auschwitz for eternity.

Though Auschwitz has become a Jewish mandala of sorts, for the most part, it functions in a perverted way. We gaze on Auschwitz, the site, or invoke its name, as a gateway to the

sacred. The last thing on our Auschwitz mind is impermanence.

Auschwitz as a gateway for the spiritual has no depth. In the Jewish imagination, Auschwitz is our fixed eternity. Auschwitz keeps returning in the same form.

Israel as a gateway for the spiritual has no depth. In the Jewish imagination, Israel is our fixed eternity. Israel keeps returning in the same form.

Auschwitz and Israel are real. Auschwitz and Israel are unreal.

As a gateway for the spiritual, Rosh Hashanah has no depth. In the Jewish imagination, Rosh Hashanah is fixed in eternity. Rosh Hashanah keeps returning in the same form.

Yom Kippur as a gateway for the spiritual has no depth. In the Jewish imagination, Yom Kippur is fixed in eternity. Yom Kippur keeps returning in the same form.

This doesn't mean that what is has to be. It's not about destroying/erasing our real/imagined place/calendar or our distinct/imagined identity. Jewish identity embraces our past and present as if they matter. As we embrace our identity, we need to release ourselves from identity's hold on us.

As we hold onto Jewish, it becomes violent and unethical. It drifts away.

Let go of Jewish. If Jewish returns, it will return in a different form.

If you let go of Jewish and it returns, you know it matters.

During these days of reflection, give the prophetic back to God. If you give the prophetic back to God and the prophetic returns, then you know the prophetic is the deepest part of you.

On Rosh Hashanah do something (un)Jewish. Give it all up.

Think Rosh Hashanah doesn't matter.

Be Still and Know
CAPE CANAVERAL

SEPTEMBER 18

THE PROPHETIC
UNDER THE BANYAN TREE

Think the prophetic. Prepare it for the coming year. Then give it up. Send the prophetic on its way.

Think the prophetic for Yom Kippur. Place the prophetic on a fasting regimen. Hope that Jewish will turn toward justice and compassion. Embody that hope. It's the only way hope exists.

Experience yourself without the prophetic. Experience yourself without Jewish. Experience yourself by giving it all away.

Create the prophetic as a mandala made of sand. Build it. Destroy it. Listen to the prophetic's transitory sound. You'll know there's no direction home.

Picture the prophetic sitting under a banyan tree. A banyan tree's roots grow down from the branches to form secondary trunks. Sit still. Let the prophetic roots nourish you.

Mourn exile. Now give exile away. If it returns, be grateful for exile's challenge.

Write an irate letter. Tell God you don't want the prophetic. Send the prophetic back to God. Address it: "Return to Sender." If the prophetic returns, the prophetic is native to you.

Write a convincing letter explaining why you don't want Jewish anymore. Address it: "To Whom It May Concern." If Jewish returns, embrace it.

Imagine exile and the prophetic as bound together. Send both on a voyage across the sea. Note where they make landfall. Exile and the prophetic always turn up somewhere.

Wherever exile and the prophetic appear, they are. If they reach someone else's shore, fine. If they reach your shore, that's fine, too.

Laugh at the absurdity of the powerful. Even their language betrays humanity.

Laugh at the absurdity of dissent. Its language conceals powerlessness.

Practice exile with intensity. Practice exile as if your life depended on it. Now recognize that your life is more than practice and more than exile.

Practice exile. Practice the prophetic. Hold fast. Let go.

David Gregory
NBC NEWS

SEPTEMBER 19

DAVID GREGORY
CAME TO MY SEDER

Miscellany. Scattered reflections during the Days of Awe. Trying to keep it light. Back to the diversion after yesterday's thought poem.

I begin on the David Gregory front, apropos of his controversial (without mentioning the words Palestine or Palestinian) interview a few days ago with Netanyahu. Around the time I had Muna Hamzeh speak in my Holocaust course, Gregory spent Passover in my home in Central Texas.

It happened like this. President Bush's vacation spot is in Crawford, Texas just a few miles from where I lived. It was during Bush's first term and he was on Easter vacation so Gregory, then Chief White House correspondent for NBC News, was there to cover the President. That year Passover intersected with Easter and Gregory looked for a Jewish home to share a Seder meal. Combing through the university directory for a Jewish Studies presence, he happened upon me.

As I remember, Gregory is from a mixed background and now identifies Jewish. My time with him was pleasant. For the most part, Gregory is more or less as he comes across on television, intelligent in a certain way, interested in the back and forth of good conversation and considerate of others. On the food scene, as a contribution to the Seder meal, he brought exquisite chocolate macaroons from a bake shop in Washington.

I'm not sure if he knew who I was and what I represented in the Middle East war of ideas before our Seder time together. If he did, he didn't let on. We discussed the Middle East a bit. Obviously he understood Israel's transgressions and showed concern for Palestinians. Yet even in private he had a newsman's presence about him. He played both sides of the issue. He didn't want to wade into the Israel-Palestine quagmire.

"Meet the Press" was Gregory's reward for playing both sides of all issues in public and private. To become successful, keep the world at bay by being non-committal on things of importance. Or impartial, depending on how terms are used in the company you keep and the company which promotes you. The reward is lots of money and status. Thinking of Gregory, though, I wonder if a life that follows those rules makes a life.

After our time together, he invited me to Crawford for a Presidential press conference. The only way to gain entry was to be part of the press or a press person's invited guest. So there I was, just yards away from President Bush. I found him as he is often portrayed, an impish prankster and the stereotypical immature middle-aged man.

Mahatma Condi was also there, standing off to the side. I remember feeling how staged these press conferences are and how the world is discussed – and decided upon – in such

flippant tones. The overall sense of the proceeding was boredom. Everyone seemed tired and out of place. Uprooted – to return to Simone Weil's theme.

It is hard for most of us to imagine Jewishness different than the Jewishness that surrounds us. We can imagine rebelling against that Jewishness. Rebelling against that Jewishness is our Jewishness. At times we're caught up short by those who question the content of our Jewishness. Other times we catch ourselves up short. We ask ourselves if the only Jewish we know is rebellion against the Empire Jewish Other.

The Days of Awe heighten everyone's suspicion. What is this one's and that one's Jewish?

But factor this in. Whenever content to Jewish is prescribed or ascribed, there's always rebellion. The attempt to define the content of Jewish inaugurates assaults on radical thought. It demands conformism to establishment power. Boundaries are established that cannot be crossed without incurring severe penalties.

When the definition of Jewish isn't up for grabs, Jewish atrophies. The more Jewish is trumpeted, the less it means. Much to do lately about the Abrahamic faiths, what with the anti-Muslim video, the death of the American ambassador to Libya, rumblings in Egypt and the Pope in Lebanon.

Can't we all just get along?

I was amazed when I heard that the recent hurricane was named Isaac. The weather storm came only weeks before the present religious storm. Of course, the religious storm is ancient; it's been with us for so long we don't even name it. When we're in the eye of the religious storm, we count our blessings. It's only a matter of time before the torrential rains and ferocious winds return.

Isaac is a Biblical talisman for being bound and being free. The Abrahamic legacy is variously interpreted along those lines The God in the Abraham/Isaac story is a forbidding/forgiving one, depending on how interpreters turn the text. As is common in the Bible, the text can be read different ways. It also has silences, jump cuts in the narrative and redactions galore.

My son, Aaron, attended a class in a seminary on the Hebrew Bible last summer. Part of the course focused on the Abraham story. We spent many an evening on what seems to be a very straight forward story. At least with modern interpretations, it isn't.

But then I often wonder about modern interpretations of ancient texts. We bring our modernity to everything and when the Bible is concerned Orientalism is often the elephant in the room. Religion does this to everyone, it seems. It skews our sensibilities and our judgment. Much like secularism does. There doesn't seem to be an exit from interpretative frameworks that are later changed or disavowed completely.

I stay away from the Abraham/Isaac story primarily because the rather ridiculous interfaith mandala gathers the three monotheistic religions under the same (modern) tent. I find the "tent" theme strange. Of late, I haven't met any of the Abrahamic faith participants that live in a tent. Mostly I meet them at conferences in mammoth hotels.

Nonetheless, sometimes there are symbolic Abrahamic Faiths' tent meetings. Usually the host complains about the complexity of renting and using such a venue. To begin with, tents are hard to find. For the tent gatherings to make sense, the rented tent has to be large enough for a crowd. Tent rentals are expensive. Other than weddings for the affluent, they're not much in demand. The modern "Rent a Tent" industry hasn't taken off yet.

The Jerusalem Abrahamic Faiths stuff is especially dumbed down. The World Parliament of Religions is rife with it. Satellite gatherings can also be the religious place to be.

At Abrahamic Faith gatherings anyone who's anyone has a religious costume. When the dignitaries appear they carry their sacred book with them. Everyone prays in their own language whether anyone around them understands their language or not. Everyone pretends they're interested in other faith prayers when they're hardly interested in their own.

As a religious fashion show it's the place to be.

In general, these gatherings aren't gateway mandalas. For the most part, they block the way forward by freezing all of us in the religious equivalent of shipping crates. Once you're packaged carefully, there's no way out until you've arrived at your destination. If spirituality is a journey, you have to be prepared to move in a variety of directions that aren't on the shipping routes.

Our good friend and cosmopolitan Jew, Edward Said, couldn't stand the Abrahamic Faiths' routine. It couldn't be more inane and farther from the Jewish prophetic Said was so drawn to. The idea that Jerusalem and the world would be better off with the monotheistic religions at the core of a political deal is ludicrous. Among other things, such a view enshrines the official leadership of these religions as religious in a meaningful way. It is more accurate to understand them as political gamers who advanced to the top rungs of the church/mosque/synagogue bureaucracy. Romanticizing these religions consigns the prophetic to the fringes of the spiritual world. Or, rather, it pushes them off the religious map altogether.

The Abrahamic Faiths movement is for the most part static. It protects religion – and politics – from the prophetic sniping at its heels. The real Jerusalem is less about the Judaism, Christianity and Islam than it is about Jews and Palestinians finding a just way to integrate their lives. Within the context of justice, religions have a place.

Meanwhile, parasailing, where people dangle from a parachute tethered to a boat, is in the news along the Florida coastline. It seems that folks are dropping from the sky on a fairly regular basis. The latest is a woman who slipped from her harness and fell two hundred feet to her death a few days ago. As you might expect, the parasailing industry is unregulated. The local news reports as a matter of fact that regulations aren't very popular in Florida.

Along the parasailing line during the High Holidays, I wonder if a representative of each faith, fully decked out in their official religious garb, could parasail in the Mediterranean and then, catching a wind current, be airlifted over Jerusalem. The citizens of Jerusalem can see the Flying Abrahams calling for peace and prayers for everyone and everything.

Visions of the Ed Sullivan show. Apropos of the relevance of the High Holidays.

Showtime
CRAWFORD, TEXAS

SEPTEMBER 20

THE NEXT FOUR YEARS

I can see that the David Gregory Seder story has legs. Good ones. You see Gregory struck me as a thoroughly decent guy. Intelligent as well. I found his intelligence, though, to be thoroughly conventional – and American. Despite his French language ability, which he displayed at a Bush news conference in Paris, Gregory's intellectual range is curious and strategic rather than deep. Though he's not one to go deep on you, if you initiate the journey, he'll follow.

Without questioning his Jewishness or his intellectual ability, his manner and presentation seemed much more in search of Jewishness than at home there. Perhaps this is generational, a product of intermarriage or even his California upbringing. Whatever the reasons, I found this striking. Felt like I was entering another world of Jewishness.

During the evening at my home, he was open and accommodating. We used a delightful child's Haggadah and Gregory was quite keen on participating. I can't say whether his promotion has changed him. I did notice the upscale grooming for his elevation to host of Meet the Press. Strange that the question of his final promotion is linked in my mind to how he appears on television. Does Gregory project the "presence" that NBC wants when Brian Williams retires?

When I went to the Bush press conference the next day, he was again quite gracious. The press conference was disturbing to me and from a distance of some years, even more so. I know that by their nature press conferences are staged. Still the stakes are so high, what with America's global role. To see Bush and members of his Cabinet close-up reminded me that they were human beings like all of us. However, the contrast between our shared humanity and the power they wielded, strikes me. To see that cast of characters is even worse.

I am not sure which is worse. The idea that Ronald Reagan used to read off note cards when he interacted with foreign dignitaries or the possibility that Bush didn't think he needed note cards.

This brings me to the present cast of characters and the next four years.

In little more than a year we've gone from Occupy's 99% to Mitt Romney's 47%. I wonder what depressing figures will come next.

When we couple Mitt's "Dependent 47" with his recorded comments about the chimera of the two-state solution and how Palestinians don't want peace or a state side-by side with Israel, I think the presidential choice is clear. Of course, I know Obama's limitations. Nonetheless.

On the other hand, there is more and more reporting on the imminent collapse of the Palestinian Authority and our sure knowledge that a second term Obama won't do much on the Israel-Palestine front. We know that the party platforms regarding Jerusalem, like their statements on God, are similar – and meaningless.

We're already working on the next four years in Middle East politics American-style. Just yesterday I was contacted for a New England speaking tour in February. Naturally, the organizers want a topical title. Off the top of my head I suggested, "The Next Four Years: Getting Ready for More of the Same?" I doubt that's a sexy enough title to attract those still left of the once growing, now declining, Israel-Palestine activist community.

I'd rather have a minyan than lie about the future. On the minyan, we need to think about the dwindling numbers and, without being ageist, the gray haired nature of those who show up at movement events. Sure there's a new generation but their numbers won't replace the old activists. This includes the church groups that have been incredibly active on the Israel-Palestine issue. Mainstream denominations which have carried the activist ball have been in a steep decline for years. There are few signs of reversing this decline.

All of this raises the issue of dissent and an institutional framework to sustain it. If dissent should have such a framework and how is always debated. Without some institutional framework dissent can't go anywhere. With institutionalization we have the proverbial NGO question of becoming enablers of what we ostensibly want to end.

I doubt that these trends will be reversed in next four years. If we're honest, activist and interested partisans have been dwindling since the early 1990s. Part of this is history – everything has been working against positive movement in Israel-Palestine. Part of it has to do with what has been offered as possible ways forward. On the Jewish side, the real issues have been deflected for decades by Jews who are naïve about Jewish power and those who actively seek to limit the discussion. On the Palestinian side, argumentation has been undermined by timidity, infighting and grandstanding. But, then, since Jews grandstand, why shouldn't Palestinians?

Yes, there has been positive movement as well, especially the deepening ties of Jews and Palestinians of Conscience. The One State conferences may or may not represent an advance. The same is true of the growing specifically named anti-Zionists networks. I'm not at all sure what this can possibly mean now since we're dealing with entrenched Israeli state power and other state powers as well. I am concerned with the lack of deep thought surrounding Jewish and Palestinian history and culture. I believe that particularity is important. It is the primary way of opening an engaged universality.

In any case, the most frustrating aspects of the contemporary Israel-Palestine discussion is that deep and superficial argumentation from all sides has failed to move the situation on the ground in a positive direction. History and contemporary politics seem to be operating under impossible historical conditions or, depending on your mindset, ominous astrological signs.

Whether the reasons for the constantly devolving situation in Israel-Palestine are

political or astrological misalignments, the "Next Four Years" theme is hold on for dear life. What's come around so many times is coming around again.

Is this assessment defeatist, as is often charged, or realistic? Either way, the world is always changing. Therefore our primary challenge is to remain engaged. Being engaged, we learn. We change. We prepare to offer our commitment when the time is ripe. If it isn't ripe in our lifetime, there is little we can do about it. Israel-Palestine is larger than any one of us. Despite our flaws and the vagaries of history, we struggle to be faithful. That is what we can control.

For now, though, I pick up where I left off, with the Flying Abrahams, our prelates from different faiths parasailing the Jerusalem skies. Think of their view of the next four years.

What do they see?

On the contemporary scene, they see how (un)unified the (exceedingly temporary) eternal capital of Israel (Palestine) really is.

Looking out across Jerusalem, they're able to see Dimona, Israel's nuclear arms facility.

Since I haven't parasailed Jerusalem, I'm not sure if they can see Iran from there. Netanyahu has colored Iran red, however, so they might at least see the Iranian red sky in contrast with Jerusalem's blue sky. Or should Jerusalem also be painted red, since the countries our Flying Abrahams view are fearful of what Israel might do with its nuclear might?

If our prelates could visualize the history of Jerusalem from the air, they might abandon their religious outfits and flee to the hills. Jerusalem's history, like the woman who fell from her parasailing harness in Florida, is a tragic story to behold. Experiencing the city's history together, our prelates might undergo a conversion. They may well become the Mahatmas of the (un)Abrahamic faiths.

Perhaps the Flying Abrahams have read the Crusader accounts of their ascent to Jerusalem. They're a must read. As you might expect, the Crusader accounts are vivid. They traveled a long way to reach the Holy Land, a tale by itself. En route, the Crusaders expropriated everything they could lay their hands on and, of course, slaughtered Jews. So when they reached Jerusalem and captured the religious shrines, the slaughter of the infidel commenced.

My favorite Crusader accounts have them standing knee deep in the blood of their religious adversaries. Truth be known, they enjoyed every minute of it. Unfortunately for them, we know what they didn't know; it would soon be their turn. The Crusader's revelry was soon repaid in spades.

One Crusader lesson takeaway for the next four years is that we shouldn't worry overly much about victory or defeat in the immediate frame. In Jerusalem's history the roles are soon reversed. Our second Crusader lesson takeaway is for the long haul and equally sobering. The avenged take equal pleasure in the slaughter of the former victors.

Like the Crusaders, Israel thinks itself immune from the predictable reversal. Now our parasailing prelates know that the victors are like that throughout Jerusalem's history. They never think the blood they're standing in will soon be their own.

There are differences, of course. History isn't just one giant repetition. The hills surrounding Jerusalem now are Israeli settlement/cities. Fleeing modern injustice is mostly urban. Urban, even in Jerusalem, is a different kind of wilderness.

This raises the always vexing issue of when settlements become cities. Answer: When settlers are there long enough, the military is strong enough and the state is determined enough to outlast and outwit the forces that oppose it. That is, until the reversal occurs

If you're not depressed by the next four years of Israel-Palestine, file the following under "The Next Hundred Years." I just finished reading George Dyson's *Turings Cathedral: The Origins of the Digital Universe*. Dyson narrates the origins of the digital universe which occurred within two history changing developments: the decoding of self-replicating sequences in biology and the invention of the hydrogen bomb. In other words, the computer/internet was born with the discovery of DNA and atomic weaponry.

For Dyson it isn't a "coincidence that the most destructive and the most constructive of human inventions appeared at exactly the same time." He postulates that "only the collective intelligence of computers could save us from the destructive powers of the weapons they allowed us to invent." The kicker is that the machines that developed the codes necessary for the creation of the digital universe were available only in the evenings and weekends. During the weekdays the computers were otherwise occupied with the development of atomic weaponry.

Lesson for "The Next Hundred Years": When you think iPhone, think nuclear weaponry.

Life lesson: What we prize is often our demise.

Dyson adds another cautionary note. The computer/internet/nuclear weapon developments occurred in of all places, Princeton, New Jersey, at the Institute for Advanced Study. This was an auxiliary University in Exile that gathered the best – Jewish – minds fleeing Nazified Europe. The result was a two-sided ledger of progress and destruction. The doomsday or paradise race was on. It's still on. Which side will win the day remains unclear.

So Israel-Palestine has to be seen in a global panoramic view. Thus the Flying Abrahams. To be deployed elsewhere as well?

Israel's Declaration of Independence
JERUSALEM

SEPTEMBER 21

RESEARCHING THE JEWISH
FUTURE IN THE ISRAEL STATE ARCHIVES

What does the prophetic say to the next four years of more of the same? Practicing exile.

What does exile mean in the next four years of more of the same? Practicing the prophetic.

What to do in exile with the prophetic in the next four years of more of the same? Continue on in our practice of exile and the prophetic.

Continuing on is the fidelity we need, the only fidelity worth its grain of salt and the only witness that makes sense in the next four years of more of the same. By continuing on the next four years of more of the same might be different. Well, it will be different if we are. As with most of life, it's a matter of degree. We don't know where the tipping point is or when it will arrive.

I return to the need for strategic depth. If everything has two sides the outcome is constantly in doubt. Viewed in historical long haul time, celebrations are momentary. So are defeats.

It's easy to sit on the proverbial fence and pretend that you're not involved. Especially if the tidal waves overturn everyone else's life boat while leaving yours intact (for the time being).

I am reminded of Noah's Ark, though this time the wealthy of the earth gather two by two to outlast the "horde" surge. When you're one of the saved, even if you're on an auxiliary boat, there's a lot of pressure to be silent. Most are silent, of course.

Shoving others overboard when need be is part of this enabling silence. We all have a "save yourself" DNA sequence deep within us.

Though occasionally it happens that just when someone is trying to hang on for dear life, they stop. They refuse to shove someone else overboard. You know what's next. Off you go, you're the one thrown into the sea. You watch the lifeboats fade into the distance.

How breathtaking it is when a person takes a stand. It's as simple as that, the prophetic is right there in front of your eyes. In the actions of another we witness hope embodied. In our own actions we witness hope made real.

During our Days of Awe, we should remember the thirtieth anniversary of the massacres at Sabra and Shatila. It turns out that there are new developments in the case. These new details bring the massacre closer to our American shores with an interesting twist.

Dealing with newly declassified documents on the Sabra and Shatila massacre, Seth Anziska points an interesting finger at the American government. The documents contain verbatim discussions, arguments and accusations between American and Israeli officials. It turns out US officials knew what was going on in the camps and confronted the Israeli government in angry tones. Led by Ariel Sharon, Israel refused to back down. The massacres continued.

Where were these documents found? In the Israel State Archives. Where was the story published? In the *New York Times*.

History is playing its subversive role. There's no confession like history. The Israel State Archives makes the American and Israeli Yom Kippur look like a child's prelude to the adult story.

Has Jewish religious life in all its guises become a child prelude to the real thing? Sharing knowledge is age appropriate, of course. Jews have regressed to the stage where the real history of our empowerment is hidden away in the Israel State Archives.

It seems that the central role of the Jewish establishment over the next hundred years will be damage control. Progressive Jews have also played that role. The challenge for Jews of Conscience is to refuse damage control. The fear on all sides is that if the truth becomes known there may be little left of Jewish.

That fear must be faced head on. When everything that surrounds Jewish is stripped away we arrive where we began – with the prophetic – the Jewish indigenous.

What has already been found is one thing. What will be found in the future is another. Like the Crusaders' accounts, preserved for history and now read with horror, our collective hair will stand on edge when the full story is told.

Which it will be. On a Yom Kippur in the future our collective history toward Palestinians will be confessed. Perhaps, even on this Yom Kippur it will be told somewhere.

Part of the story was discovered in Israel. Part of the story was published in New York.

History eventually goes global. Jewish history is not exempt.

Interesting, who would have thought that the Israel State Archives would be the place where the history of the Jewish state was turned upside down?

Researching the Jewish future in the Israel State Archives. At first it seems strange. Then it doesn't.

Michael Oren
ISRAELI AMBASSADOR TO THE UNITED STATES OF AMERICA

SEPTEMBER 22

THE AMERICANIZATION
OF ISRAELI POWER

My history lesson for the day, from an unknown admirer, via email. As you read it and learn remember, it's better than a death threat.

> Regarding your book about "Israel and Palestine," "Palestine" is a historically illegitimate European name for Israel dating back to the Romans briefly renaming Israel "palaestina" and the British later anglicizing it into "palestine" during the British Mandate. Palestine does not appear even once in the Hebrew Bible, Christian Bible nor even in the Quran, while Israel appears 2500 times. Your history lesson for the day.

Thank you "Michele" for reminding me how entangled the Israel-Palestine issue is.

The *New York Times is* at least one step ahead of my unknown admirer when it defines the Israeli diplomat, Michael Oren, aka Michael Scott Bornstein, as "the man in the middle."

So thinks the *New York Times*. However, what we find in Oren's biography is that though functioning as Israel's ambassador to America, he's really an American. After all, he was born in New York and raised in New Jersey. All his university degrees are from American universities. His father served in the Korean War. His wife is from San Francisco. Why, then, such a *Times* fuss about Oren's perfect American accent?

He's an American, stupid!

I'm not delving into the double loyalty debate which sounds an awful lot like the Obama Birther issue. I don't want to go Donald Trump's level, and besides, when I hear comments like "Israel is our 51st state" or references to politicians as "Our Senator from Tel Aviv," I think stupid. I also think anti-Jewish.

My point is much more complicated and important than that silliness. To start, and apropos of the High Holidays, the *Times* reports Oren attending highly politicized Rosh Hashanah celebrations with side trips to an Israeli arm producer in Maryland and J Street in Washington. Like the term Palestine, Rosh Hashanah is a tangled web for sure.

Here's the *Times's* take:

> He has run up to Washington for damage control. He has spent hours with reporters making Israel's case against Tehran. He went to a Rosh Hashanah party celebrating the Jewish New Year at Vice President Joseph Biden Jr.'s house. He had the White House chief of staff and hundreds of others over

for Rosh Hashanah at his house. He went to ribbon-cutting ceremony in Maryland to open the North American headquarters of an Israeli military contractor. He even made a quiet trip to press his arguments about Iran at J Street, the dovish Jewish lobbying group.

Talk about politicizing the Jewish calendar. This is the same accusation that the Jewish establishment often makes about Jewish dissidents. As in, how dare you talk about the need for a collective confession on Yom Kippur?

In reality, we're talking about which kind of politics the High Holidays are played for rather than whether Rosh Hashanah and Yom Kippur are politicized. If you ever want a text book case for the intersection of religion and politics, here it is.

Also note how high Jewishness rates on the Washington food chain. Vice President Biden – as far as I know he isn't Jewish – hosts a Jewish New Year's gathering. Obama's chief of staff, Jacob (Jack) Lew, an Orthodox Jew, attends the New Year's bash at Oren's residence. Then there is the ribbon cutting at the Israeli military contractors. What kinds of armaments are being made there?

J Street is a "quiet" visit, though it's difficult to understand why. J Street is so mainstream Michael Lerner was forbidden entry there.

In a nutshell, there you have it. An American Jew becomes Israel's ambassador to the United States. With his perfect American accent he hobnobs with the American political elite, reciprocating Rosh Hashanah party favors. He makes sure that the Israeli military is on American shores. On the QT he meets with J Street Israel enablers. Wonder of wonders, then, America's "unshakable" support for Israel.

Would Palestinians, Muslims and every other religion, people and nationality change places with Israel in the Washington circus? Of course, they would. Would they have the internal critique generated by Jews of Conscience over the years? An interesting question. Yet the issue isn't what could or should be. We have to stay with the High Holiday facts on the ground.

Establishment Jewish influence on American foreign policy is here to stay. Israel support by the United States government is here to stay. Obama is correct when he brags that the American-Israeli relationship has never been stronger. He could add that the relationship has never been more technologically sophisticated, more integrated or more empowered than it is now.

In the next four years look for more of the same on the High Holidays – whoever is president.

So tell me, which entanglement is worse, more detrimental and decisive. Is it my new email admirer who can't find Palestine in the Bible or our sophisticated elite that enables Israeli power?

The strange thing is that once upon a time – when those of us of a certain age were

growing up – recognition of our High Holidays at the national level was important. It made us feel accepted in America.

Once upon a time, the Jewish southpaw, Sandy Koufax, sat down on Yom Kippur. He refused to pitch in the first game of the 1965 World Series. Koufax's statement: Jews are part of the American mosaic.

Now our "acceptance" has a much more militant tone. Michael Scott Bornstein is one link in the Americanization of Israeli power. He represents the militarization of American Jewish life.

The charge of double loyalty should be reinterpreted. The question for Jews has always been which side of the Empire Divide we choose. The two choices – empire or community.

When Sandy Koufax sat down for Yom Kippur he stood up for the Jewish community. When the powerful flock to the (American) Israeli ambassador's residence they stand up for empire.

The question isn't the Ambassador's American English. The question is what became of Michael Scott Bornstein.

That question provides a snapshot of the American journey from community to empire. It is highly charged and infinitely more important than the English ability of a born and bred American.

Israel State Archives
JERUSALEM

SEPTEMBER 23

THE JEWISH CIVIL WAR
INTERVIEWS

I've always loved reading interviews. Once in a while I'm interviewed. Looking back over the interviews I've given is fun – and depressing. I have some interviews going back to the mid-1980s. Reviewing them is enlightening.

The video interviews interest me most because they visualize the styles of the day. The fun part is looking at younger versions of my aging self. The depressing part is they cover the same ground as they do now. The only difference is that everything, and I mean everything, is substantially worse.

Sometimes I'm asked to respond to questions in writing. I just completed one which I include below. Since it is for a Brazilian audience, it will be translated and published in Portuguese. The venue is the Jesuit Universida de do Vale do Rio dos Sinos (Unisinos) located in Sao Leopoldo, Rio Grande do Sul, Brazil. Haven't been there but traveling Jewish can be accomplished in many ways.

I wonder if our ever expanding *Encyclopedia Prophetica* should contain the hundreds, perhaps thousands of interviews on Israel-Palestine over the decades. The originals of the interviews can be collected in the Israel National Archives. One day the interviews might be unearthed by a researcher determined to document the traces left by Jews of Conscience.

The *Jewish Civil War Interviews*. A stand-alone book?

The Israel State Archives file classification: "Fragments of the Jewish Prophetic in the Golden Age of Constantinian Judaism." (FJP – GACJ) Or: "The Jewish Civil War (1967 –): Jews of Conscience." (JCW – JC)

Perhaps there are other interviews on the subject in Portuguese as well. I'll ask if the publishers can add this shout out in the publication:

> The interviewed Jewish scholar asks that you send any interviews like this in Portuguese to the Israel National Archives. He thinks it is important since they might be discovered by a researcher who seeks to trace the signs of Jews of Conscience who are challenging Jewish power today and who are exiled from the Jewish community. Thus they are not being accorded their important historical status for the future. Understandably, he fears the disappearance of their witness from Jewish history and world history. The author believes that the indigenous of the people Israel is the prophetic and that Israel's prophetic witness nourishes the prophetic witness of other peoples, including those of us in Brazil who embrace liberation theology.

When it comes out in Portuguese I'll publish it here as well. I want to make it difficult for the Israel National Archives to lose track of it. As well, since most of my readers don't read Portuguese it might function a bit like John Cage's "silent," *4'33"* composition. The (un)readability of the text might awaken us to our own text.

Of course, there may be objections all around to publishing an interview that can't be understood by most readers. What a waste of space! But think about the possibilities. How about publishing it on Yom Kippur – to be read aloud in synagogues around the world? In Brazil and Portugal it could be read in Arabic. That would be interesting, don't you think? Or better yet, perhaps Arabic should be the language of choice for our Yom Kippur faithful in the United States. What an uproar that would bring. It might occasion a Zion Square lynch update on the Rabbis for Jewish Rights website.

Arabic as the dominant language in American Jewish community on Yom Kippur. What would Michael (B)Or(e)n(stein) have to say to my Seder compadre, David Gregory, in American English, about that?

Here it is, then, the interview, as yet (un)translated. Think of it as a snapshot of Jewish life. For the Israel National Archives, Cape Canaveral, Florida, High Holidays, 2012.

> **Q** - In your opinion, is the analogy of what happens between Israelis and Palestinians in the region with the South African apartheid meaningful? Why?
>
> **ME** - I am not concerned with analogies. In history, analogies lead us astray. I view the world through the lens of Jewish history. Segregating a people and treating them as if they don't belong in their own country is wrong. It is wrong in South Africa. It is also wrong in Israel. Palestinians have a right to be free in their own homeland.
>
> **Q** - The conflict has a political and geopolitical motivation in its origin, hence the organization of the modern Zionist movement. Today, are there theological aspects used to support the actions taken by Israel?
>
> **ME** - From the beginning Zionism was mostly secular but there has always been a religious wing of Zionism. As with secular Zionism, the religious wing was diverse. This included spiritual Homeland Zionists like Martin Buber who argued that Jews and Palestinians should share Palestine. Today, most religious Zionists use the state to further their messianic claims exclusively for Jews. Having said that, Jewish religiosity is more difficult to characterize than Christian religiosity. The division in Jewish life between the religious and the sacred is nuanced once you move beyond the simple categories of belief and non-belief. Thus, I would argue that religious and secular, state and homeland Zionism have historical-religious aspects. Dissent within Jewish life, especially regarding Zionism and the state of Israel carries the same historical-religious theme. For the most part, of course, Jews simply argue

as Jews. Nonetheless Jewish argumentation is always colored by a sense of peoplehood and destiny. I would call the ground of this deep encounter with Jewishness historical-religious.

Q - What is the relationship between religious Zionism and political Zionism? Nowadays, are they different? In which moments do they mix themselves?

ME - Religious and political Zionism are mostly quite separate. They also work together toward certain goals. One common goal is domination of the land and politics in the expanding state of Israel. Another common goal is that the land of Israel is for Jews alone. Both religious and political Zionists believe that Jews have to be privileged in Israel and Palestinians pose a threat to Jewish sovereignty. Of course, there are gradations and divisions. For the most part, religious and state Zionists diverge on fundamental issues of Jewish destiny and agree on the practical elements of Jewish ascendancy.

Q - How do you analyze the role of religion in the conflict between Israelis and Palestinians?

ME - The conflict between Jews and Palestinians in Israel-Palestine is primarily political. The conflict is about land, peoplehood, statehood and the resources to maintain them. Of course, religion is present as well. Obviously Jerusalem is central to the three monotheistic religions – this shared religious heritage heightens the political drama. As in other parts of the globe, religion tends to follow the tenor of political situations. Since Jerusalem and Israel-Palestine in general are militarized, Judaism and Islam are as well. If the political situation is demilitarized, Judaism and Islam will follow. Because of the demographics and other factors Christianity plays a limited role in the Israel-Palestine political equation.

Q - What is the position of the various streams of contemporary Judaism in relation to the conflict? In general, has the international Jewish community a clear position in front of Israeli actions in the Middle East?

ME - In general yes, the Jewish community follows what I call a Constantinian line. In the last decades a Constantinian Judaism has formed which supports Israel without question. When there are questions, they are muted to maintain Jewish solidarity. Alongside Constantinian Jews are Jews of Conscience. Jews of Conscience break with Constantinian Jews. They see the Jewish community's alliance with empire as betraying the very concept of what it means to be Jewish. There is a civil war in the Jewish community between these two groups. Of this civil war, there is no end in sight

Q - What is the meaning of "Just Peace" and what is its relationship with the Israeli-Palestinian conflict?

ME - The questions of questions! The international consensus is two states for two peoples, Israel alongside Palestine. The reality is that Israel has taken so much of Jerusalem and the West Bank that few believe that a two-state solution is possible any longer. Some argue for a one-state solution where Jews and Palestinians live side by side within a state with equal citizenship regardless of ethnic or religious background. Neither scenario is likely in the near future. Today, we have one state, Israel, which dominates the land from Tel Aviv to the Jordan River. There are millions of Palestinians within Israeli control; they are without the fundamentals of citizenship and equality.

Q - In your opinion, is a direct dialogue between the Palestinian National Authority (PNA) and the state of Israel the shorter way to achieve peace in the region? Or may the UN as a representative and interventional institution be the most effective way? Why?

ME - Neither will work. It's a matter of power, which Israel has and Palestinians don't. There isn't any power that is able or willing to push Israel back to its 1967 borders. The UN is powerless.

Q - How do you theologically explain the conflict in the Middle East? In your opinion, is it possible to make an interpretation of the sacred texts in the light of what is happening today in the region?

ME - I doubt sacred texts will do much good in the Middle East or elsewhere. Living the prophetic is what we can do. Though the prophetic is doomed to failure, prophetic failures open the possibility of change in the future. Every peace plan known to humanity has been tried in the Israel-Palestine conflict. What we need now is the truth. Let the prophetic chips fall where they may.

John Mearsheimer
UNIVERSITY OF CHICAGO

SEPTEMBER 24

MY (UN)INVITED EXCHANGE WITH
JOHN MEARSHEIMER

Continuing on my interview theme – to be deposited in the Israel National Archives, of course – I am cutting in on an interesting email exchange that was posted yesterday. The email exchange was initiated by Jerome Slater, University Research Scholar at SUNY (Buffalo) and involved the One-State/Two-State solution. It was joined by John Mearsheimer, Professor of Political Science at the University of Chicago, Youssef Munayyer, Executive Director of the The Jerusalem Fund for Education and Community Development and its educational program, the Palestine Center, and Stephen Walt, Professor of International Affairs at Harvard University's Kennedy School of Government.

The exchange is quite interesting. The conclusion I draw from the exchange is that no one knows what's going to happen in the future.

The featured cast of characters is familiar. You can catalogue exchanges of this kind by the decade. Just throw out the names that were the flavor then and you'll know the years the exchange occurred. I suppose everyone does their bit, then someone new arrives.

I've been around for a long time but never made the big leagues. I have the advantage of joining the discussion without an invitation. I can say what I have to say and leave it at that.

Of the exchanges I found Mearsheimer's the most interesting. Or perhaps the most telling. Therefore in my (un)invited appearance I interact with the points he made. My responses to Mearsheimer:

> **JM** - I think the main problem with your argument is that there is no way the US is going to put serious pressure on Israel to accept a two-state solution. Obama tried and failed miserably; it wasn't even close.
>
> **ME** - Yes clearly Obama has failed as other presidents before him. Clearly Obama's sympathies lean toward Israel. Then there is the political factor of Jewish support. Add the Clintons and there you have it. The only movement on Israel during Obama's first term is closer to Israel.
>
> **JM** - I might add that to create a viable Palestinian state would require us to put enormous pressure on Israel, because we would have to reverse so many facts on the ground and because the hardliners are so powerful in Israel. In my opinion, there is no chance this is going to happen. We now have and will continue to have for the foreseeable future a Greater Israel.

ME - This is an obvious point that anyone with any political savvy affirms. However, the emphasis on "hardliners" is misplaced. The political and economic consensus in Israel is take as much land as can be taken and weaken as far as possible Palestinian presence on all fronts. This is not a hardline position. Jerusalem and the West Bank – with a surrounded and weakened Gaza – has been Israeli policy for decades. Why reverse such a policy if it can be carried out successfully?

JM - And by the way, as time goes by, it will become even more difficult to move toward a two-state solution as the settlement enterprise will grow even larger.

ME - Agreed. But this has been understood by all parties, once again, for decades. The settlement enterprise or rather the Israelization of Palestine is continuous. Indeed as the settlement enterprise has grown larger, Israel as a state has grown with it. It is more accurate to understand the situation as the expansion of Israel rather than the expansion of settlements. It is also more useful since calling the expansion of the state of Israel the expansion of settlements gives the illusion that settlements can be stopped and reversed. In the main, this isn't going to happen for a variety of reasons. The most important reason is that a settlement reversal would be seen as an assault on Israel as a state.

JM - On the one-state solution, I think there is no question that Israeli Jews will mightily resist democracy inside Greater Israel. That situation will cause all sorts of problems for the Israelis and give them powerful incentives to expel the Palestinians. I worry a lot about that outcome and hope that the Palestinians have the good sense not to play into Israel's hands.

ME - Yes the expulsion card comes up once in a while, usually around wars and the rumors of war. I do agree that the "democracy within Greater Israel" card is a non-starter. Again, this isn't due to the hardliners unless you define the consensus within Israel as hardline. Only an extremely small percentage of the Jewish population of Israel wants to live in a state where Palestinians are equal citizens. Even those who advocate it or think that it might be possible would ultimately seek to contain this possibility. The idea that the Jews of Israel would agree to live in the Arab Middle East within a unified state where Palestinians are equal citizens is a rhetorical illusion. If it came down to the choice of full democracy or expulsion, Israel would choose expulsion. So far the strategy of containment has warded off the need to make that choice.

JM - You think there is a good chance that Greater Israel can maintain itself for the foreseeable future, even if it is not a democracy and is indeed an apartheid state. After all, they have been able to maintain the occupation all these years. You may be right; one does marvel at how Israel has been able to avoid serious

sanctions for its past behavior toward the Palestinians.

ME - The marvel of marvels is explainable by looking at historical and balance of power factors. Nonetheless, it is a marvel because everything seems to break Israel's way. Of course, Israel has helped things break its way. The combination of historical and political factors with intentional action is what's truly remarkable about Israel's ability to keep on keeping on. Think what a boon September 11th was for Israel. Iran is Israel's current gold mine.

JM - Still, I think you are wrong. The world has changed and is changing in ways that will make it impossible over the long term to maintain an Israel that is an apartheid state, and here I am talking the next thirty or so years. Very briefly, here are my reasons.

JM - 1. Israel has benefitted greatly from the illusion that there will be a two-state solution; that will soon be over.

ME - Yes, Israel has benefitted from that illusion. But now that the two-state illusion is over there doesn't seem to be any further movement. Rather, the "movement" – whatever it really was – has stopped. Or is what we have more or less the same "movement" we've had for decades?

JM - 2. Greater Israel will be (is) an apartheid state and that will be hard to miss and very difficult to defend — I would argue impossible over the long term.

ME - This has been argued for years. Think back a decade when the Apartheid Wall began. The argument was that with the building of the Wall no one could deny what Israel was doing. Therefore the Wall would be the end of Israeli expansion. Now think of the Lebanon war that followed and the invasion of Gaza that followed Lebanon. Each time Israel's ability to maintain its international stature was at an end. Lo and behold, Israel maintained its ability to function as a state. The obviousness of Israel's apartheid hasn't stopped Israel. One could argue that it hasn't even hurt Israel.

JM - 3. The face of Israel is undergoing a fundamental transformation with the steady drift to the right, the growing racism, and the growing numbers of ultra-orthodox. That, coupled with apartheid, will make it hard for Israel to sell itself as a "Western society," as it has done so well in the past.

ME - Regarding the Palestinians which is the issue here, it is difficult to argue a change over time with regard to Israel's actual policies. Certainly, the rhetoric is stronger and overt Jewish religiosity plays more of a political role than in Israel's early years. One can argue the decline of ethical standards in the Israeli military as well though Palestinians who experienced their dispossession in Israel's founding and beyond might dispute this. Racism may have changed

its face to some extent, what with the highly charged settler and religious rhetoric. However, Israel is based on Jewish supremacy. What is commonly called racism today was there from the beginning. On the "Western society" front these issues, too, have changed without changing. Since the West has perceived Arabs and the Middle East as its own resource playground – and still does – why can't Israel continue to sell itself as Western?

JM - 4. The internet makes it almost impossible to miss what is going on in Israel.

ME - Agreed. However, the full internet impact has been true for more than a decade. Notice any changes on the ground that reflect that increased exposure?

JM - 5. Israel's "new historians" have made it clear what the Israelis have done and are doing to the Palestinians and that has generated a huge amount of sympathy for the Palestinians around the world. Israel in the past was very adept at selling itself as the victim. Now they look like brutal victimizers and the Palestinians look like the victims.

ME - No question this is right. Israel as the victim is in deep background. Palestinians as victims are in the moral ascendancy. Yet again, there is no political movement forward that reinforces that perception. As well, the Jewish victim factor can come back into play quickly if in fact Israel was in danger or under assault. More than the historical Holocaust or nuclear weapons, "victim Israel" is Israel's political wild card. Under duress, it can be played with alacrity. Does anyone think the European or American governments would allow Israel to go down?

JM - 6. The lobby is powerful, but it now has to operate out in the open and engage in smash-mouth politics. That is not good; as Steve Rosen said, "A lobby is like a night flower; it thrives in the dark and dies in the sun."

ME - It may not be good. It may not be bad. When lobbies like AIPAC are in the shadows they have a certain kind of power. They do fear coming into the open. In the light, a lobby like AIPAC either dies – or thrives. From my perspective, AIPAC is stronger today than ever. It is doing quite well in the light of day.

JM - 7. The American Jewish community is hardly monolithic and it contains a substantial number of people who are deeply critical of Israeli behavior and willing to voice their opinions. I believe those numbers will grow over time; Peter Beinart is a harbinger of things to come.

ME - Peter Beinart is the flavor of the month and by that I don't mean to disparage him or his thought. You can mark Jewish dissent by certain names that have also been flavors of the month, sometimes years, even decades. Think of all the known Jewish dissidents who have emerged over time, then

think of the political movement on the ground. True those deeply critical of Israeli policies are more numerous and more willing to say it. However, like the illusion of the internet, the importance of Jewish dissent on the political level is highly overrated. The Jewish establishment decided a long time ago to take their issues to the broader public and diverse political stake holders. Jews haven't been important to the Jewish establishment on Israel for decades.

JM - 8. The Holocaust is receding into history and it will become increasingly difficult for Israel and its supporters to invoke that horrific tragedy to provide Israel with cover.

ME - The Holocaust is indeed receding in history and, in the main, the argument about Israel has shifted to a Holocaust future. Obviously this invokes the historical Holocaust but the Holocaust future needs to be probed for its political significance. Instead of using the Holocaust as a political litmus test for supporting Israel, the fear of a future Holocaust is the political lever used today.

JM - 9. Elites in the Arab and Islamic world are becoming more Westernized and are much better able to engage in politics in the West than they were in the past.

ME - Elites in the Arab and Islamic world have been Westernized for decades. It does seem to me that they are becoming more sophisticated in their political engagement. Part of this might be the growing Middle Eastern diaspora communities in the West. Nonetheless, politics is politics and economics is economics. The status and wellbeing of the Westernized elite around the world is deeply integrated into the West. Thus it is in their interest that the West continues to dominate and that they play their part in that domination. Obviously, this has to be negotiated and sometimes these Western elites fail. With the power dynamics in the world today, thinking that these elites will move beyond placating the Western powers- that-be is an illusion.

JM - 10. The Arab world is likely to become more democratic and more educated over time and that is likely to make countries in the Middle East more critical of Israel. This is what is now happening in Egypt.

ME - I'm not sure about this – it seems like we're falling into the Western colonial trap i.e. "education" – however that is to be defined – makes the world go round. The more important factor in regional and global politics is self-interest. As long as the Middle East is Euro and American-centric then Israel will receive a free pass no matter what the rhetoric is. If the region goes Asian, then it will depend what they want in return. The criticism of Israel in the Arab world has been there from day one. If anything, Israel – partly because of Europe and America – has become an accepted, even needed, power in the region. In the main, Arab governments do not want Israel to disappear as the

scramble for power would then be on. If Israel disappeared or was severely disciplined, Palestine might emerge as a vibrant and empowered state. No one in the region wants that.

JM - 11. There is an important precedent that many will point to so as to delegitimize Greater Israel and make the case for turning it into a real democracy: South Africa.

ME - South Africa, the great example often trotted out for various, mostly, rhetorical reasons. There are some reasons that it should be. There are other reasons it shouldn't be. Israel is an apartheid state but that shouldn't convince us that Israel is a candidate for a South African transformation. I doubt this to be the case. The reason is what is missing in these discussions – the Jewish factor. The Jewish factor is a sense of Jewish destiny and aloneness. This is truly what makes Israel different. With this in mind, Israel's calculations for end game scenarios are different than other nations, including South Africa. As well, rarely discussed is how Palestinians would fare if such a transformation took place. If you look at South Africa transformed, notice the persistence of deep socio-economic and ethnic divisions. The hope is that with economic developments these divisions will disappear. I'm not so sure. Anyway, in relation to Israel-Palestine the end of Israeli apartheid does not in any way guarantee a free and equal Palestine.

JM - For all these reasons, I don't think it will be possible for Greater Israel to maintain itself as an apartheid state over the long term. Again, this is why I am fearful that Israel will pursue expulsion. Of course, I may be wrong about all this, but I don't think so.

ME - Quite a note to end on, though it does bring us back to the beginning. Israel is practicing a policy of expansion and containment, the very same policy it has pursued since its birth. There has never been an extreme political centrist push to finish the job. Political, economic and military practicalities and perhaps some vestige of Jewish ethics have oriented Israel toward a slower and efficient way of dealing with its perceived rights and needs. Why start now with a more extreme policy when the tried and true has been working and is deemed acceptable by the international community? By acceptable, I mean Israel has not been stopped. Military interventions against other countries violating international law or Western interests are manifold. Why not a military intervention against Israel? The reason: Israel's policies are judged to be within the acceptable range. Barring any significant change in that acceptability, Israel will continue with its policy of expansion and containment.

B'Tselem
JERUSALEM

SEPTEMBER 25

B'TSELEM
AND THE END OF JEWISH HISTORY

As Yom Kippur draws ever nearer, thoughts about what confession means – and doesn't mean. Typically, we think confession purges the past. We begin again with a clean slate. I have come to think that confession is more about the future. Yom Kippur is about the future – as it could be.

Yesterday I had a conversation with a friend who sees confession and the future as linked with helping others in need. Though she doesn't want those in need abandoned, she isn't too high on the "helping" option. Reason: the world out there is dangerous and, for the most part, meaningless. Self-deception lurks as well. The desire to help others often masks our need to be rescued. Altruism isn't everything it's cracked up to be.

The end result of this logic? Give what you can but don't endanger what you have. What you give away won't be returned.

Those who have been through the wars where collusion and lies reign can hardly deny this logic. On the personal side, lessons are there to be learned. What we give of ourselves and what we hold back are concerns with regard to intimacy. So, too, on the public scene.

Hannah Arendt divided the world into private and public realms, essentially signing on to my friend's position. I wonder, though, when we venture within or outside are the private and the public so divided they exist in separate worlds?

A few years ago at the Carter Center, I touched on this topic in a discussion with Mitri Raheb, the Palestinian Christian pastor in Bethlehem. The Carter Center was hosting its annual Human Rights conference. The Jewish side of things was represented by me and the director of B'Tselem, the longstanding, pioneering and most prominent Israeli human rights organization.

B'Tselem is an important organization. When B'Tselem is mentioned we think of an organization that documents human rights violations by Israel and by doing this protects the human rights of Palestinians. Moreover, B'Tselem does this to help move Israel to a two-state solution. In this way they are quite like Rabbis for Human Rights, which I also admire and have written critically of.

I view B'Tselem in a somewhat different light. Though it seems B'Tselem's focus is on the immediate violation of human rights, the most important work it does is historical in nature. B'Tselem is documenting the end of Jewish history as we have known and inherited it.

By the "end of Jewish history," I mean the ethical framework of Jewish history. What I mean by "as we have known and inherited it" is that Jewish history will continue but in a way that Jews of Conscience cannot embrace.

Founded in 1989 during the first Palestinian uprising, B'Tselem is creating a significant, detailed and devastating indictment of the Golden Age of Constantinian Jewish life. I'm sure that the Israel National Archives is collecting their documentation. These files will stand alongside the materials documenting the ethnic cleansing of Palestinians in Israel's founding and, among other things, the recently discovered transcripts of conversations concerning the Sabra and Shatila massacres. B'Tselem's investigations and publications should also be included in my proposed *Encyclopedia Prophetica*.

Several years ago I discussed my take on B'Tselem with the chair of their Board. I expected push-back. She thought for a moment, and then told me I was right. At the Carter Center, the director of B'Tselem couldn't understand a word I was saying. She's still stuck in the "Jewish rescue" mode.

B'Tselem's website description of itself is fascinating in this regard. The first thing it wans to do is to ensure Jews that publicizing Israel's human right's violations accords benefits to Jews and to Israel. I believe that B'Tselem is being honest with itself – just like Rabbis for Human Rights is honest with itself. Honest, that is, up to a point.

Read their response to the rhetorical question they pose: "Don't you worry that you are making Israel look bad?

> B'Tselem's primary goal is to ensure that Israel respects human rights in the Occupied Territories and fulfills its obligations under international law. Publicity has often proven effective in improving Israeli policies and for this reason we are obligated to publicize policies that harm human rights and run counter to Israel's legal obligations. While B'Tselem reports on some of the least attractive aspects of Israeli policy, in doing so we highlight some of the best aspects of Israeli society. B'Tselem is part of Israel's vibrant, civil society, working in spite of the difficult security situation to improve our society from within. We are proud to represent this part of Israel to a world which is all too often unaware of it.

B'Tselem's reflection of itself is true to its intentions. They also argue how effective they are in working with the Israeli government and army. In effect, after all these years, B'Tselem, like Rabbis for Human Rights, can be judged as enablers of the occupation as others have in the issue of the role of NGO's in Israel-Palestine. But, at least in relation to B'Tselem, its intention is only a superficial understanding of what they are doing, historically speaking.

This brings me back to Mitri Raheb. I first met Mitri in 1984 as he was just starting out. A more humble person you can't find. Because he is so humble, I thought that, unlike other Palestinian Christians who appealed to the West, he wouldn't build an organizational mini-empire.

On the humility side, I was right. On the organizational side, I was wrong. Primarily through his German contacts, Mitri has an important and productive presence in Bethlehem. Obviously, his important work is dependent on the outside for finances. This outside connection also brings his organization some protection from Israeli authorities.

Despite Mitri's work, the political and economic situation in Bethlehem is disheartening. If we had a slow motion tape of the developments in and around Bethlehem since I first visited Mitri, we'd note substantial changes for Palestinians all around. All of them are negative. This includes the Wall that snakes around the city. Yet this is only the most visible sign of a Palestinian city under siege.

In the almost twenty-five years I've known Mitri, he has always been kind and considerate. At the Carter Center, I also experienced a rougher edge. In a short discussion about aid and hope, I noticed the edge. Mitri dismissed the idea that Palestinians would be rescued by outside forces, no matter their good intentions. To set a more hopeful tone, I mentioned President Carter and his support for Palestinian rights. Mitri's demeanor remained the same.

President Carter attended all the conference sessions and almost wept when he spoke on the plight of the Palestinians. He is quite an advocate to have. However, Mitri, his congregation, city and people have had many "friends" voicing their support for years. This includes B'Tselem. Where had this support brought Palestinians?

When a people is abandoned to the extent that even those who help can't do much of anything besides voice moral support, a cynicism about history and humanity can become the norm. Standing on the "helping" side, our arguments against cynicism are limited.

I wonder if Mitri has lost faith in humanity.

As a Christian he follows a messiah who suffered for humanity and thus "redeemed" creation. Does the continual plight of the Palestinians test his faith in redemption?

Do Jews of Conscience who land on his doorstep restore his faith in humanity or, in their weakness and limitations, do they challenge it even more?

Mitri on Yom Kippur. Think of the confession needed which might bring about a different future – if it was acted upon. We know it is not forthcoming. Worse, though, is the following: If such a confession was forthcoming would the city of Bethlehem be liberated?

B'Tselem is documenting the end of Jewish history as we have known and inherited it. Being collected in the Israel National Archives.

B'Tselem is documenting Mitri's end, too.

What will Bethlehem be like when the curious researcher arrives somewhere down the historical road?

Yom Kippur's confession is about the future we refuse to embrace.

The Confession That Isn't
CAPE CANAVERAL

SEPTEMBER 26

THE DAY
WITHOUT A FUTURE

Yom Kippur has arrived. I am done with thought poems and deflection.

Yom Kippur is the most hypocritical day of the Jewish calendar. This is true of all holy days of the great world religions and, no doubt, the lesser ones as well. Citing the hypocrisy of Yom Kippur is a cheap shot. Too obvious.

Critical thought and action are more important than reading sacred texts and chanting prayers. When piety serves the continuation of empire it's worse than meaningless. It's a form of blasphemy.

The sacred texts and prayers of most religions subvert empire pretensions of the powerful. Yet in a curious transposition, subversion becomes a form of legitimatization. Against the meaning of the text, the powerful become agents of good. In their own minds, of course.

Historically speaking, Christians are global experts in textual inversion. Squaring the teachings of Jesus with empire is more than difficult. It's impossible.

Some think the current inversion experts are Muslims. On the historical scale, Jews have entered the distortion sweepstakes only recently. Once on the scene, though, we've taken the plunge. Rosh Hashanah at the Big House is illustrative. Yom Kippur without mentioning the ethnic cleansing and occupation of Palestinians is another.

It isn't just Israel-Palestine where the confession is needed. The day after I sent off my interview to Brazil, I received another invite from a city nearby where the interview is being translated. They're going to be holding a forum creating a Kairos Brazil document. So getting ready for my travel to Brazil, I picked up a copy of a book on Jewish history. I found these passages of (un)Israel-Palestine confessional interest for Yom Kippur.

But first a short Yom Kippur "Jews in Brazil" history lesson to set the stage.

The history of the Jews in Brazil is one of displacement and success. The thumbnail sketch finds Jews present in Brazil from the beginning of European settlement in the Americas. Jewish presence accelerated when the Inquisition reached Portugal in the 16th century. The arrivals were mostly Sephardic Jews fleeing the Inquisition in Spain and Portugal to the religious freedom of the Netherlands. At that point, Brazil was under Dutch control.

The development of Brazil's sugar industry was accelerated by Portuguese Jews. More Jews arrived when the Brazilian constitution of 1824 granted freedom of religion. With the rubber boom in the nineteenth century, Moroccan Jews began arriving. Then there

was Jewish immigration with the rise of the Nazis in Europe. In the 1950s, another wave of immigration brought thousands of North African Jews to Brazil.

The book on Jewish history is by Marc Lee Raphael. I happened on his comments about the other side of Brazil's – and America's – Jewish immigration success story. The first is on Jews and the slave trade in Brazil. The other is even closer to home:

Jews also took an active part in the Dutch colonial slave trade; indeed, the bylaws of the Recife and Mauricia congregations (1648) included an imposta (Jewish tax) of five soldos for each Negro slave a Brazilian Jew purchased from the West Indies Company. Slave auctions were postponed if they fell on a Jewish holiday. In Curacao in the seventeenth century, as well as in the British colonies of Barbados and Jamaica in the eighteenth century, Jewish merchants played a major role in the slave trade. In fact, in all the American colonies, whether French (Martinique), British, or Dutch, Jewish merchants frequently dominated.

This was no less true on the North American mainland, where during the eighteenth century Jews participated in the 'triangular trade' that brought slaves from Africa to the West Indies and there exchanged them for molasses, which in turn was taken to New England and converted into rum for sale in Africa. Isaac Da Costa of Charleston in the 1750's, David Franks of Philadelphia in the 1760's, and Aaron Lopez of Newport in the late 1760's and early 1770's dominated Jewish slave trading on the American continent.

The tangled web of Jewish history is an important Yom Kippur theme. It won't be heard in most synagogues today. We're the poorer for it. Because the confessional reckoning is refused, our ability to change direction in the future is diminished.

Every day without a reckoning is a day without a future. So it is with Yom Kippur.

When piety serves the continuation of empire, reading sacred texts and chanting prayers is blasphemy.

But then Isaiah already encapsulated this thousands of years ago. It's even read in synagogue on Yom Kippur:

> To be sure, they seek Me daily,
>
> Eager to learn My ways.
>
> Like a nation that does what is right,
>
> That has not abandoned the laws of its God,
>
> They ask Me for the right way,
>
> They are eager for the nearness of God.
>
> "Why, when we fasted, did You not see?
>
> When we starved our bodies, did You pay no heed?"

Because on your fast day

You see to your business

And oppress all your laborers!

Because you fast in strife and contention,

And you strike with a wicked fist!

Your fasting today is not such

As to make your voice heard on high.

Is such the fast I desire,

A day for men to starve their bodies?

Is it bowing the head like a bulrush

And lying in sackcloth and ashes?

Do you call that a fast,

A day when the Lord is favorable?

No, this is the fast I desire:

To unlock the fetters of wickedness

And untie the cords of the yoke

To let the oppressed go free

To break off every yoke.

Feigned fasts. Isaiah, an original Jew of Conscience, knew it well. The Jewish prophetic won't let Yom Kippur go down easy.

MAPS, ILLUSTRATIONS & PHOTOGRAPHS

MAPS, ILLUSTRATIONS & PHOTOGRAPHS

Cover Photograph - Marc H. Ellis
Part One, Part Two & Part Three - Marc H. Ellis

JULY

- 5 - Marc H. Ellis
- 6 - Dennis Sabo / shutterstock.com
- 7 - Marc H. Ellis
- 8 - Tim B. Gilman
- 9 - globalresearch.ca
- 10 - Marc H. Ellis
- 11 - huffingtonpost.com
- 12 - Chad Collins / ecclesio.com
- 13 - APIC
- 14 - Marc H. Ellis
- 15 - ifamericansknew.org
- 16 - Giovanni Girolano Savoldo
- 17 - paxonbothhouses.blogspot.com
- 18 - Benjamin West
- 19 - Tristan Tan / shutterstock.com
- 20 - Marc H. Ellis
- 21 - Marc H. Ellis
- 22 - Dan Dennison
- 23 - Justin McIntosh
- 24 - Marc H. Ellis
- 25 - thelostogle.com
- 26 - Philip Bird / shutterstock.com
- 27 - Haaretz Archive / Reuters
- 28 - Joy Adhikary
- 29 - Gil Tibon
- 29 - NASA
- 30 - Lipowski Milan / shutterstock.com
- 31 - Ryan Rodrick Beiler / shutterstock.com

AUGUST

- 1 - Tim B. Gilman
- 2 - Frikota / shutterstock.com
- 3 - Marc H. Ellis
- 4 - Unknown / Bundesarchiv Bild
- 6 - 61freedomriders.org
- 7 - Marc H. Ellis
- 8 - Marc H. Ellis
- 9 - oisc.wordpress.com
- 10 - Marc H. Ellis
- 11 - Picture Alliance
- 12 - Marc H. Ellis
- 13 - Benny Brunner
- 14 - Mopic / shutterstock.com
- 15 - Tomasz Pielesz
- 17 - The All-Nite Images
- 18 - Tim B. Gilman

19 - Marc H. Ellis
20 - Tim B. Gilman
21 - Marc H. Ellis
22 - Marc H. Ellis
23 - Marc H. Ellis
24 - Kobby Dagan / shutterstock.com
25 - washjeff.edu
26 - strangemaps.wordpress.com
27 - faithhousemanhattan.org
28 - Rachel Corrie Foundation
29 - peace.maripo.com
30 - Susanne Scholz
31 - Ryan Rodrick Beiler / shutterstock.com

SEPTEMBER

1 - AP / Haaretz / Columbia University Press
2 - ebay.com
3 - greatthoughtstreasury.com
4 - Marc H. Ellis
5 - AFP
6 - Aaron Francis
7 - Tim B. Gilman
8 - libertyportraits.com / Marc H. Ellis
9 - The Family of Rabbi David Forman
10 - Yasuhiro Yoshioka
11 - Marc H. Ellis
12 - John Anderson
13 - Harvard University Archives
14 - Jeff Janowski / augusta.com
15 - Robin Klein
16 - Anne Frank Fonds Basel
17 - Marc H. Ellis
18 - Marc H. Ellis
19 - NBC News
20 - Jason Reed / Reuters
21 - archives.gov.il
22 - Susan Tusa / Detroit Free Press
23 - Nir Keidar
24 - Varsha Sundar / The Chicago Maron
25 - b'tselem.org
26 - Marc H. Ellis

ABOUT THE
AUTHOR

Marc H. Ellis is retired University Professor of Jewish Studies and Director of the Center for Jewish Studies at Baylor University.

He is the author and editor of more than twenty books including *Toward a Jewish Theology of Liberation, Unholy Alliance: Religion and Atrocity in Our Time, Future of the Prophetic: Israel's Ancient Wisdom Re-Presented* and, most recently, *Burning Children: A Jewish View of the War in Gaza* and *Exile & the Prophetic: Images from the New Disaspora.*

Professor Ellis's writings have been translated into more than a dozen languages and he has lectured around the world. Currently he is writing an almost daily commentary series, *Exile and the Prophetic,* which can be found at mondoweiss.net.

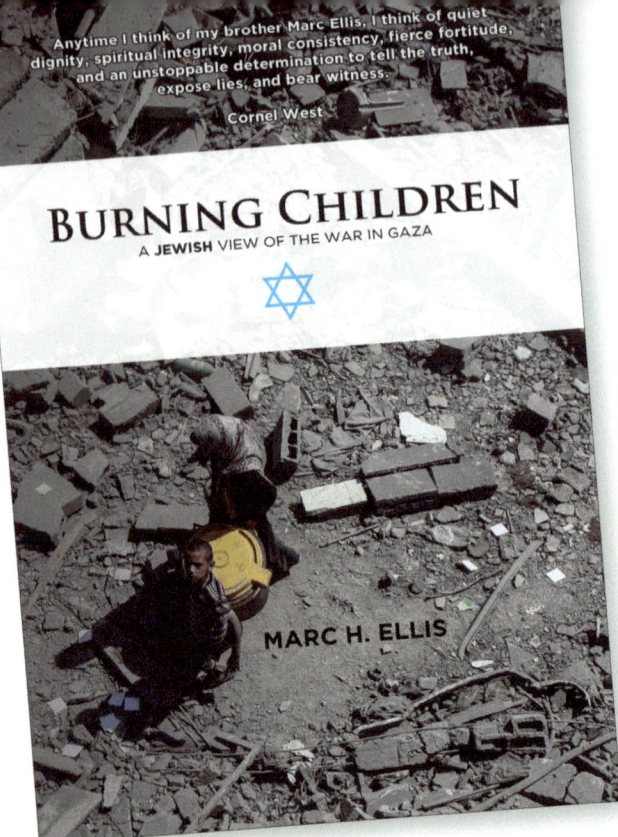

"Marc Ellis provides a vital contribution to solving one of the few remaining intractable problems of our time.

He shows that the voice of prophecy has not been silenced in the Jewish community.

We will all be the poorer if this voice is not heeded, but how wonderfully enriched if it is."

Archbishop Desmond Tutu

This collection of commentaries, written during the recent Gaza war as it unfolded, represents an attempt of one Jew on behalf of Jews of Conscience everywhere to come to grips with the state of Israel as it is rather than what it purports to be. Though written from a geographic distance, one feels the pain Palestinians experienced as a challenge to Jewish history. Have Jews survived the Holocaust only to recreate scenes of horror Israel now visits upon the Palestinian people? Or is there a way forward for Jews and Palestinians beyond mutual recrimination, displacement and war? Using the burning children of the Holocaust as the core of Jewish ethical post-Holocaust life, these commentaries ask Jews, the state of Israel and all those in solidarity with Jews and Jewish history to hold Israel accountable for its assault on Gaza and provide a vehicle for a future where Jews and Palestinians live together in justice and peace.

Artistic, Beautiful, Stunningly Quirky...
Totally Ellis... Street Photography at it's finest.

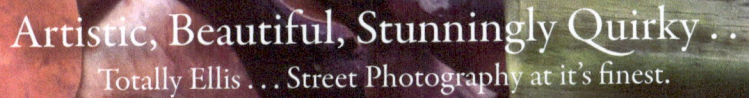

**EXILE &
the PROPHETIC**
IMAGES FROM THE NEW DIASPORA

Marc H. Ellis

*I have been traveling to Cape Canaveral and taking photographs
on the beach since I was a child.*

*So when I returned to the Cape to live a few years ago,
I resumed my avocation.*

www.ingramcontent.com/pod-product-compliance
Lightning Source LLC
Chambersburg PA
CBHW041350290426
44108CB00001B/1